Steve passionately and practically teaches us how to rightly handle and interpret the word in ways that bring healing, hope, and life.

ANDY MAHONEY, PASTOR OF VILLAGE GRACE CHURCH, PORTLAND, OREGON

Years ago, a woman I knew struggled to separate God's voice from the voice of her abusive pastor-uncle. She believed God was disappointed with her fear, until she realized the condemnation she heard in Scripture wasn't divine—it was human, distorted by abuse. It took years to reclaim the Bible from that voice. If you've had similar experiences—if Scripture has been used to wound or silence you—Steve's book is a lifeline. With wisdom, compassion, and scholarly rigor, he walks beside survivors, exposing misused texts and restoring a picture of God as protector, healer, and advocate for the abused. Start with one passage or one chapter—this is a book to heal with, not rush through.

PHILIP G. MONROE, CLINICAL PSYCHOLOGIST, OWNER OF LANGBERG, MONROE & ASSOCIATES, AND FOUNDER OF GLOBAL TRAUMA RECOVERY INSTITUTE

To Heal or Harm is a much needed and deeply healing resource. Having been married to a "pastor" who used his Bible training to twist Scripture and control me, I know firsthand how disorienting and spiritually damaging this misuse can be. Reading this book helped me uncover hidden areas in my heart that still needed healing. More importantly, it helped me reconnect with the true heart of God—his justice, his compassion, and his great love for the abused. This book is a gift to survivors and to anyone seeking to understand the healing power of Scripture when it is rightly handled.

NAGHMEH ABEDINI PANAHI, AUTHOR OF *I DIDN'T SURVIVE: EMERGING WHOLE AFTER DECEPTION, PERSECUTION, AND HIDDEN ABUSE*

Though the Bible leaves no doubt in its condemnation of abuse, Christian circles often become a safe harbor for abusers and an unsafe haven for the traumatized. A reexamination of our thinking concerning Scripture and abuse is long overdue. Thankfully, Steven Tracy offers an essential resource in this pursuit. My soul was stirred again to be a channel of hope and healing.

BRAD PELLISH, EUROPEAN CHRISTIAN MISSION INTERNATIONAL

Many who suffer under the weight of spiritual abuse not only walk away from their church communities but also from their faith, hearts broken and beliefs in ruins. What makes this pain especially heavy is that it comes at the hands of those called to shepherd—Christian leaders—who misuse the very Scriptures meant to bring healing and hope. *To Heal or Harm* thoughtfully dismantles the distorted theology that enables spiritual abuse and brings

Scripture back into its rightful, life-giving context. I wholeheartedly commend this resource to anyone seeking understanding, healing, or hope in the face of such harm.

DR. DARRELL PULS, AUTHOR OF *LET US PREY: THE PLAGUE OF NARCISSIST PASTORS AND WHAT WE CAN DO ABOUT IT*

As a clinical psychologist who has walked alongside survivors of abuse for over thirty years, I am deeply grateful for the support and insight offered by *To Heal or Harm*. Free from clichés, oversimplifications, and platitudes, the author's profound respect for Scripture brings both relief and release to those impacted by traumatic harm—and to those earnestly seeking to make wise, responsive decisions in alignment with God's word. It is a much-needed resource for Christian leaders, behavioral health professionals, and anyone pursuing freedom, safety, and healing.

LAURA ANNE ROBERTS, LICENSED PSYCHOLOGIST, OWNER-PARTNER OF CORNERSTONE CLINICAL SERVICES, MILWAUKIE, OREGON

As the founder of a trauma-informed counseling center that walks daily with survivors of abuse, I cannot overstate the significance of *To Heal or Harm*. I have seen firsthand how Scripture can be both a source of profound healing and, tragically, a weapon of harm. *To Heal or Harm* compassionately addresses this complex duality with theological depth, clinical awareness, and pastoral sensitivity. For those who have felt unseen, silenced, or retraumatized within spiritual settings, this book offers clarity and hope. I am deeply grateful for this resource and will be recommending it widely to my clients, colleagues, and community.

REBEKAH STINES, LICENSED PROFESSIONAL COUNSELOR AND FOUNDER OF HEARTAFIRE COUNSELING SERVICES

Scripture has too often been weaponized against wounded souls, heaping shame on those most in need of healing. *To Heal or Harm* rightly divides the word of God, revealing both God's heart for the oppressed and his disdain for abuse. Dr. Tracy addresses the church's failure to protect the vulnerable while illuminating God's desire for true restoration and the inherent dignity of all people. I highly recommend this both for those harmed and those trying to help.

LESLIE VERNICK, RELATIONSHIP COACH, SPEAKER, AUTHOR OF *THE EMOTIONALLY DESTRUCTIVE RELATIONSHIP* AND *THE EMOTIONALLY DESTRUCTIVE MARRIAGE*

Trauma healing begins when wounds are recognized, not ignored or suppressed. Today's painful reality is that spiritual authorities and Bible teachers often reject or silence experiences of pain and injustice, misusing Scripture in harmful ways. In this broken world, Dr. Tracy's book offers truth and hope to abuse survivors and their supporters, providing hermeneutically sound interpretations of Scripture to foster healing, advocacy, restoration, and resilience.

REV. DR. SANGHOON YOO, FOUNDER OF THE FAITHFUL CITY, ASSISTANT PROFESSOR, HUNTINGTON UNIVERSITY

This book is a gift to survivors and those who care for them. Tracy dismantles commonly distorted perspectives of Scripture that have caused deep harm in many of our churches, offering a redemptive framework for understanding God's heart through the Bible. *To Heal or Harm* is a valuable resource for pastors, mentors, advocates, and anyone seeking to walk with integrity, grace, and wisdom alongside those who carry the wounds of abuse.

CALEB E CAMPBELL, LEAD PASTOR OF DESERT SPRINGS BIBLE CHURCH, AUTHOR OF *DISARMING LEVIATHAN: LOVING YOUR CHRISTIAN NATIONALIST NEIGHBOR*

Nearly all the accounts of abuse that survivors have disclosed to me were made exponentially more excruciating by a parent or pastor's misuse of Scripture. In *To Heal or Harm*, Steve Tracy empowers survivors to reclaim God's word as medicine rather than poison and equips all believers to rightly interpret the Bible. This is essential reading if the church is to offer protection for the vulnerable and healing for the abused.

CHRIS DAVIS, LEAD PASTOR OF GROVETON BAPTIST CHURCH, AUTHOR OF *BRIGHT HOPE FOR TOMORROW: HOW ANTICIPATING JESUS' RETURN GIVES STRENGTH FOR TODAY*

Untwisting Scriptures to reveal God's heart is my passion and mission, so I'm always grateful when other men and women of God undertake it too. I love how *To Heal or Harm* addresses specific twisted Scriptures to help the abused walk in clarity, hope, and freedom and goes further to show who God really is and why we can trust him. This book will be a boon and a blessing to many.

REBECCA DAVIS, AUTHOR OF THE *UNTWISTING SCRIPTURES* SERIES

To Heal or Harm is a vital and timely resource in the fight against abuse stemming from the misuse of Scripture. With clarity, theological depth, and pastoral sensitivity, Steven Tracy confronts the so-called poison passages and offers biblically grounded, redemptive interpretations that reflect the true heart of God. He exposes false teachings with courage while unveiling the healing power of Christ's love as revealed throughout Scripture. This book is not only a corrective to distorted theology but also a balm for those wounded by it. Every pastor, counselor, teacher, and advocate should keep an extra copy on hand as an essential reference—equipping them to support the abused and challenge those who twist Scripture for power and control. I look forward to sharing this book with others—what a great and much-needed resource.

INGRID FARO, PROFESSOR OF OLD TESTAMENT, NORTHERN SEMINARY, AUTHOR OF *DEMYSTIFYING EVIL: A BIBLICAL AND PERSONAL EXPLORATION* AND *REDEEMING EDEN: HOW WOMEN IN THE BIBLE ADVANCE THE STORY OF SALVATION*

To Heal or Harm is a beautiful gift for those who have endured oppression and harm through distorted interpretations of Scripture. If you, or someone you know, has had God's beautiful message to you used as a weapon of control, I hope you will read this book. It will help you untangle the confusion that arises from the misuse of Scripture and provide insight into the true heart of God.

JOY FORREST, FOUNDER OF CALLED TO PEACE MINISTRIES, AUTHOR OF *CALLED TO PEACE: A SURVIVOR'S GUIDE TO FINDING PEACE & HEALING AFTER DOMESTIC ABUSE* AND *THE CALLED TO PEACE WORKBOOK*

This timely book exposes the shame of those who misuse Scripture to justify the abuse of victims and in the process deepen the victims' physical and psychological trauma. The anecdotes of those who have been on the receiving end of Bible bashing are heart wrenching. But this book offers far more. Dr. Tracy highlights how God sees, hears, feels, grieves, rescues, heals, and restores. He unveils the healing role of Scripture and God's demand for justice and mercy and includes illustrations of compassionate ministry to those who have experienced trauma. Highly recommended.

DAVID E. GARLAND, PROFESSOR EMERITUS, GEORGE W. TRUETT THEOLOGICAL SEMINARY, BAYLOR UNIVERSITY

Like Jesus's own mission, the purpose of Scripture is to transform and give life, but in the wrong hands the Bible has too often been twisted in order to steal, kill, and destroy. Too many people have been traumatized by Christians who have weaponized Scripture. Tracy has written a bold and necessary corrective, calling out harmful readings of Scripture and comforting the abused with the real message of the gospel, a message of the grace of God, the love of Christ, and the healing power of the Spirit. If you want to rightly handle the word of truth, read this book; it is the closest thing to a "safety manual" for the Bible I have ever read. And it is desperately needed.

NIJAY K. GUPTA, JULIUS R. MANTEY PROFESSOR OF NEW TESTAMENT, NORTHERN SEMINARY

In a world of extremes, Steve offers a needed reminder: Scripture is meant to heal, not harm. This book equips pastors, survivors, and families to recognize the abuse of Scripture and rediscover God's heart to heal and restore. Read it. Find freedom. And be healed.

DANIEL KNUTSON, LEAD PASTOR OF HOPE CITY CHURCH

Steve Tracy offers us all a beautiful gift. *To Heal or Harm* helps those of us who have hurt and been hurt when Scripture is used to protect those in power rather than to faithfully serve the flock. In a time when it may be tempting to move away from Scripture because of its harmful applications,

to HEAL *or* HARM

Scripture's Use as Poison or
Medicine for Abuse Survivors

STEVEN R. TRACY

ZONDERVAN
REFLECTIVE

ZONDERVAN REFLECTIVE

To Heal or Harm
Copyright © 2026 by Steven R. Tracy

Published by Zondervan, 3950 Sparks Drive SE, Suite 101, Grand Rapids, MI 49546, USA. Zondervan is a registered trademark of The Zondervan Corporation, L.L.C., a wholly owned subsidiary of HarperCollins Christian Publishing, Inc.

Requests for information should be addressed to customercare@harpercollins.com.

Zondervan titles may be purchased in bulk for educational, business, fundraising, or sales promotional use. For information, please email SpecialMarkets@Zondervan.com.

ISBN 978-0-310-12144-2 (audio)

Library of Congress Cataloging-in-Publication Data
Names: Tracy, Steven R. author
Title: To heal or harm : scripture's use as poison or medicine for abuse survivors / Steven R. Tracy.
Description: Grand Rapids, Michigan : Zondervan Reflective, [2025] | Includes index.
Identifiers: LCCN 2025009566 (print) | LCCN 2025009567 (ebook) | ISBN 9780310121305 paperback | ISBN 9780310121312 ebook
Subjects: LCSH: Bible--Criticism, interpretation, etc. | Bible--Hermeneutics | Healing--Religious aspects--Christianity
Classification: LCC BS511.3 .T724 2025 (print) | LCC BS511.3 (ebook) | DDC 220.6--dc23/eng/20250801
LC record available at https://lccn.loc.gov/2025009566
LC ebook record available at https://lccn.loc.gov/2025009567

Cover design: Thinkpen Design
Cover photo and art: © FamGrafis / Shutterstock; Greg Jackson
Interior design: Kristen Sasamoto

Printed in the United States of America

25 26 27 28 29 30 TRM 6 5 4 3 2 1

To Celestia,
my soulmate, kingdom partner, and model
for suffering with grace and joy

CONTENTS

CONTENTS

PART 3: THE HEALING ROLE OF SCRIPTURE

FOREWORD

Every day, we wake up with a choice to make: to bring healing or harm to the world. This is one reason many of us begin our day reading and meditating on God's Word, which Dr. Steve Tracy calls "God's Magnificent Love Letter." This letter from above encourages and equips us, heals our sores, and renews us daily, while on the spiritual journey to our eternal home.

But reading Scripture is not enough in the effort to bring healing and not harm to the world. Grievously, there are far too many accounts of people, including Christian leaders, intentionally or unintentionally using the Scriptures in such a way that they cause harm. Such harm is even more grave when the recipients are victims of abuse. What is needed is a manual that will train us to read and apply Scripture rightly on this life-threatening subject. That is what you will find here in *To Heal or Harm: Scripture's Use as Poison or Medicine for Abuse Survivors.*

Dr. Tracy diagnoses the clinical problem of spiritual malpractice in which Scripture is misinterpreted and in turn causes further damage to victims of abuse. However, he does not leave it there. He puts on a clinic not simply on how Scripture is misused but also on how it is to be used properly in addressing various forms of abuse.

This exemplary work, which I believe God will use to bring incredible healing to people worldwide, reminds me of that Zondervan classic, *How to Read the Bible for All Its Worth* by Gordon Fee and Douglas Stuart. In this new Zondervan volume, one learns *how to read the Bible on the subject of abuse for all the victims' worth.* Those who have ears to hear will learn principles on how to rightly divide the Word of truth on the subject of abuse.

Dr. Tracy operates like a masterful surgeon using a scalpel to make precise incisions in order to bring healing. His practice stands in stark contrast to the manifold examples he judiciously and objectively presents of how Scripture has been misapplied like a dagger to bring much harm to abuse victims.

I have had the misfortune or good fortune, as the case might be, to witness various medical leaders treat my adult son Christopher, who endured a catastrophic brain injury several years ago. My entire family continues to suffer the aftereffects, including what I refer to as personal residual trauma. What I look for in a medical leader is someone who manifests clinical precision and compassionate care. It brings healing to my soul when I observe a doctor, nurse, or therapist treat my son holistically. The clinical and empathic, the objective and subjective dimensions, are equally essential to effective medical care.

The same is true in the spiritual realm. Fortunately, or providentially for us, Dr. Tracy operates holistically in his engagement of Scripture. Another way of putting it is that he proceeds chapter by chapter to clearly demonstrate the three main components of biblical and theological soundness: orthodoxy, orthopraxy, and orthopathy.

We evangelicals often give pride of place to *orthodoxy*—that is, right teaching. While vitally important, we also need to ensure adherence to *orthopraxy*—that is, right practice. Last but by no means least, though often neglected, is *orthopathy*—that is, right affection or passion. Just like the book's account of the Mayo Clinic doctor who treated Steve's wife and ministry partner Celestia, Steve manifests these qualities in tending to those in need of healing. A good medical doctor and a good biblical scholar both model competence, compassion, and courage to advocate for those entrusted to their care to ensure they get the necessary help.

So not only will you find in the pages that follow *how to read the Bible on the subject of abuse for all the victims' worth* (right teaching), but you will also find that the book in your hands or on your screen will help you learn *how to apply the Bible on the subject of abuse for all the victims' worth* (right practice). If that weren't enough, you will also find incredible attention given to the heart! In other words, you will learn *how to experience God's heart on the subject of abuse for all the victims' worth* (right passion).

By no means a fringe issue for a cottage industry, many of us will be amazed to find while reading *To Heal or Harm* that the Bible addresses the subject of abuse at great length. Similarly, we will likely be overwhelmed to find how often abuse occurs in the church, and similarly how often Scripture is used to shame and silence abuse victims. So Dr. Tracy's competence, compassion, and courage to address this critically important and timely subject will go a long way to equipping us to ensure that abuse victims are no longer relegated to the fringe or pushed out the church door.

I have already highlighted this book's treatment of victims' worth. "God's Magnificent Love Letter"—Scripture—goes to great lengths to show that society at large and religious communities in particular readily mistreat and devalue abuse victims. Similarly, from beginning to end in *To Heal or Harm*, including the strategically placed appendices, we will come away realizing how God's heart breaks for abuse victims, whom he so dearly loves. So, too, I pray we will come away wanting to join God's movement to accompany Jesus, the master physician, in restoring and healing broken hearts and lives by God's Spirit.

This work is the culmination of years of Dr. and Mrs. Tracy's painstaking, love-filled therapeutic work with Mending the Soul Ministries. Join the movement on how to read, apply, and experience God's heart on the subject of abuse for all the victims' worth.

Paul Louis Metzger, PhD,
author of *More Than Things: A Personalist Ethics for a Throwaway Culture*, Professor of Christian Theology & Theology of Culture, Multnomah Biblical Seminary/Jessup University

ACKNOWLEDGMENTS

In many respects this book is the culmination of decades of study of Scripture and interactions with trauma survivors. Thousands of people have played a role in the insights reflected in this book. In the 1980s and 1990s family and friends helped fund my seminary and PhD education, giving me knowledge and tools to interpret Scripture. While that training was decades ago, I will never cease to be grateful for their sacrificial support. Over three decades of teaching at Phoenix Seminary, my students have blessed me with their insights and hard questions, greatly sharpening my understanding of Scripture. But all the theological precision in the world is of very limited value unless it is applied to the real world we live in, a world filled with blood, tears, and scars. Thus, the thousands of abuse-trauma survivors with whom my wife, Celestia, and I have interacted and served have been the greatest imaginable blessing. Many of their stories and insights are recounted in this book. Words are inadequate to express my admiration for the survivors whom Celestia and I have gotten to love, here in the US and around the world. They model what it means to apply the promises of Scripture to hard, painful situations. Beloved Congolese brothers and sisters have particularly taught me what it means to stand on God's Word when your entire world is falling apart, you do not enjoy a single day without trauma or life threats, and you have nothing but Jesus and his word to cling to. Their faith has deepened my faith. I am more obedient to and trusting of Scripture due to their testimonies.

The staff and board of Mending the Soul ministries have been extremely supportive of this book project in numerous ways. Thank you. A special note of thanks goes to my beloved family. Our three children, in their own respective and very costly ways, have lived out numerous principles articulated in this book, particularly God's heart for those shattered by abuse. Elizabeth, Abby, and Luke, your lives and your love are an incredible source of joy. This book would have been much different without you in our lives. Most of all, I am grateful for Celestia, my life partner of almost fifty years. Other than the Congolese, I have hardly ever seen anyone cling as tenaciously to Jesus and to Scripture as you do. Your deep understanding of God's Word has taught me so much. I am exceedingly grateful for how you have taught me to stand on God's truth no matter what the price or the hard circumstances. You are my rock and my soulmate. The best is yet to come!

PROLOGUE

At the outset of this book, I want to acknowledge that I have been uniquely blessed and shielded. In light of my gender, theological training, and ministry-leadership history, I have rarely had Scripture weaponized against me. I have had a voice that was respected and listened to (sometimes much more than I deserved). I am painfully aware, however, that my experience is not shared by most Christians. Many of my spiritual brothers and especially my sisters have suffered deep, long-lasting wounds from distorted biblical interpretations. Their convictions have been chronically discounted and their voices silenced. They have been dogmatically told by others that God's Word teaches what it actually does not teach. And these rigid misinterpretations have crushed them. Cheryl is one of those women. I am grateful she has agreed to write this prologue. It gives a most helpful, real-life example of how God's Word can be distorted by the people and communities who appear to most revere Scripture. We will come back to Cheryl's story several times in this book.

I deeply respect Cheryl for her intimate walk with Jesus. It was actually her love for Jesus and respect for his Word that made her especially vulnerable to others' destructive distortions of Scripture. But there is much more to her story, including a beautiful, redemptive conclusion. I'll now let Cheryl recount her experience with Scripture—for harm and for healing.

CHERYL'S STORY

"If I want to find an abuser, I go to church!"

These words, emphatically stated by my attorney, Diana, hung in the air between us as I looked at her quizzically. Mumbling something incoherently, trying to manufacture a tepid defense of faith communities, I was nearly paralyzed at the bluntness—and sadly, the harsh truth—of her declaration.

I had come to Diana amid a painful separation from my husband, after leaving a marriage of more than twenty years filled with every form of abuse, including physical, emotional, verbal, financial, sexual, and spiritual. Raw from the trauma of decades of abuse and overwhelmed with the chaos created as my narcissistic husband raged against me and anyone who tried to help or protect me, Diana quickly became not only my legal advocate but also a friend. And she always, always called things as she saw them.

As hard as I tried to develop a response to Diana's bold assertion, I was both instantaneously aware of its accuracy and profoundly saddened at its legitimacy. In Diana's mind, her comment was supported by years of family law experience and helping clients like me. As she listened to the details of my husband's seminary training, participation in various church ministries, and insatiable hunger for leadership opportunities while simultaneously severely abusing me at home, she knew she had seen this scenario many times before in her lengthy legal career. Although the specifics of each case varied, the bottom line was the same—abusers used God and the Scriptures to justify inflicting the most abhorrent behaviors on their families. Diana shared stories with me of nameless clients and their abusers who, like my husband, tormented their spouses and then cloaked it under religiosity, as if God condoned it. One client was not just figuratively beaten with the Bible but physically pummeled with a giant hardcover volume, even while suffering from a severe, life-threatening illness. The horror of that imagery was inescapable.

Later, after my time with Diana and completing years of counseling, I would speak with other survivors or their caregivers either as a Mending the Soul (MTS) small-group facilitator or presenter at a live training. I often referred to my story as "The Tale of Two Redemptions," because God reached down not once but twice to release me from imprisonment. The first time he redeemed me was as a young child, from the captivity of my own personal sin into salvation through faith in his Son. The second time was as a forty-plus-year-old woman from the bondage of a destructive marriage to a malignant, narcissistic abuser.

You see, I was imprisoned in a marriage with a man who had systematically deconstructed my original God-given design through decades of abuse. He used his extensive study of Scripture to excuse and even justify the abuse. My husband served in various church positions (paid and volunteer) over many years. He received adulation from those who saw only his public persona and not the ugly, behind-closed-doors reality.

Abuse had been a part of my life from the earliest age, long before meeting my husband. My father's sexual abuse began well before I could speak. When I inadvertently disclosed the abuse at age seven, my mother temporarily kicked my dad out of the house. I felt responsible for the drama and fallout, assuming I had done something bad. When my mom allowed my dad to move back in after fake tears and promises of change, the abuse continued well into my teens. Amid this chaos, God redeemed me the first time.

For several years, he was my refuge and safety when life was scary. I felt his love and protection despite my home environment. That would soon change.

My mom ultimately gathered the courage to leave my dad when I was a teen. By that time, however, I was full of shame and experienced a warped view of God as my heavenly Father. Although I had deep gratitude for Christ's provision of salvation and held tenaciously to my faith, the early joy and comfort were overshadowed by a sense that God must have thought I deserved the abuse because he did not intervene to stop it. I began to feel wholly unlovable, worthless, and disgusting. I later learned that my abuse as a child would prove to be fertile ground for revictimization as an adult.

Before that, however, Satan was already hard at work, desensitizing me to spiritual abuse through an unhealthy church system that was extremely legalistic. Rules developed around "standards" supposedly required to conform to God's law and earn his favor. Verses were twisted to support toxic theology, and shaming was routinely used to enforce obedience to extrabiblical requirements. Compliance with spiritual authorities was mandatory and unquestioned. My own youth pastor, who was not an abuser and more of a dad to me than my own, corroborated the teachings even though his intent was not malicious. He used to teach me that when he said, "Jump!" I should say, "How high?" He quoted, "To obey is better than sacrifice," from 1 Samuel 15:22 as a reminder that we were to obey *him* as our spiritual leader. Practically cultic in nature, the church's senior pastor was viewed as God's human representative, and we were told to "not touch God's anointed" regardless of his private or public behavior.

Because of an inaccurate view of the fall of man and a manufactured theology focused on female submission, misogyny reigned in the community. Women were perceived as "less than" and more prone to wickedness. Wives were taught to be under the "umbrella of authority" and to be completely submissive even to the point of self-harm or hurt to their children, because God would ultimately reward them for their suffering. The church taught "no divorce for any reason" or for sexual infidelity only, and it was the wife's responsibility to preserve the marriage regardless of the cost because "God hates divorce."

It was in the youth group in this same church where, at age sixteen, I met and began dating my future husband who planned to be a pastor. Biblical distortions and cultlike thought indoctrination would define our relationship and continue to twist my view of God. Married at age nineteen, my husband's abuse began soon after the wedding, even though he was a seminary student preparing for ministry. Verbal and emotional abuse quickly escalated into physical and sexual abuse that became increasingly worse and more traumatic. Because of my natural tendency toward people-pleasing and compliance, combined with my traumatic childhood and church system, I made every effort to learn how to be a submissive and sacrificial wife.

Along with my husband's increasing "knowledge" of Scripture came profound pride and the belief that he must serve as priest and cultic intermediary for me, his "foolish and sinful" wife. He alone established my spiritual reality and convinced me that God honored his hypocrisy and malevolence when he determined it was "deserved" or there was "no other way to get through" to me. He said he could see why my father would choose to abuse me. My own sense of worthlessness motivated me to accept these statements as truth. After seminary we moved to Dallas, where my husband would work on two more theological degrees. The violence and sexual assaults escalated, accompanied by frequent emotional and verbal attacks. I was already showing signs of post-traumatic stress disorder. No opportunity to question or disagree with my husband existed. Despite regular instruction at church, personal Bible study, and two years of Bible college myself, I was frequently told that I did not know what I was talking about when approaching spiritual matters. My husband stated I had not learned the original languages as he did, that I was influenced by my unbelieving family or had been deceived by my "desperately wicked" heart, or was just plain "kooky."

He cleverly managed my perception of God and the Bible. When I shared verses that I thought were comforting or encouraging, I was told they were not meant for me. When I stated that I felt certain emotions during a disagreement or even a prompting of the Holy Spirit that diverged from my husband's opinion, I was instructed to give chapter and verse. If I could not, my concerns were derided and dismissed. If I offered a passage, I was told my interpretation was faulty. I was reminded that I had not studied Scripture as he had and therefore had no right to question his explanation or justification of his behaviors. Although I loved God intensely, God seemed as contradictory and scary to me as my abusers—occasionally loving but also frequently explosive, harsh, unpredictable, neglectful, and callous. His Word was not providing comfort to me but instead was ammunition for my abuser. I could not trust God and tried to remain under the radar.

After twenty-three years of abuse and trauma in the marriage, I carried out my expected duties but often moved through life vapidly as a member of the walking dead, both emotionally and spiritually. I distrusted that God ever really valued or cared about me as an individual. The reawakening to God began slowly in early 2008 as I timidly again entered the world emotionally as a result of participating in a Mending the Soul group and starting faith-based and trauma-informed counseling that included a healthy biblical philosophy. Like a limb experiencing blood flow after falling asleep, my whole life seemed painful and raw. I began facing the truth of what had happened during my childhood and marriage. Dreams disintegrated, fantasies dissolved, and waves of emotions surfaced that felt so overwhelming I could barely breathe. I feared I would not survive the upheaval.

God's presence in the process was unmistakable. Try as I might to dismiss or explain it away, God had again clearly directed my path to him through a series of extraordinary circumstances that I could not begin to engineer—circumstances that impacted me directly, only me. Even so, I resisted his love and fought against the messages he was giving me that I was valued and cherished by him. Just for who I was and just as I was. He accepted me, imperfections and all. He saw me. And he wanted me, not to hurt me, but because he treasured me.

Obeying God ultimately resulted in the need to separate from my hostile and unpredictable husband to ensure physical and emotional safety. My version of the story would have ended differently—my husband would have repented, stopped being abusive, and the marriage restored. My husband instead hardened his heart, and divorce followed. God continued to soften and heal my heart. Bit by bit, my image of God was transformed from that of a scary, sadistic, and vindictive punisher to that of a loving, compassionate father. I saw how my ex-husband's abuse and my sinful idolatry of him resulted in a shallow and distant relationship with the Lord. I learned that God did not need my perfection but wanted my heart. I placed the sins of idolatry, people-pleasing, and perfectionism on the altar and began to rest in his shalom.

As my knowledge and understanding of God grew, so did my desire to know him more. For the first time, I craved time in his Word and prayer and couldn't get enough. Realizing the depths of his grace has taken my relationship with him to a level deeper than I have ever experienced in all of my Christian life. In this process, I realized that God loved me and did not view me as a big mistake or a waste of perfectly good DNA. Despite a lifetime of abuse, he had protected my original design that my ex-husband worked so hard to destroy and that I came to hate. I learned that God not only saw value in me but actually cherished me.

God has given me life again, along with hope, joy, and peace.

Several years later, God brought into my life the exquisite gift of a loving and caring husband who has been a healing balm to my children and me. He and I will soon celebrate five years of marriage and are savoring the delights of grandparenting together.

In the chapters to follow, Dr. Tracy unpacks the role and power of Scripture and contrasts the harmful use and misuse of God's Word with its intended healing use. May the Holy Spirit illuminate your mind and heart while reading this book, and may you know that your commitment to truth and growth will help others experience the healing power of God.

Cheryl M. C., abuse survivor
Chandler, Arizona

INTRODUCTION

Perhaps you can relate to some portions of Cheryl's story. Even if you did not experience the malevolence and harm she suffered, chances are you have been harmed in one way or another by the misuse of Scripture. In fact, virtually all of us have at some time been given (or created) erroneous interpretations of God's Word. Many of these flawed readings are generated by non-abusers with good motives. Regardless of the character and motives of those who misconstrue Scripture, misreadings can cause great harm. Only when God's Word is properly interpreted can it consistently be a source of life and health. Hence, my goal in this book is to give the reader, particularly laypeople who lack formal theological training, a template for correctly interpreting Scripture for themselves. To further this goal, I will apply key interpretive principles to various biblical passages most commonly misused against survivors. Additionally, I will survey key passages that are most helpful for survivors, passages that are more often overlooked than misread. I deeply desire my audience to confidently form and live out their own biblical convictions. While laypeople are my primary audience, pastors are a close second. After three decades of training pastors, I have found that most of them fervently desire to interpret Scripture faithfully and shepherd their flocks well. But as I myself experienced over fifteen years of pastoral service, Scripture and abuse can be complex. With the best of intentions one can misread Scripture and harm the vulnerable people entrusted to one's spiritual care. I pray that this book will guide pastors in understanding and applying critical biblical texts to their congregations.

The book is organized into three parts. Part one lays the foundation for the rest of the book by overviewing the nature and richness of Scripture and then giving six foundational principles for sound biblical interpretation. Part two surveys key biblical texts most commonly misused against survivors. These texts are organized topically, with a chapter devoted to each topic: passages on marriage, children, the church, abuse victims, and spiritual life. We will look at how key biblical texts have been misused and then discover what those texts do and don't mean. We will not simply look at how these texts have been harmfully misused but will also see how the biblical passages are applicable to and helpful for survivors. Part three surveys key biblical texts and themes that are most helpful for abuse survivors' protection and healing. Part three is organized into three chapters: God's response to abuse; God's mandate to protect the vulnerable and care for the abused, and God's commitment to heal, redeem, and restore. Finally, I have included two appendices to provide additional practical resources. From ancient times to the present, women have often been viewed as inferior and thus are not treated with the dignity and value they deserve as image bearers of God. Thus, I provide a concise biblical overview of the value and dignity of women. We have found this to be a very helpful teaching tool in our trainings. The second appendix catalogues some of the most common lies believed by abuse survivors, along with some of the most helpful biblical truths to counter these lies. At the end of the book, you will find extensive endnotes. Out of respect for you, my readers, lay and specialists alike, I wanted to thoroughly document my sources and provide suggestions for additional resources. Since I have given examples of what I consider erroneous interpretations, I want my readers to be able to assess for themselves whether I have fairly cited and summarized the views of others.

Finally, it might be helpful for me to give a brief explanation of our ministry. Several times in the book I refer to "Mending the Soul" (MTS). This is the Christian nonprofit God led Celestia and me to launch in 2003 when we were overwhelmed at the lack of biblically and psychologically integrated resources to help abuse survivors and their caregivers. It has been one of our greatest joys to bring Celestia's psychological training and twenty years of professional counseling experience and my pastoral experience and academic training together to create resources we ourselves lacked in our early ministry years. The stories in this book have primarily come from our own experiences with abuse survivors and are based on actual events. In many instances I have changed various details to protect the anonymity of those involved. In some cases, stories are composites of two or more actual events.

May God use this work to decontaminate biblical passages that have been poisoned against you and allow you to experience more of the beauty and healing power of Scripture. To that end, let's now explore the beauty and character of Scripture in the following chapter.

Part 1

THE ROLE AND POWER OF SCRIPTURE

Chapter 1

THE RICHNESS OF SCRIPTURE

God's Magnificent Love Letter

Within the Scripture there is a balm for
every wound, a salve for every sore.
—CHARLES H. SPURGEON

The Holy Scriptures are our letters from home.
—AUGUSTINE OF HIPPO

The law of the LORD is perfect,
refreshing the soul.
The statutes of the LORD are trustworthy,
making wise the simple.
The precepts of the LORD are right,
giving joy to the heart.
The commands of the LORD are radiant,
giving light to the eyes. . . .
They are more precious than gold,
than much pure gold;
they are sweeter than honey,
than honey from the honeycomb.
—PSALM 19:7–8, 10

Yosemite National Park is no stranger to danger. Yet the discovery of the bodies of three family members—a father, mother, and baby—along with the family dog in August of 2021 was particularly troubling. There were no obvious signs of what led to their mysterious deaths on the Savage Lundy Trail. Speculation ranged from foul play to a lightning strike, exposure to poisonous gases from abandoned mines, illegal drug use, or poisoning by toxic algae blooms. Several months after their bodies were found, authorities unraveled the mystery. The family had died of dehydration and hyperthermia. They had set out to hike a dusty trail with little shade on a particularly hot day. They simply ran out of water, resulting in tragedy.

Water is essential to human life. We cannot live without it. Paradoxically, this critical, life-giving resource is often a source of death. According to the World Health Organization, water-related diseases are one of the leading causes of illness and death, particularly for children. For example, in 2017, 220 million people required treatment for schistosomiasis, an acute and chronic disease caused by waterborne parasitic worms. We need water to live, but the water we drink can kill or maim us. What a dilemma! So it is with Scripture. God's Word is essential for a vibrant spiritual life. Scripture is a lamp for our feet and a light for our path (Ps 119:105). It brings peace and protects us (Ps 119:165). It is worth more than gold and sweeter than honey (Ps 19:10). Yet this essential resource can fill us with disease and, given enough time, destroy us.

Scripture warns of people who destructively "distort" the Scriptures (2 Pet 3:16). Perhaps the starkest example of Scripture twisting, which could have had disastrous consequences, is the temptation of Jesus recorded in Matthew 4:1–10. Three times Satan came to Jesus and repeatedly quoted (misquoted) Scripture to tempt Jesus. We should note, of course, that each time Jesus responded with Scripture, again showing how powerful and life-giving Scripture is when properly applied. So, the crux of the issue is this: How can we properly understand and apply Scripture so that it becomes soul medicine instead of heart poison? In this chapter, we will survey the richness of Scripture so that we can better appreciate its power and beauty. This will prepare us for the next chapter, which will guide us in correctly interpreting Scripture.

THE CHALLENGE OF TRUSTING

When I was ten years old, my family drove to Yellowstone National Park. We were excited to see rugged mountains and stunning meadows full of wild animals. While our family shared many memorable days together, we also shared something else—a flu virus that passed from person to person throughout the entire trip. To this day, over fifty years later, I vividly remember enjoying my favorite dessert one evening after dinner—a frosty strawberry shake—and a few hours later, losing that tasty shake because of the violent onslaught of the flu. While I thankfully recovered in just a couple of days, it was many years before I again wanted a strawberry shake. The mere thought of a strawberry shake made my stomach flip-flop. I had developed a visceral aversion to my favorite drink. After all, that drink was innately, with little or no intellectual analysis on my part, linked to a miserable sickness. I shied away from shakes and refused to drink them. In somewhat similar ways, since all abuse survivors have experienced tremendous pain from what people have done to them, they often come to distrust others in subtle and complex ways. Social scientists have found that childhood abuse (all forms) is associated with increased levels of distrust and a diminished ability to discern those who are trustworthy.[1]

Similarly, adult abuse trauma often results in an exaggerated distrust of others. This seems to be the dynamic at play in Psalm 116, a thanksgiving psalm occasioned by an unidentified threat to the psalmist's life ("The cords of death entangled me, the anguish of the grave came over me," v. 3). The writer goes on to confess "in my alarm I said, 'Everyone is a liar'" (v. 11). Actually, not everyone is a lying, untrustworthy scoundrel. But in the midst of life threats, that is how this psalmist felt.

The superscription of Psalm 142 indicates that it is a psalm of David written when he was hiding in a cave from his pursuers. The psalm again indicates that it was written in a time of life-threatening trauma ("rescue me from those who pursue me, for they are too strong for me," v. 6). Most commentators believe this refers to David hiding in the cave of Adullam or En Gedi, recorded in 1 Samuel 22 and 24. In this psalm David again declares "no one is concerned for me . . . no one cares for my life" (Ps 142:4). But the two biblical accounts of David hiding in caves reveal that he had *not* been abandoned by all his peers. Others *did* care about him, and some *were* trustworthy. In the incident at the cave of Adullam, as soon as David escaped to the cave "his brothers and his father's household heard about it," and "they went down to him there" (1 Sam 22:1). He had actually not been abandoned but had trustworthy family members joining him. Likewise, in the cave of En Gedi, David was not alone, as some of his men were in the cave with him (1 Sam 24:3). Furthermore, when King Saul entered, David's men were ready to attack Saul on his behalf (1 Sam 24:7). In both instances, David had trustworthy people in his life, but apparently the abuse trauma he had experienced had eroded his basic trust in others. In short, Psalm 142 accurately records David's feelings of being deserted by everyone around him, though the biblical account of David's life suggests he hadn't been abandoned. David, like most trauma survivors, struggled to trust others. To begin to address abuse survivors' struggles to trust the voice of God found in Scripture, we need to survey the nature of Scripture.

THE NATURE OF SCRIPTURE

In my junior year of college, Celestia and I were separated the entire academic year. We were deeply in love and committed to advancing our relationship—long distance, sight unseen. This was the 1970s, decades before cell phones and the internet were invented. So we communicated the old-fashioned way—by writing letters. Every day we were apart we wrote a love letter to each other. Those daily epistles were my lifeline to a girl I dearly loved but couldn't see or touch. Her letters, covering an endless variety of topics, assured me of her love for me and kept deepening my understanding and appreciation of her. So it is with our Creator, the lover of our souls. He has given us his Word, the Bible, to speak to us, to deepen our understanding of him and the world he has created, and to deepen our intimacy with him. Let's now unpack the nature and intent of Scripture.

Inspiration

Historically the Bible has been considered a "holy book" by Jews and Christians. In the Mishnah, an ancient collection of rabbinic oral traditions, the Hebrew Scriptures are said to be unique for they "defile the hands" (by virtue of their holiness in contrast to human sinfulness), unlike other respected books.[2] Christians, through the centuries, have referred to the Bible as the "Holy Bible." Where did the idea of the Bible being holy come from? The Bible actually describes itself this way. In 2 Timothy 3:16–17 the apostle Paul asserts that "all Scripture is God-breathed and is useful for teaching, rebuking, correcting and training in righteousness, so that the servant of God may be thoroughly equipped for every good work." The Greek word Paul uses here for Scripture is *graphē*, from which we get the English word *graphic*, which refers to that which is expressed by writing. In ancient secular Greek literature *graphē* had a general meaning of "that which is written." But in the New Testament *graphē* has an exclusive technical meaning of "sacred Scripture."[3] The language Paul uses in 2 Timothy 3:16 to describe Scripture is very telling, for he says it is *theopneustos*, literally "God-breathed." In 2 Peter 1:20–21 we find a similar, more detailed explanation of the nature and origin of Scripture. Peter says that "no prophecy of Scripture came about by the prophet's own interpretation of things. For prophecy never had its origin in the human will, but prophets, though human, spoke from God as they were carried along by the Holy Spirit."[4] In other words, Scripture has two authors, divine and human, with the former (the Holy Spirit) guiding and carrying along the latter. While authored by humans, Scripture is ultimately authored by God himself. It is an authentic message from our Creator. *Scripture isn't just a collection of books about God; it is a book from God.* It is his love letter to us.

This helps explain why over and over Scripture itself claims to be an authentic message from God. Over and over the Scriptures declare "God says," "the Lord says," etc. The writers of Scripture understood that when the humans wrote Scripture, God was speaking through them. For instance, Hebrews 1:5–12 describes things spoken in the Old Testament by David, the sons of Korah, and other psalmists as having been spoken by "God."[5] Peter describes Paul's writings as "Scripture" (2 Pet 3:15–16). Paul, in 1 Timothy 5:18, quotes Luke 10:7 and calls it "Scripture." Furthermore, Jesus calls the Old Testament writings the "Scriptures."[6] The biblical authors repeatedly indicated they knew their message was the Word of God. For instance, in 1 Corinthians 14:37 Paul states, "If anyone thinks they are a prophet or otherwise gifted by the Spirit, let them acknowledge that what I am writing to you is the Lord's command."[7] In short, when we read the Bible, we are not just reading a great literary work. We are reading the very words of God. It is his sacred word to us.

Authority

Authority is the right and power to command obedience. Authority can be delegated or inherent. My junior high math teacher's authority was delegated (she was a meek pushover but still had the authority to send us to the office and to determine our grades). My junior high PE teacher's authority was inherent (he was big and scary). Christ's earthly authority was delegated from the Father (John 8:28, 54; 14:10), but he also had inherent authority due to his relationship with the Father (Matt 7:28–29; Luke 4:36; 8:24–25). So the Scriptures have derived authority since they come from, and point to, God (2 Tim 3:16–17; 2 Pet 1:19–21), but they also have inherent authority as God's appointed self-disclosure. Hebrews 4:12 affirms the inherent authority of Scripture: "For the word of God is alive and active. Sharper than any double-edged sword, it penetrates even to dividing soul and spirit, joints and marrow; it judges the thoughts and attitudes of the heart." While the Bible is literature, it is not like any other book. It has unique power and a uniquely authoritative voice. Thus, it is the supreme authority to continually direct our life. As Psalm 119:9–10 states, "How can a young person stay on the path of purity? By living according to your word. I seek you with all my heart; do not let me stray from your commands."

It is important to recognize that Scripture stands supreme over every human authority (religious, domestic, political, etc.). This is a particularly powerful principle for abuse survivors since they have experienced, in some way or another, the abuse of human authority. I can't begin to count the number of stories I've heard about abusive authority figures—husbands, teachers, pastors, parents, etc.—making declarations and commands that were as unbiblical as they were harmful. I vividly remember a charismatic pastor in the northwest. He planted a church that quickly grew into a dynamic and trendy organization. He was publicly praised for his dynamic leadership and effective mentoring. However, for those who stayed in ministry with him, they came to see a very dark underbelly. This pastor controlled and dominated his congregation, dictating every aspect of church life and of his individual congregant's lives. For instance, he pressured individuals to quit their jobs to move close to the church because that was the "godly" thing to do. He counseled husbands to rule their wives in a heavy-handed manner, directing matters big and small in their marriages. He reveled in "knowing" what God's will was for their lives and frequently told them so, demanding that they obey his spiritual authority. After a few years of his spiritually abusive leadership, the church was in upheaval and eventually split.

Years later, many of those young couples were still disillusioned and deeply wounded. When Celestia and I counseled those whose lives had been shattered by this spiritually abusive pastor, it was quickly apparent that most of them had been deceptively manipulated into assigning all biblical interpretation over to this pastor.

He had conditioned them to believe he was the ultimate benevolent authority in their lives. His opinions and declarations trumped their own convictions and understandings; he alone knew the "correct" meaning of Scripture.

This is precisely when the authority of Scripture is such a powerful, corrective truth. Scripture stands over all other human authority. While God has established human authorities (e.g., Rom 13:1–2; 1 Pet 5:5), they are always penultimate. God's voice, expressed through his Word, must always be *the* final authority in our lives. In Jesus's day, the scribes, Pharisees, and Sadducees were the reigning spiritual authorities. Pharisees were particularly scrupulous in their interpretations of the Hebrew Scriptures. Some New Testament scholars believe the word "Pharisee" comes from a Hebrew word meaning "the specifiers"—that is, those who had the correct, most precise understanding of God's Word.[8] They prided themselves on their knowledge of Scripture and developed extensive traditions regarding the meaning and application of Scripture. While Jesus affirmed some of their beliefs, such as the resurrection (Matt 22:23–33), he staunchly rejected many others, refusing to accept teachings and traditions he knew went against Scripture (Mark 7:1–13). Likewise, the apostles were commanded by the Sanhedrin, the most authoritative Jewish body, not to teach about Jesus. In response, they confidently declared, "We must obey God rather than men" (Acts 5:29 ESV). And so must we, regardless of how dogmatic those human voices are.

For those who have experienced spiritual abuse and have had Scripture weaponized against them, the sacredness and authority of Scripture may offer more terror than comfort. So it is important that we further clarify the nature of sacred Scripture. It is a divine love letter! After spending decades in the evangelical church, I've seen Scripture most frequently perceived as a rule book or a theological manual. Scripture does contain a wealth of theological truth, and it is an authoritative message from God regarding moral behavior. I am convinced, however, that Scripture first and foremost is a love letter from God himself. Lest you're tempted to roll your eyes over such a description, let me tell you why I use this description.

Divine Intent—Restoration

By *love letter* I am describing the *divine intent* of Scripture—to communicate God's message to fallen humans in order that they might experience blessing through restored relationship with him. From Genesis to Revelation, the Bible is a book of divinely initiated redemption. It proclaims restoration of the shalom (wholeness, health, flourishing, perfection) that was shattered by the fall (Gen 3). Immediately after Adam and Eve rebelled, God offered unexpected hope. Genesis 3:15 declares that the seed of the woman (Jesus) would crush the head of the serpent (Satan). And a few verses later we get our first glimpse into the costliness of redemption and the restoration it would bring. Despite Adam and Eve's failure to own their rebellion, God graciously eases their shame by providing animal-skin garments to cover their nakedness (Gen 3:21). Blood had been shed on their behalf. Eden had been shattered, but God was already working to redeem and restore. The rest of Scripture develops this theme, from God calling and establishing a covenant with Abraham so that through him and his descendants all people on the earth would be blessed (Gen 12:3), to the covenant with David, through whom God promised to establish an eternal kingdom (2 Sam 7:12–16), to the coming of Christ, the descendant of David who would redeem, deliver, and restore, guiding "our feet into the path of peace" (Luke 1:79). In other words, Christ came to restore all that had been broken and lost in the fall. This restoration culminates at the return of Christ with the establishment of the new heavens and new earth, in which all things will become new, complete perfection will be established, and God will dwell intimately with his people for all eternity (Rev 21–22).[9] Yes, the Bible is a holy book written by a holy God. And, shockingly, that holy God initiated a most costly plan to redeem fallen humans and restore everything lost in the fall. This holy God loved us before we loved him (Rom 5:8; 1 John 4:19). He desires to bless, redeem, and restore. It is worth noting here that the biblical passage most frequently alluded to in the Bible itself is Exodus 34:6–7a: "The LORD, the LORD, the compassionate and gracious God, slow to anger, abounding in love and faithfulness, maintaining love to thousands, and forgiving wickedness, rebellion and sin."[10]

Restoration summarizes the overarching message of Scripture. This is important for abuse survivors to understand because they are typically filled with shame and develop (with the "help" of their abusers) distorted perceptions of Scripture and of themselves, believing the core message of Scripture is judgment and divine anger. One helpful and concise statement of this overarching theme of restoration is by Michael Goheen and Craig Bartholomew in *The True Story of the Whole World: Finding Your Place in the Biblical Drama*.[11] They write, "While justly angry, God did not turn away from a world bent on destruction but turned his face to it in love. With patience and tender care the Lord set out on the long road of redemption to reclaim the lost as his people and the world as his kingdom."[12]

Blessings

Once we recognize Scripture as God's love letter to redeem and restore, we can better understand the beautiful ways Scripture describes itself. For instance, Psalm 119, the longest chapter in the Bible, offers by far the most detailed description of Scripture (170 of the 176 verses of this psalm explicitly refer to Scripture). It is composed of twenty-two stanzas of eight verses each. Using an acrostic in which the first verse of each line starts with the same letter of the Hebrew alphabet (in ascending sequence through the

22 stanzas), the psalmist praises God by noting the beauty and blessing of God's Word. The author uses eight different Hebrew words for Scripture. You may notice that many of these words—"law," "commands," "precepts," "decrees"—have a somewhat negative connotation in our culture. They signify what you can't do, have, or experience. They implicitly impugn. But this dour connotation is the opposite of the biblical author's perspective. He boldly, repeatedly proclaims God's Word as a source of stupendous, rich blessings. Derek Kidner is spot-on in titling Psalm 119 "the rich and precious jewel" of Scripture.[13] The summary result of zealously following Scripture is identified in the first two verses of the chapter—blessing (Ps 119:1–2).[14] "Blessed are those whose ways are blameless, / who walk according to the law of the LORD. / Blessed are those who keep his statutes / and seek him with all their heart." The blessings of Scripture are then unpacked over the following 174 verses. The author of Psalm 119 notes so many different blessings of Scripture that they are challenging to catalog. Scripture, when lived out,[15] results in life (vv. 144, 159), comfort (vv. 50, 76), freedom (v. 45), liberation (v. 133), strength (v. 81), peace (v. 165), knowledge and good judgment (v. 66), wisdom (v. 98), light (v. 105), guidance (v. 130), moral victory (v. 9), and removal of shame (vv. 6, 39).

Is it any wonder that the psalmist declares God's Word an invaluable treasure (Ps 119:162), sweeter than honey (v. 103), and a source of great delight (v. 16)? Satan, however, fiercely resists this message. He cunningly strategizes to get us to believe the same lie that Eve fell for in the garden of Eden—namely, that God's Word can't be trusted because he really doesn't have our best interest at heart. If obeyed, his commands will cause us to experience a diminished life.[16] Actually, the very opposite is true. God's Word reflects his desire to bless us. Satan wants us to doubt and disobey God's Word in order to destroy us. As Jesus declared, "The thief comes only to steal and kill and destroy; I have come that they may have life, and have it to the full" (John 10:10).

It is absolutely essential to understand God's Word, including his commands, in terms of God's desire to bless us. Cornelius Plantinga, in *Not the Way It's Supposed to Be*, one of the best books in print on the doctrine of sin, brilliantly makes this connection. He starts by asserting that God's desire for creation is best understood through the concept of shalom. Sin violates not just the character of God but shalom itself. Plantinga says:

> In the Bible, shalom means *universal flourishing, wholeness, and delight*—a rich state of affairs in which natural needs are satisfied and natural gifts fruitfully employed, a state of affairs that inspires joyful wonder as its Creator and Savior opens doors and welcomes the creatures in whom he delights. Shalom, in other words, is the way things ought to be.
>
> God hates sin not just because it violates his law but, more substantively, because it violates shalom, because it breaks the peace, because it interferes with the way things are supposed to be. (Indeed, that is why God has laws against a good deal of sin.) God is for shalom and *therefore* against sin.[17]

God's Word is the only path to shalom, which brings us back to the dilemma experienced by survivors. How can you trust the Word of God when it was weaponized against you to perpetrate, rationalize, or minimize abuse? Given the all-too-common practice of church leaders failing to protect the abused while defending abusers, one might reasonably assume that the Bible must be poisonous and therefore not to be trusted. Thankfully, this is not the case; Scripture has much to say about and to faith leaders who abuse their power. Before we move on, let's briefly mention a few essential truths regarding abuse and Scripture.

Abuse and Scripture

Scripture Addresses All Forms of
Abuse in Hundreds of Passages

Unhealthy families (biological and spiritual) enact "codes of silence." They tenaciously refuse to acknowledge or address painful, costly issues such as abuse. It is stunning to see a family ignore a grandfather's lewd jokes and inappropriate touches or a Christian school sweep abuse allegations against one of their teachers under the rug. Even more shocking is the number of churches that refuse to protect victims instead of one of their own who is perpetrating the abuse. This travesty of justice is intolerable and does more damage than we can possibly quantify. And if abuse is *not* addressed by the very churches that claim Scripture to be God's inerrant, authoritative Word, it implies that Scripture must have little or nothing to say about abuse.

Over the past decade, I've polled thousands of seminary students and conference attendees, asking how many have heard a single sermon or Sunday School lesson on domestic violence or physical abuse. While physical abuse is the category of abuse addressed most in Scripture, I have never had more than 7 percent of a group of Christians say they have heard a single sermon on physical abuse or domestic violence—*not one.* Typically, it's less than 5 percent of the audience, even though there are hundreds of passages excoriating physical abuse. *How can this be?*

The characteristics of physical abusers and the effects of their abuse receive extensive treatment in Scripture.[18] God also acknowledges and condemns sexual abuse in explicit detail in numerous passages. For instance, Genesis 19:4–5 describes attempted male gang rape; Genesis 34 records the rape of Dinah by a foreign prince; 2 Samuel 11 chronicles the power rape of Bathsheba by King David; 2 Samuel 13 gives a detailed account of the incestuous rape of Tamar by her brother; Judges 19 traces the fatal gang rape of a Levite's concubine by village men. In addition, numerous passages address verbal and spiritual abuse as well as neglect.

While churches and families struggle to address abuse, God's Word does not. And the Bible's frankness in addressing abuse makes it a most compelling resource for survivors.

Scripture Offers Unique, Life-Giving Instruction to Abuse Survivors

Many well-known and loved passages of Scripture were written in the context of abuse in order to encourage and guide survivors. For instance, Psalm 119, which we just reviewed, was written in a context of abuse and threat. "Though rulers sit together and slander me, your servant will meditate on your decrees. Your statutes are my delight; they are my counselors" (vv. 23–24).[19] In other words, when human voices are untrustworthy and abusive, God's voice in Scripture becomes particularly precious and powerful. The psalmist's declaration of the beauty and blessing of God's Word was not written from an ivory tower by a sleepy and detached theologian but by an abuse survivor grappling with the pain and trauma of life threats, destructive slander, and persecution. God's Word was an essential resource for abuse survivors in ancient Israel, as it is for survivors in twenty-first-century America.

Scripture Acknowledges and Harshly Condemns Abuse

Scripture severely denounces abuse in all segments of society, especially in communities of faith. Surveys of Christian women who have experienced domestic violence reveal that what these women most want from the church is: (1) the church's recognition that violence against women and children is a problem even in the church; (2) a straightforward condemnation of domestic violence from the pulpit. Scripture's acknowledgment and condemnation of abuse serves as a tremendous validation to survivors. Let's look at a few examples.

To build a case that all humans are sinful and therefore need a Savior, the apostle in his letter to the Romans asserts that physical and verbal abuse is universal and widespread in the human race. Citing several different Old Testament texts, Paul specifically argues that

> Jews and Gentiles alike are all under the power of sin. As it is written: "There is no one righteous, not even one.". . . "Their throats are open graves; their tongues practice deceit." "The poison of vipers is on their lips." "Their mouths are full of cursing and bitterness." "Their feet are swift to shed blood; ruin and misery mark their ways, and the way of peace they do not know." (Rom 3:9–10, 13–17)

Logically, based on Paul's line of reasoning, to deny the prevalence of abuse and resultant suffering throughout all cultures is to implicitly question universal sinfulness and the need for Christ's sacrifice. In other words, abuse is a primary and essential biblical topic. You cannot deny or minimize abuse without minimizing and denying biblical teaching. Scripture gives multiple examples of abuse perpetrated by men, women, Jews, gentiles, priests, princes, kings, soldiers, and commoners. Numerous passages of Scripture give candid accounts of abusive spiritual leaders, including the patriarch Abraham, his wife Sarah, King David, and various Hebrew priests and prophets.[20] One of the stated qualifications for a church elder is that he is not an abuser (1 Tim 3:3). Not only does the Bible candidly acknowledge the prevalence of abuse, but it soundly condemns it.

Scripture declares that God detests abuse and unrepentant abusers (Ps 5:5–6; 11:5). For instance, not only did God strike the abusive sons of Eli dead (1 Sam 2:16–17, 22, 25; 4:17), he also killed

Eli for not stopping their blasphemous abuse (1 Sam 3:13). Some of Jesus's harshest words are directed to those who harm children: "If anyone causes one of these little ones—those who believe in me—to stumble, it would be better for them to have a large millstone hung around their neck and to be drowned in the depths of the sea" (Matt 18:6). Jesus also had incredibly harsh words for faith leaders who manipulate the Scriptures to spiritually abuse those in their care:

> Woe to you, teachers of the law and Pharisees, you hypocrites! You shut the door of the kingdom of heaven in people's faces. You yourselves do not enter, nor will you let those enter who are trying to. (Matt 23:13)

> Woe to you, teachers of the law and Pharisees, you hypocrites! You are like whitewashed tombs, which look beautiful on the outside but on the inside are full of the bones of the dead and everything unclean. In the same way, on the outside you appear to people as righteous but on the inside you are full of hypocrisy and wickedness. (Matt 23:27–28)
> *You snakes! You brood of vipers! How will you escape being condemned to hell? (Matt 23:33)*

While it is tragic in our post #MeToo society that abuse continues to be ignored and condoned in all sectors of society, God's Word unequivocally and repeatedly acknowledges and condemns it. And this recognition and condemnation is a great aid to abuse survivors.

Scripture Gives Robust Guidance and Tools for Survivors
Almost half of the 150 psalms are lament psalms in which the writer cries out in his pain to God—and most of the time, that pain was caused by abusers. The lament psalms offer a template for how to honestly pray to God when your heart is breaking from abuse,

particularly when God doesn't seem to be answering your prayers (Pss 13; 74). Most of the time victims suffer while perpetrators abuse with apparent impunity (Pss 10; 73). The lament psalms are meant to be used in various settings. They are categorized as individual and communal, and they can be used for personal healing and in group settings when an entire organization or church or people group has experienced abuse.[21] Lament is one of many powerful biblical resources for those in pain.

Scripture Cannot Be Legitimately Used to Justify Abuse or to Condemn Victims

Scripture repeatedly decries the misuse of power by abusers (e.g., Eccl 4:1–3; Mic 2:1–2) and highlights God's delight in justice and mercy for their victims. God is the one who "executes justice for the oppressed" (Ps 146:7 ESV). He is a "father to the fatherless, a defender of widows" (Ps 68:5). Toward those who "oppress the poor and needy and mistreat the foreigner, denying them justice" God declares, "I will pour out my wrath on them and consume them with my fiery anger, bringing down on their own heads all they have done" (Ezek 22:29, 31).

Tragically, the robust biblical teaching on justice and mercy for the abused is often ignored or denied by evangelicals. *This perverts God's truth and poisons his Word.* Several years ago, I was contacted by a professor at Arizona State University who asked if I would participate in a public forum on abortion. There would be two pro-life and two pro-choice speakers. I agreed to speak and prepared a thirty-minute presentation titled "Abortion, the Marginalized, and the Vulnerable: A Social Justice Perspective for Reducing Abortion."[22] The room was crowded, and for the most part the interaction was respectful and enlightening. (The university hired armed guards to attend the event, anticipating that this volatile topic might elicit hostile reactions from attenders.) I packed as much as possible into my allotted half hour, drawing from robust biblical teaching on the reality of abuse and oppression and the moral imperative of extending justice and mercy to the vulnerable, the born and the unborn. After the forum concluded, the professor who had organized the event came and thanked me for my presentation. While I appreciated her gracious comments, it is customary to thank speakers, so it wasn't unexpected. Her following comments, however, stopped me in my tracks. She lowered her voice and stated, "I grew up in the church. I was in youth group every week. But when I started asking what the Bible says about poverty, oppression, and justice, I was shamed and told I was a terrible Christian to ask such questions. I left the church decades ago and have never been back. *But if I had heard the kind of presentation you gave tonight on biblical justice and mercy, I might never have left the church.*" Her comments were heartbreaking. And her treatment by church leaders was inexcusable. Scripture repeatedly decries the misuse of power by abusers and highlights God's delight in justice and mercy for their victims.

Clarity

Books on the theology of Scripture typically include the doctrine of the "clarity of Scripture." Ironically, theologians often call this doctrine the "perspicuity of Scripture." I have to chuckle that theologians use a term like *perspicuity*, which many people don't clearly understand, to say that the Bible is clearly understandable. Regardless, let's start with what *clarity* doesn't mean before moving on to what it does mean. The clarity of Scripture doesn't mean that all of Scripture is equally clear and easy to interpret. After all, Peter acknowledged that some of Paul's epistles "contain some things that are hard to understand, which ignorant and unstable people distort" (2 Pet 3:16). Nor does the clarity of Scripture mean that one can come to any biblical text and immediately understand it. In 2 Timothy 2:15 Paul commanded Timothy to "be diligent to present yourself approved to God as a worker who does not need to be ashamed, accurately handling the word of truth" (NASB). Properly interpreting Scripture requires diligent effort. So what does the clarity of Scripture mean? In a nutshell, it means that the truths needed for salvation and living a godly life are sufficiently clear in Scripture for all to understand and follow. This implies that Scripture is for all people; it is not reserved for the educated or the intellectuals. Scripture is sufficiently clear to be taught to children (Deut 6:4–7). It can make "wise the simple" (Ps 19:7). The big picture of Scripture is not hidden but clear and accessible to all who will receive it. The clarity of Scripture should give us great encouragement to come to God's Word, knowing that God's message is available to us. It is not remote and esoteric. God wants to speak to us. His Word gives us a clear voice to follow. This encouraging truth was articulated by Moses, as he sought to guide the often-straying Israelites:

> Now what I am commanding you today is not too difficult for you or beyond your reach. It is not up in heaven, so that you have to ask, "Who will ascend into heaven to get it and proclaim it to us so we may obey it?" Nor is it beyond the sea, so that you have to ask, "Who will cross the sea to get it and proclaim it to us so we may obey it?" No, the word is very near you; it is in your mouth and in your heart so you may obey it. (Deut 30:11–14)

CONCLUSION

Forty-five years ago, I married Celestia, my high-school sweetheart and girl of my dreams. I thank God daily for her. She is one of the godliest and most compassionate women I have ever met. She is truly one of God's favorites. (If that sounds audacious, consider the fact that no less than five times in his Gospel the apostle John called himself the disciple whom Jesus "loved"; see John 13:23; 19:26; 20:2; 21:7, 20.) Celestia's relationship with Jesus is deeply intimate. She knows she is God's beloved. She talks to God and hears from him as very few I've ever known. And she powerfully blesses those around her, particularly those who are hurting.

Yesterday, as I get to do often, I observed her skillfully guiding and consoling our African staff, who were suffering overwhelming secondary trauma after witnessing another unimaginable child-abuse case. Ironically, Celestia's spiritual wholeness and vibrancy have come through brokenness and pain. Early in our marriage when I was still in seminary and we were newly minted parents, she had a catastrophic skiing accident in which she shattered her left arm. Bone debris and breaks had annihilated her elbow and erased the normal nerve channels connecting her hand function to her brain. When she woke in the recovery room, she could not move or feel her arm or hand; it was paralyzed. That initial fall precipitated frequent major orthopedic surgeries that have continued to the present.

We now know that she has a rare, genetic, connective tissue disease as well as nerve dystrophy developed as a consequence of her severe medical trauma. She lives with constant chronic pain. Virtually no one outside our family has any concept of the challenges she faces every day. Celestia boldly asserts that God has used her broken body to tether her heart to his. God's Word to my beloved is precious. He has used his love letters to heal, direct, console, and empower her. It is truly miraculous to see.

Before each surgery, Celestia asks God to give her an *anchor* Scripture she memorizes before those long hospitalizations. This becomes her conscious meditation before succumbing to the anesthesiologist's induced sleep. Her mind is focused on God's words chosen just for her. She then wakes in peace. Scripture is her strength. Scripture settles her anxious thoughts. Scripture is her courage. Scripture is her truth. Scripture is her joy. Not surprisingly,

Celestia's daily meditation on all those love letters is the bedrock for her extensive trauma care and training experienced by hundreds of thousands of abuse survivors worldwide.

We want that for you. To learn to trust God's Word as your absolute truth and to love it as your source of healing power and transformation, to allow it to lift your eyes from your painful circumstances or past to his face of love. God uses our pain when it is offered to him. He speaks and heals us through his Word.

So how exactly do we properly interpret the Bible so that it can become a source of life and healing? What principles can guide us when Scripture is weaponized against us? The next two chapters will answer these questions.

Chapter 2

PRINCIPLES FOR INTERPRETING SCRIPTURE: PART 1

In religion, what damned error,
but some sober brow will bless and approve
It with a text, hiding the grossness
with fair ornament?
—SHAKESPEARE, *THE MERCHANT OF VENICE*

Now the Berean Jews were of more noble character
than those in Thessalonica, for they received the
message with great eagerness and examined the
Scriptures every day to see if what Paul said was true.
—ACTS 17:11

While I attended numerous public and Christian schools over many years, one of the most memorable was my Christian high school. I attended a public grade school in the late 1960s, a time of great social upheaval in the United States. Junior high was chaotic and confusing. I was very intimidated by the secular school environment in which very few of my peers seemed to share my Christian beliefs or values. So I was excited to attend a small Christian high school that required all students to profess a personal faith in Christ and attend a local church. Bible classes were woven into the curriculum. On top of daily Bible classes, we had chapel twice a week. Surely, such Bible saturation would result in shared theological convictions. After all, we were reading the same Bible. So, I was quite unprepared for the lunchtime "Bible wars," in which students heatedly argued for their pet doctrines by adamantly quoting Bible verses. I was shocked to discover how many diverse and often contradictory doctrines could be "proven" by Scripture. I eventually discovered that the problem was not Scripture. God doesn't contradict himself. Instead, the problem is that unless you have a solid template for interpreting Scripture, you can use the Bible to "prove" anything. In this and the following chapters, I will give a basic overview of biblical interpretation and explain several essential interpretive principles.

A WORD OF ENCOURAGEMENT

Before we get into the details, I want to encourage lay readers, particularly those who have been intimidated by church leaders. Having been a pastor and seminary professor for decades, I know how easily those of us with advanced biblical and theological training can (intentionally or unintentionally) intimidate others. For instance, how can you disagree with a pastor's interpretation when he declares, "In Greek or Hebrew, it means _____"? Of course, we need well-trained biblical teachers to help us better understand Scripture. That is why I wrote this book. But every Christian has the right to study God's Word for themselves and form his or her own convictions. As I often tell my seminary students, "Don't believe what I'm teaching you just because I [or your pastor or the textbook author] says it is the truth. Search the Scriptures for yourself and see if what I'm saying harmonizes with what God tells you from his Word. Develop your own well-informed biblical convictions and stand on them." This is precisely the perspective found in Scripture itself. For instance, when Paul came and proclaimed the gospel (biblical truth) in Berea, Luke declares that "the Berean Jews were of more noble character than those in Thessalonica, for they received the message with great eagerness and examined the Scriptures every day to see if what Paul said was true" (Acts 17:11). In other words, the Bereans were not intimidated into just accepting the interpretations of Paul, a former Pharisee and expert in the Hebrew Scriptures. They formed their convictions based on their own study of the Scriptures. This harmonizes well with what John told his disciples when he said:

> I am writing these things to you about those who are trying to lead you astray. As for you, the anointing you received from him remains in you, and you do not need anyone to teach you. But as his anointing teaches you about all things and as that anointing is real, not counterfeit—just as it has taught you, remain in him. (1 John 2:26–27)

The "anointing you received from him" most likely refers to the Holy Spirit, whom Jesus promised to send to his disciples (John 14:16). Furthermore, Jesus promised that the Holy Spirit would indwell believers and guide them "into all the truth" (John 14:17; 16:13). It seems John's audience was contending with an early form of false teaching, which by the second century came to be known as Gnosticism. *Gnosticism* comes from the Greek word for "knowledge." These teachers denied that Jesus took on human flesh (see John's refutation of this in 1 John 1:1–3) and that they, the spiritual leaders, had a special "knowledge" that others didn't possess.

Thus, the uninitiated laypeople needed to get the truth from these exceptional, hyperspiritual leaders. John's response to this is, "No, you don't need human teachers to give you the truth. You have the Holy Spirit in you; he is the ultimate teacher." Since the Holy Spirit is the One who inspired the Scriptures (2 Pet 1:20–21), we must look to the Spirit to speak to us through God's Word. God gives human teachers to bless the church (Eph 4:11–12; 1 Tim 3:2), but they do not have the final say. Immerse yourself in God's Word, apply the principles of sound biblical interpretation, humbly listen to the Spirit and other believers, including teachers, and then form your own convictions. You will answer to Jesus, not your pastor, spouse, or any other human being. Your allegiance is to Jesus.

NECESSARY PREREQUISITES

Reliance on the Holy Spirit

In theology, we refer to the doctrine of "illumination," which refers to the Holy Spirit's work in the believer's life to clarify the meaning and personal life application of Scripture. We need the Spirit to guide us in understanding and living out God's truth—this is his role in the life of a believer. For instance, Jesus told his disciples, "I have much more to say to you, more than you can now bear. But when he, the Spirit of truth, comes, he will guide you into all the truth" (John 16:12–13). Paul also affirms the believer's reliance on the Spirit to understand and value God's truth:

> What we have received is not the spirit of the world, but the Spirit who is from God, so that we may understand what God has freely given us. This is what we speak, not in words taught us by human wisdom but in words taught by the Spirit, explaining spiritual realities with Spirit-taught words. The person without the Spirit

does not accept the things that come from the Spirit of God but considers them foolishness, and cannot understand them because they are discerned only through the Spirit. (1 Cor 2:12–14)

In other words, *we must rely on the Spirit who gave the Scriptures to help us understand and apply them in wise ways.* Biblical interpretation ought not be a purely intellectual exercise, for the student must possess and be in tune with—listening to, reliant on, yielded to—the Holy Spirit (Gal 5:25; Eph 5:18; 1 Thess 5:19). Now we can better understand Cheryl's experience recounted in the introduction. Her husband had advanced biblical training, but his stone-cold heart, evidenced by his perverted, abusive behavior, *prevented* him from interpreting and applying Scripture correctly.

Years ago, when I attended a fine evangelical seminary, I received a poignant lesson in biblical illumination. In the course of my seminary training, four of my professors tragically left the faculty—a biblical-language professor committed suicide; a Bible scholar committed sex crimes; a counseling professor was disciplined for having sexual relations with a client; a spiritual-life professor's marriage fell apart. All four were excellent, highly trained educators with extensive knowledge of Scripture. Yet each story proves that biblical interpretation is not merely an intellectual exercise. *Everyone* must rely on the Holy Spirit to understand and apply God's Word.

A final principle related to illumination is this: *the biblical interpretations of someone clearly violating Scripture are not to be trusted. Do not be intimidated or persuaded by biblical arguments from abusers or their defenders.* You have a divine guide (the Holy Spirit) who will lead you through God's Word.

A Humble Receptive Posture

It is not sufficient simply to criticize the text: we must now let the text criticize us.[1]

It is common for seminary professors and some pastors to attend professional conferences where individuals give academic presentations on their research and interact with the audience. Often the presentations are boringly technical, creating a subdued audience. I'll never forget a notable exception several years ago. The conference room was absolutely packed. Those of us crammed into the room anticipated this presentation to be lively and stimulating. The professional society hosting the conference was composed of many liberal biblical scholars, so this lecture promised to be controversial. We were not disappointed. The well-known New Testament scholar presented his paper on Pauline sexual ethics. The presenter took the biblical text seriously and, for thirty minutes, skillfully unpacked it. After concluding his presentation, he responded to comments and questions. One of the first respondents argued that the presenter's findings were deeply flawed because he had failed to utilize what she considered a most fundamental principle for reading Paul's letters—namely, a "hermeneutics of suspicion." (A "hermeneutics of suspicion" is an approach to literary interpretation in which the reader comes to the text with suspicion, assuming the text reflects destructive patriarchy and/or attempts by those in power to maintain their control. Those who champion this principle view the Bible as essentially "guilty until proven innocent.") To my surprise, the presenter agreed with the respondent that reading the Bible with a hermeneutic of suspicion is essential. However, he redirected the suspicion to a different object. He confidently but graciously asserted that we should be consistently suspicious of our own sinful tendencies. He confessed that he found it far too easy to explain away biblical texts he didn't want to obey and suggested we best read Paul, or any other biblical author, with a humble "hermeneutics of suspicion" toward *our* sinful hearts and a hermeneutics of *trust* toward Scripture.[2] It was early in my academic teaching career when I heard this sage advice. I've never forgotten it.

What does a humble, receptive posture entail? This type of surrender flows out of a sober recognition of our human tendency to control the meaning of a text to suit our desires instead of allowing the text to critique and guide us. We should be sobered by our innate capacity to distort truth to suit our own purposes.

A Joyful Recognition That God Continually Speaks to His Children

Many passages affirm this truth, but one of my favorites is in John 10:3, where Jesus, the Good Shepherd, says the sheep "hear" (the Greek here is present tense, suggesting ongoing action) the shepherd's voice, "and he calls his own sheep by name and leads them" (ESV). As we saw earlier, Jesus promised to send the Holy Spirit, who would indwell believers, speak to them God's truth, and remind them of Jesus's words (John 14:26). The Holy Spirit speaks to us through the words of Scripture. In this respect, the Bible is absolutely unique. While I have always loved books and have a large and diverse personal library, there is no other book like the Bible. I have countless "inspiring" books in my library, but only the Bible is God's holy inspired Word. So, when you come to Scripture, prayerfully *ask* and *expect* God to speak to you. Or, more precisely, ask God to give you the discipline to create solitude and sensitivity to hear his voice.

A Self-Awareness of How Culture Taints Our Reading of Scripture

Having spent extensive time in various cultures outside my own, I am sobered at how insidiously and thoroughly our culturally acquired biases cloud biblical interpretation. For instance, on our first trip to the Democratic Republic of the Congo in 2007, we were astonished at the widespread reports of pastors and bishops beating and raping their wives. Women in this culture were virtually enslaved people, expected to work the fields, care for the children, cook, clean, and satisfy all their husbands' physical and sexual desires. The entrenched patriarchy of their culture was so thoroughly embedded that the numerous passages that affirm the value and dignity of women and heavily qualified male leadership simply didn't sink in. And yet these faith leaders read their Bibles and believed they were following God's Word. Culture had tainted Scripture, and they didn't realize it. Yet, on that same trip, we had fascinating, convicting conversations about generosity, greed, and care for the elderly with these same African leaders. They couldn't fathom how American Christians owned large homes, often with empty bedrooms, and did not house the vulnerable and needy, including the elderly. They asked why American Christians didn't obey the Bible. They forced me to think much more deeply about my own cultural misreadings of Scripture.

A few years later, our African friends' negative critique was driven home when my frail father-in-law recounted a story about traveling alone. He was suffering from an intestinal ailment, and while walking through the airport accidentally soiled his trousers. He was very embarrassed and looked for a restroom where he could clean up. An African immigrant who worked at the airport saw him, immediately took him to the toilet, and gently helped him clean up. This humble immigrant came from a culture in which the elderly, even if they are strangers, are highly valued and respected. He didn't think twice about going out of his way to aid an elderly stranger in need. We don't know if this man was a believer, but I do know that few Christians raised in America would respond in such a loving, honoring manner. Our cultural conditioning has clouded Scripture. When we interpret the Bible correctly, we must do so humbly, with a surrendered heart.

HERMENEUTICAL PRINCIPLES

In ancient Greece, Hermes was the gods' herald or messenger. He was a winged god who travels quickly from heaven to earth (or earth to the underworld) to bring messages. The name "Hermes" is connected to the Greek word *hermēneuō*, which means "to interpret" or "to translate" (John 1:42; 9:7). A compound form of this verb is used in Luke 24:27 when Jesus, after his resurrection, talks to some of his disciples and "beginning with Moses and all the Prophets, he *explained* to them what was said in all the Scriptures concerning himself." *Hermeneutics* is the interpretation or explanation of Scripture. It is an art and a science. Hermeneutics is an art or skill requiring abilities developed through practice. Hermeneutics is a science that involves the application of specific principles. This and the following chapter will now focus on six of the most essential hermeneutical principles.

Clarify the Context

It was a warm spring in 2007, and our first trip to Africa. It was our team's "baptism by fire." We were in the Democratic Republic of the Congo. According to our host, we were conducting one of the first abuse trainings ever given to Congolese pastors. The language, sights, sounds, and foods were quite foreign to us, as were some of the biblical interpretations.

The previous day we had a lively interaction regarding male-female relationships. Before this day's teaching session began, one of the Congolese pastors gave a short devotional. I can still remember him. He was smartly dressed, probably in his only suit and dress shirt. He was utterly focused and earnest in addressing the assembly. He read Psalm 45:10–11 which states: "Hear, O daughter, and consider, and incline your ear: forget your people and your father's house, and the king will desire your beauty. Since he is your lord, bow to him" (ESV). He made immediate application of this text to the women, declaring: "Listen and consider, you wives. God's Word requires you to bow down to your husbands. Your husband is your lord. You must obey all his commands. You are to serve him and follow him without question. This is what God's Word declares." Since the devotional was translated from Swahili into English, it took a moment for us to realize what he was saying. We were shocked at how he interpreted this text. He had clearly objected to the previous day's teaching about marriage and was issuing what he felt was a biblical corrective. As horrified as we were at this interpretation of Psalm 45, what basis did we have to say that his Congolese interpretation was inferior to ours?[3] After all, the biblical text does tell the woman to bow down to the husband as her lord. This African pastor didn't miss the words of the text; instead, he missed the context in which those words are found.

The first rule of hermeneutics is to clarify the context, immediate and extended. What is the broad (extended) context of Psalm 45:10–11? We see at the very beginning of the psalm in verse one that it is addressed to the king. This is a "royal psalm" addressed to the king (cf. v. 5, 8, 10, 15). More specifically, the occasion is the king's wedding day. So, the broad context of Psalm 45 is not marriage in general but a *royal marriage in particular*. It doesn't address how wives, in general, are to relate to their husbands but how this royal bride was to relate to her monarch husband (v. 9). In terms of the immediate context of these verses, we should note that the queen is to bow down to her husband "for he is your lord" (v. 11)—that is, her royal earthly sovereign. Such a command in ancient Israel makes sense, for the king was the royal ruler of the nation and to be given great respect and honor. (The NIV translates v. 11 as "honor" instead of "bow down," but these two renderings have a very similar meaning.) Jewish kings had power and authority that none of their peers possessed—so commanding the king's bride to bow and give the king honor as the king is understandable and proper in this setting. But taking it out of this context and making this a rule for all wives in all cultures to follow is a gross violation of Psalm 45 and the principles of sound hermeneutics.

Let's make a few additional observations about the immediate context of these verses (vv. 10–13). Far from making this royal bride a lowly servant, she is esteemed. She is described as "glorious" in her chamber (v. 13) and worthy of great honor, for the people of Tyre (a mighty city) will come to give her gifts and seek her favor (v. 12). This observation from the immediate context helps to balance out and clarify the command for her to honor her husband, for she is also honored. Psalm 45 gives us a good case study on properly clarifying context to interpret Scripture.

It has been said that the first three rules of hermeneutics are: context, context, context. While it is a bit of an overstatement, it highlights the importance of this principle. Sadly, this is one of the most ignored principles of hermeneutics. Often, Christians simply quote Scripture without considering the context, as if merely because a statement is in the Bible it must reflect a biblical truth. However, the Bible contains many statements that accurately account for what was said or done without endorsing those words or actions. In this sense, *you can find many things in the Bible that are not biblical.*

For instance, several years ago, I was listening to a Christian radio station, and their "power verse" of the day was Job 5:19: "From six calamities he will rescue you; in seven no harm will touch you." While this might initially seem like a beautiful promise to claim, this ministry used it inappropriately and harmfully. It reflected what we call the "prosperity gospel" and teaches that obedient Christians with faith will always experience physical and financial blessing and healing. They will not suffer.

The context of this verse is a statement by Eliphaz, one of Job's accusers. The broad context of this verse is a speech by Eliphaz condemning Job, asserting that Job must be experiencing severe trials due to hidden sin: "Who, being innocent, has ever perished? . . . Those who plow evil and those who sow trouble reap it" (Job 4:7–8). The immediate context is a warning to Job that he should repent of his sin in order that God would heal and bless him (5:18). This is the context for "no harm touching you."

What a horrible false indictment this was against Job, who had experienced unspeakable trauma and simultaneous loss of his health, property, and loved ones (1:13–2:8). His trauma included grotesque abuse by two different marauding bands who slaughtered his servants and stole his livestock (1:14–17). Eliphaz was arrogantly declaring that Job's suffering was self-induced, but if Job would just repent his problems would be over. Yet God himself condemned this twisted theology. At the end of the book of Job, God declares his great anger against Eliphaz and the other false comforters "because you have not spoken the truth about me, as my servant Job has" (Job 42:7). In ignoring the context of Job 5:19, this radio station used a "power verse" not to declare truth, but a harmful lie.

Let Scripture Interpret Scripture

This is the second most important rule of hermeneutics. Sometimes it is called the "analogy of faith." For Protestant Christians, this means that Scripture, not tradition or a body of authoritative church leaders, is the best interpreter of Scripture. Another way of looking at this is to say that we must always compare Scripture with Scripture to develop a truly biblical perspective on a given issue. It is easy to overlook or minimize this principle, but given the richness of Scripture, it is essential. The Bible contains sixty-six books written in three languages over hundreds of years by dozens of authors in widely varied cultures. Thus, it reflects widely varying perspectives that must be harmonized.

The underlying principle is that *God's Word is true and trustworthy because God is true and trustworthy*. As the prophet Samuel declared to King Saul, who was seeking to avoid the consequences of his grievous disobedience, "He who is the Glory of Israel does not lie or change his mind" (1 Sam 15:29). For unrepentant sinners (including abusers like Saul), this truth is terrifying because it means God cannot be manipulated; his Word can't be changed to serve our selfish whims. This truth is a tremendous comfort and blessing for those seeking to follow God's Word.

We can count on God's Word to be true. But we must use sound hermeneutics, including letting Scripture interpret Scripture, to determine the meaning of a particular passage. We must not present a verse or two as the totality of biblical truth on a given topic. Otherwise, we can teach harmful "biblical" admonitions that crush those who receive them. This is precisely what the Pharisees did. Their mistruths were "heavy, cumbersome loads" that were callously put "on other people's shoulders" (Matt 23:4).

If two verses appear to contradict each other, continue to study Scripture to gain the bigger picture. For instance, Proverbs 26:4 says not to answer a fool according to his folly, but the next verse says the opposite: "Answer a fool according to his folly." Clearly, these two verses describe somewhat different matters. It may be that verse four is giving the general principle of not responding to a fool so that you don't become "like him," while verse five gives the exception to this rule. Sometimes fools need to be responded to openly so that they and those around them are given a reality check and do not become wise in their own eyes. These verses are both true but incomplete in themselves. One verse helps to clarify the other.

Christian leaders cause great harm when they issue unqualified warnings based on a single verse of Scripture. We'll illustrate by noting other examples of various verses seemingly contradicting each other while addressing different aspects of a given issue. In Matthew

5:22–23, Jesus says that the one who is angry with his brother or sister "will be subject to judgment" and that the one who calls his brother or sister a fool "will be in danger of the fire of hell." I've often heard this text used to condemn abuse survivors who are angry at their unrepentant abusers. Is this a fair indictment? Not if we compare Scripture with Scripture!

In other Gospel texts, we find that Jesus himself was angry with the Pharisees (Mark 3:5), and elsewhere he called them fools (Matt 23:17). In all three of these passages, the Greek words for anger (*orgizō/orgē*) and fool (*mōros*) are the same. But clearly they must not be describing precisely the same things or else Jesus would be committing the very sins he condemned.

The prohibition against anger and calling your brother or sister a fool in Matthew 5:23 is qualified with the additional prohibition against calling your brother or sister *Raca*, which was an ancient Aramaic word of insult. Jesus did call the Pharisees fools because that was what they were. However, he did not demeaningly, gratuitously insult them. Nor should abuse survivors today. The prohibition in Matthew 5:23 is directed at a particular kind of insulting anger; it is not a prohibition against all anger. We must not make premature conclusions about a biblical ethic of speech or anger based on a single (or a few) verses. Scripture clarifies Scripture. (We will have more to say about anger in subsequent chapters.)

Let's give a different example. How do we understand the causes of poverty? Are the poor simply lazy, as many political conservatives seem to believe? Or are they merely victims of oppression, as many political liberals seem to think? We can make either argument by looking at select verses about poverty. Proverbs 28:19 says those "who work their land will have abundant food, but those who chase fantasies will have their fill of poverty." Proverbs 10:4 says, "Lazy hands make for poverty, but diligent hands bring wealth." And Proverbs 23:21 says, "Drunkards and gluttons become poor." Based on these verses, we might conclude that the rich are virtuous, and the poor are lazy, foolish, and indulgent. These verses do give us a partial picture of poverty. Sometimes, it does result from lack of industry, refusal to delay gratification, and abuse of alcohol. And sometimes people are rich primarily due to their excellent character and industry. But that isn't the whole picture. Proverbs 22:16 notes that some people oppress the poor to increase their own wealth. (This is very similar to James 5:1–5, which condemns the rich for building their wealth by oppressing and defrauding the poor.) The same book of Proverbs states that the empty field of the poor would yield a harvest, but "injustice sweeps it away" (Prov 13:23). Proverbs 18:23 condemns the rich for responding harshly to poor people's pleas for mercy. Wealth doesn't always result from good character; sometimes it is the result of abusive evil. Clearly we cannot just cite a few verses in Proverbs to have a biblical perspective on poverty and wealth. So it is with every other biblical truth. We must compare Scripture with Scripture to get a fuller, correct understanding.

Methodologically, how do we best apply this hermeneutical principle of letting Scripture interpret Scripture? As we saw with the principle of clarifying the context, it is best to start with the Scripture surrounding a given text, then look at texts in the same book, and then texts on the same topic in other biblical books written by the same author. Ultimately, we can and should allow all Scripture to interpret all Scripture. Still, there are fewer cultural, literary, and other differences between texts in the same book or books written by the same author. Here is a simple example in the same biblical book. In 1 Corinthians 14:34, Paul says: "Women should remain silent in the churches. They are not allowed to speak." At first blush, this appears to be a watertight prohibition. Thus, some churches tragically muzzle women in church based on this text. However, a quick survey of 1 Corinthians shows this is incorrect since Paul gives guidelines for women prophesying and praying in the assembly

(1 Cor 11:5, 13). Other Scripture in this same book shows that Paul is not giving a universal prohibition against women speaking but a limited one.[4]

One of the simplest, most straightforward ways to let Scripture interpret Scripture is to do word studies on a given topic, including synonyms and antonyms in the English Bible translations. Some excellent biblical-research software programs such as Accordance, Olive Tree, and Logos can allow one to do simple and in-depth word studies, including the Greek and Hebrew words used in Scripture. One of the most accessible, free resources for basic word studies of various English Bible translations is found at biblegateway.com. Using this tool to do an English word study of a given biblical theme is a great way to start using Scripture to interpret Scripture.

Look for the Plain, Literal Sense of the Passage

In the early 1990s, a radio broadcaster and evangelist named Harold Camping began proclaiming that based on his study of Scripture, the exact date of Christ's return was going to be September 6, 1994.[5] This was the first of a series of failed predictions he issued over the course of fifteen years. He initially gathered a substantial global audience and received millions of dollars in donations. Through using a highly creative, nonliteral hermeneutic he found the "church" in biblical references to Judea, Jerusalem, Hezekiah, and the disciples' boat (referenced in John 21), and he came to reject much historical Christian teaching and developed novel, bizarre interpretations. For instance, he argued that based on Revelation 18:4—"'Come out of her, my people,' so that you will not share in her sins, so that you will not receive any of her plagues"—all true believers must leave the local church or they would be subject to the plagues God was about to send on the earth.

Furthermore, he argued that God had destroyed the church, the Holy Spirit was no longer working in it, and no one in the current church could be saved. (While countless people were supposedly saved through his ministry.) Camping's unbiblical teachings caused turmoil, discouragement, and pain for numerous individuals and families. It generated great ridicule from unbelievers. Camping became well-known in the 1990s because he had access to an extensive radio broadcasting network to spread the toxic fruit of his erroneous hermeneutic. There are countless lesser-known leaders whose interpretations have been gravely harmful and abusive. Unfortunately, this type of reading of the Bible is not new and goes by the label *allegorical* or *spiritual* interpretation.

In the history of Christian hermeneutics, there has been a long and unfortunate tendency to look for and even prioritize allegorical (sometimes called "spiritual") interpretations. The Protestant Reformation brought a renewed emphasis on the literal sense of Scripture, but unbridled allegorizing continues to create harmful misreadings.

By the early third century, two interpretive schools had arisen in the church: the literal interpretation, championed by the school of Antioch in Syria, and the symbolic, championed by Origen, based in Alexandria, Egypt.[6] By the fifth century, the allegorical hermeneutic won out, allowing Christian theologians to find biblical support for a wide range of doctrines not plainly taught in Scripture. These allegorical interpretations are sometimes impressively creative and far removed from the actual biblical text, as is the case with Origin's imaginative reading of the parable of the good Samaritan. He interpreted Adam as the man beaten and robbed, Jerusalem as paradise, Jericho as the world, etc. While the truths Origin found in this passage are affirmed elsewhere, his interpretation is far removed from the text.

However, other allegorical interpretations are starkly at odds with the rest of Scripture. For instance, some allegorical interpreters read the account of Bathsheba going to King Solomon to advocate for her son, Adonijah, found in 1 Kings 2:19, and conclude it teaches that Mary, the mother of Jesus, is the queen of heaven who intercedes for us today.[7] The obvious problem with this type of allegorical hermeneutic is that there is little or no control. Interpreters can discover virtually any meaning they desire to find. Making matters worse, many allegorical exegetes insist that their interpretation is more spiritual and can only be perceived by spiritually mature people. This hermeneutical strategy and posture are ripe for abuse, for if one disagrees with the given interpretation then that person is accused of not being spiritually mature. This is a perfect strategy for spiritual abuse and is often used by cults.

The word *allegory* comes from a Greek word that means to speak symbolically. There is undoubtedly symbolism in Scripture. Jesus taught through parables, and various New Testament writers appeal to Old Testament figures symbolically (e.g., the brazen serpent in Num 21:9 applied to Christ in John 3:14; the Passover leaven applied to Christian purity in 1 Cor 5:5–8; the bread and wine of communion being Christ's body and blood in 1 Cor 11:24–26). In Galatians 4:24, Paul says that Sarah and Hagar, mothers of Isaac and Ishmael, can be understood allegorically to refer to the old and new covenants. Sound hermeneutics recognizes there is symbolism or allegory in Scripture.

Three Guidelines for Allegory

1. Unless there are clear grounds to do otherwise (as with a figure of speech, such as "the end of the earth"), *allegorical readings are always built on literal readings*. While Paul understood Sarah and Hagar symbolically, he didn't deny they were literal historical women. Similarly, while some New Testament writers give a "fuller sense" to an Old Testament text (e.g., Matt 1:23; Heb 9:6–28), they never negate or demean the literal meaning of the Old Testament text.

2. Good biblical or contextual reasons must exist to understand a passage allegorically. Not all Scripture has a symbolic meaning.

3. The plain, literal meaning must not be treated as inferior to the symbolic or allegorical meaning.

There is great danger in prioritizing "spiritual" nonliteral interpretations, particularly when they alter or contradict the literal meaning. For instance, the church fathers developed a tragically negative view of marital sex. This partially resulted from misreading Paul's positive description of singleness in 1 Corinthians 7:25–40. However, one of the most significant hermeneutical influences was their allegorization of the Song of Solomon. They rejected and declared blasphemous a literal reading—erotic, romantic poetry describing the emotional and physical love of a husband and wife. Instead, they insisted that the Song of Solomon could only be read allegorically as a description of God's love for his people.

On the contrary, while Song of Solomon is poetry, it bears no marks of allegory. *It is said to be Solomon's song (1:1) sung to his bride (4:10)*, and no other biblical writers interpret it as allegorical. Furthermore, the erotic descriptions of the two lovers' bodies make no sense as allegorical descriptions of God's love for his people. A literal reading affirming the beauty of marital sexual intimacy harmonizes perfectly with other biblical passages (Gen 2:24–25; Prov 5:15–20; 1 Cor 7:1–5).

Nevertheless, for almost fifteen centuries of church history, the allegorical reading of Song of Solomon was the dominant Christian view. It led to a significant depreciation of sex in marriage, reflected by ancient church leaders such as Peter Lombard (ca. AD 1100–1160), who declared that when a marital couple had sex, the Holy Spirit left the room. This metaphorical understanding allowed the church father Augustine (ca. AD 354–430) to insist that marital sex hinders prayer and to declare that the godlier a husband and wife are, the earlier they will agree to stop having any sexual intimacy.[8] We are still today dealing with the destructive fallout of the church fathers' denigration of marital sex. *Bad hermeneutics have harmful consequences.*

More on the Plain, Literal Sense

By "plain, literal" sense we are not suggesting that there is no metaphorical language in Scripture but that we should interpret literally unless there are clear indications to do otherwise (figures of speech, etc.). In looking for the plain, literal sense, we should pay attention to the specific words the author uses, ultimately in their original language. Bible commentaries and lexicons can help us with word meanings. In doing this, we should beware of teachers who assert that the "root" or "real" meaning of a given word is such and such unless they can show that the "root" meaning is used in Scripture the way they say it is. Words mean what they mean in the context of their usage. (Greek and Hebrew lexicons are a great help in showing what biblical words mean based on their usage.)

Let's illustrate the danger of pressing "root" meanings while ignoring context of usage. Suppose your son comes home from school and says his teacher praised an oral report he had given in class, telling him he did a "nice job" and that it was an "incredible presentation." Would you tell your son that the teacher had doubly insulted him because the English word *nice* comes from the Latin word *nescius*, which means "ignorant" or "foolish," and the word *incredible* comes from two Latin words meaning "not credible"? Of course not!

While this is the correct etymology of *incredible* and *nice*, it is irrelevant to modern English. The teacher was not shaming the student for a foolish report, because words mean what they mean in the context of how they are used. Contextually, these words were used to give a compliment. So it is with Greek and Hebrew words in the Bible. Failing to recognize this principle can lead to destructive interpretations. For instance, I have heard many pastors assert that *hypotassō*, the Greek word often used in the New Testament for the wife's submission to her husband, was a military term from two Greek words meaning "to rank under," "to set under" (Eph 5:21–22). They argue that wives are to submit to their husbands as a private submits to a higher-ranking officer. (Some go as far as to define *biblical submission* as a wife simply saying, "yes sir," much like a soldier would obey a commanding officer promptly, fully, and without questioning his orders.) Needless to say, such an understanding of marital submission from this faulty definition of *hypotassō* is ripe for abuse. And it is thoroughly unbiblical. To "rank under" tells us little about how this word is used in the New Testament. In fact, a military understanding of *hypotassō* flies in the face of the way the word is used in the New Testament. Unlike higher- and lower-ranking military members, husbands and wives are generally equal in skill and knowledge. Husbands and wives are in an intimate covenant relationship. Soldiers are not. Husbands and wives are called to submit to each other. Soldiers of different ranks are not. Husbands are not given military-type authority over their family members. In short, we must pay attention to how words are used to determine their meaning.

Finally, we should note that "plain, literal meaning" involves paying careful attention to what the passage is saying and affirming and not reading into the passage something that is not there. For instance, Rebecca Davis recounts that even when she was an adult with children of her own, her spiritually abusive mother would subject her to long, shaming rebukes when she felt Rebecca did not share her pet beliefs.[9] Rebecca's mother used Scripture to condemn her. She often quoted Proverbs 22:28 to prove that Rebecca had no biblical right to disagree with her parents: "Do not move an ancient boundary stone set up by your ancestors." The only way one can read this text as condemning an adult child for having their own convictions, which differ from their parents, is to deny a plain, literal meaning to this passage. Nothing in this verse suggests that "ancient boundary stone" is not a literal boundary stone. Period. The broader context of Proverbs confirms and clarifies this, for Proverbs 23:10 says, "Do not move an ancient boundary stone or encroach on the fields of the fatherless." Moving boundary stones was a literal theft from a neighbor (Deut 27:17; Job 24:2), not a metaphorical dishonor of a parent. Identifying the plain, literal meaning of the passage will deliver us from countless harmful misreadings of Scripture. And it can deliver us from toxic shame when Scripture is weaponized against us.

The hermeneutical term for what Rebecca's mother did in reading into Scripture something that is not there is called *eisegesis*, literally "reading into" the text meanings that are not there and not supported by the text. Let's apply the concept of *eisegesis* to Psalm 23:4. In this well-known, beloved passage, David speaks of God, the good shepherd, and his "rod and staff." Several times over the years I have heard pastors teach on this text and assert that in ancient Israel, shepherds would often use their staff to break the legs of wayward sheep. As one commentator argues:

> He took the wayward lamb, which refused to follow his voice, and gently laid its hoof on a big rock and held it so that it could not retract the leg. He then took his staff and gave that leg such a whack that the bone was broken! At that point the lamb could not even keep up with the flock, so our Shepherd had to carry that little rascal on his own shoulders from pasture to water and back again. Every day.
>
> You know about bonding. That's what happened. Remember the pictures in Sunday School of "Jesus and the Lost Lamb"? He's probably on his way to (or from) breaking a leg. Because he loves that little rascal. And he wants it to follow him when they move around. Because that lamb is an integral part of his breeding and flock development programme.[10]

One pastor, building on this absurd interpretation, declares to other pastors that they must be leg breakers of their flocks: "This is the difficult part of the calling for you elders. You are called to teach us the ways of righteousness, and when we stray, it is your job, sirs, to break our legs and bring us back into the flock."[11] This interpretation has no actual basis in ancient Jewish shepherding practices or in the text of Psalm 23. Jewish commentaries on Psalm 23 never give this interpretation of "rod." Most significantly, this "leg breaking" interpretation contradicts the context, for the psalmist says, "Your rod and your staff, they comfort me" (v. 4). A rod used to break legs would be a source of terror, not comfort. This reading is a clear case of eisegesis, reading something into the text that isn't there. Interpretations that make God out to be an abusive shepherd are destructive and unbiblical.

We have now seen three essential principles for interpretation: clarify the context; let Scripture interpret Scripture; look for the plain, literal sense of the passage. In the next chapter, we will look at the final three essential rules for interpreting Scripture properly.

Chapter 3

PRINCIPLES FOR INTERPRETING SCRIPTURE: PART 2

Victims of physical abuse are often beaten so severely that their true identities are unrecognizable, or scarred so deeply in their psyches or spirits that their true selves cannot emerge. Similarly, this is what happens when we misinterpret Scripture. The meaning and message of Scripture becomes obscure, its authentic nature cannot easily be recognized, it is not allowed to speak its deepest truths, and its voice is muted, throttled or silenced.

—MANFRED BRAUCH, *ABUSING SCRIPTURE*[1]

Do your best to present yourself to God as one approved, a worker who does not need to be ashamed and who correctly handles the word of truth.

—2 TIMOTHY 2:15

It is truly incredible how many contradictory messages people claim to find in Scripture. Only by applying sound hermeneutical principles can we avoid making Scripture say what God never intended it to say. This next principle is exceedingly helpful in protecting us from dangerous interpretations.

IDENTIFY THE MOST LIKELY
MEANING OF THE AUTHOR

Some have labeled this the principle of authorial intent. In other words, seek to determine what the biblical author was intending to communicate.

It was one of those meetings every pastor dreads. John's wife, Sherry, had called the church in tears, informing us that her husband had just declared he was divorcing her and moving in with his girl-friend. She pled with me to talk to John and bring him to his senses (oh, that I had that kind of pastoral power). I promptly called him, and he reluctantly agreed to meet at a local restaurant. At the outset of our conversation, he unabashedly confirmed that he was leaving his wife and two young children to move in with his mistress. When I asked how he could reconcile abandoning his family with biblical teaching, he cited John 10:10 ("I came that they may have life and have it abundantly," ESV) and declared, "This verse means to me that whatever I need to do to have an abundant life is okay with God. I'm not happy right now, and I need to live abundantly. God understands and accepts that." I was stunned. This very intelligent dentist had developed his own unique hermeneutical system that justified adultery by giving it a biblical rationale. While John's rationalization of immorality and family abandonment was extreme, the way he got there by a "private meaning" hermeneutic is quite common.

A word of clarification is in order. Sometimes, when people say, "This is what this verse means to me," they are really saying, "Here is how I apply this verse in my life." That is well and good. Personal application of Scripture is essential. But to be precise, the application is not meaning but is based on textual meaning. One of the key principles for correctly interpreting biblical texts is to identify the most likely meaning of the author. I say "most likely" in recognition of the fact that we cannot get inside someone else's mind. But this does not leave us without any clues. By carefully considering the author's literary context, culture, and specific words, we can generally obtain a reasonable sense of what the author intended to communicate.[2]

Identifying the author's most likely meaning protects against inaccurate "private" interpretations. It also protects against "woodenly literal" interpretations, which are not credible. For instance, in Matthew 13:31–32 Jesus refers to the mustard seed as "the smallest of all seeds." In Mark's account, it is called "the smallest of all seeds on earth" (Mark 4:31). But we know from modern botany that the orchid seed, not the mustard seed, is the smallest of all seeds. This apparent biblical *error* disappears when we consider the most likely meaning of the author. The mustard seed was the smallest seed sown by first-century Palestinian farmers, which was surely Jesus's (and Matthew's) point. When Luke describes Pentecost and says that in Jerusalem that there were "God-fearing Jews from every nation under heaven" (Acts 2:5), he isn't making a strictly literal statement. Every nation on the earth did not have Jews. Rather, when we consider the cultural context, Luke the author is surely referring to every country of the Jewish diaspora. Similarly, we read in Genesis 41:57 that during the famine "all the world came to Egypt to buy grain from Joseph." It is historically and logistically indefensible to assert that people from every nation on planet Earth came to Egypt. That is *not* Moses's point. Rather, he is viewing the world from his vantage point—that is, "all the eastern Mediterranean region."[3]

Coming back to John 10:10, we must begin with the context to help us discern the author's intended meaning. Jesus had healed a blind man on the Sabbath and had confronted the Pharisees for their spiritual blindness. In the Hebrew Scriptures, the relationship between God and his people is described in terms of the relationship between the shepherd and his sheep (e.g., Ps 23). The Davidic Messiah is also described in Scripture as the shepherd of Israel (Ps 78:70–72; Ezek 34:23–24). Furthermore, Israel's spiritual leaders were often condemned by God for being false shepherds who abused rather than nurtured and protected the flock of God (Jer 23:1–4; Ezek 34:1–10). These shepherds did not feed the people God's truths, which resulted in their people becoming lost, wounded, and sick (Ezek 34:3–4; Zech 10:2–3).

These Old Testament themes surely informed Jesus's words in John 10. In John 10:7–10, Jesus contrasts himself with the false shepherds who only care for themselves and are destructive thieves. He claims to be the true shepherd who cares for and nurtures his sheep, giving them abundant life because of the sacrifice of his life (John 10:11). John, the author of this Gospel, wants his readers to clearly understand that there are two paths, one bringing life and the other bringing destruction and death.

Abundant life is found only in following Jesus, the true shepherd. There is no conceivable universe in which the author of John 10:10 could have meant that abundant life is found in doing whatever one wants to do, even if that means violating the law of God, breaking a marriage covenant, and abandoning one's children. This interpretation grossly violates the principle of authorial intent. "Private meaning" hermeneutics often lead to severe distortions with destructive consequences. Sound hermeneutics require identifying the biblical author's intended meaning.

RECOGNIZE THE LIMITS AND FUNCTIONS OF OLD TESTAMENT LAW

A critical and often unaddressed hermeneutical issue is the role of the Mosaic law in the life of the New Testament believer. Christians have historically affirmed the Bible's verbal, plenary inspiration—all portions of Scripture and all the words of each portion are inspired by God. However, just because all Scripture is divinely inspired does not mean that all Scripture must still be obeyed. For instance, God specifically told Peter that the Old Testament dietary laws were no longer binding for New Testament era believers (Acts 10:9–16). The book of Hebrews teaches that the Old Testament sacrificial system found its fulfillment in Christ (Heb 7–10). In establishing a new covenant, God "has made the first one obsolete" (Heb 8:13).

New Testament (i.e., new covenant) believers no longer obey the Mosaic commands regarding sacrifices. But how about the hundreds of other commands and prohibitions in the Mosaic law, which are recorded in Exodus, Leviticus, Numbers, and Deuteronomy? Are Christian parents obligated to circumcise their boys? Can a father nullify his adult daughter's vows? Are Christian couples obligated to obey Mosaic menstrual purity laws? These are not merely academic questions.

Decades ago, I attended several of Bill Gothard's weeklong seminars. I was a teenager and remember Gothard making numerous Mosaic laws binding on believers with absolutely no discussion of which laws weren't to be obeyed. The tacit reasoning seemed to be that if it was a command found in the Old Testament, it must still be followed. Period. This approach to Scripture is confusing at best and ripe for abuse at worst. It often (as with Gothard) facilitates a highly legalistic, harmful understanding of the Christian life. However, if the teacher or preacher is quoting Scripture, laypeople are often reluctant to challenge such teaching.

A more recent example of the harmful misapplication of Mosaic law to New Testament believers is given by biblical patriarchist and Vision Forum founder Doug Phillips. Phillips argues, based on Numbers 30, that fathers have the power to nullify a vow made by their wives or daughters when he says:

> The father is the head of the home. They [adult daughters] are
> not to act outside the scope of their father as long as they're

under the authority of their fathers, fathers have the ability to nullify—or not—the oaths and vows. Daughters can't just go out and independently say, "I'm going to marry whoever I want." No, the father has the ability to say, "No, I'm sorry, that has to be approved by me." She can't even go out and represent him on a business level unless the father says, "Yes, you're authorized and approved by me."[4]

In addition to ignoring numerous biblical texts that contradict his theological model,[5] Phillip's patriarchy is gratuitously predicated on New Testament believers still being under the Mosaic law. So, let's briefly examine whether this is the case. It is essential to understand that God graciously established a covenant with the children of Israel. Through his servant Moses, God gave the children of Israel guidelines to govern individual and community life. Their obedience to the 613 commands contained in the Mosaic law reflected their obedience to the covenant and, ultimately, to Yahweh himself. But the prophets promised that one day God would establish a new covenant with his people, not written on stone tablets but written on human hearts (Jer 31:31–34). This does not impugn the old covenant reflected in the Mosaic law, for God, the good lawgiver, gave that to his people. It was a critical part of salvation history and is God's inspired word and includes his commands to Israel. But it was not the final word in God's redemptive plan.

Being God's word, the Mosaic law has much to teach us about the character of God and his desires for his people. As Paul states in Romans 15:4, "Everything that was written in the past was written to teach us, so that through the endurance taught in the Scriptures and the encouragement they provide we might have hope." We gain countless insights from Mosaic laws that we are not obligated to obey. For instance, Paul cites the law of not muzzling livestock when they are treading grain (Deut 25:4) and applies it to spiritual leaders being compensated by their congregations for their labor (1 Tim 5:18). While not being under this specific law, believers gain helpful insight from it.

Here is the fundamental principle regarding which commands we must obey: *New Testament believers are not obligated to follow a specific Mosaic law unless it is reiterated in the New Testament.* Many Mosaic commands are reiterated. For instance, nine of the ten commandments (all but Sabbath keeping) are reaffirmed in the New Testament. But hundreds of them are not and are not morally binding for the believer.

Not all evangelicals agree with this hermeneutical approach to the Mosaic law.[6] For instance, many categorize the Mosaic law into moral, civil, and ceremonial laws, arguing that New Testament believers must only follow the ethical or moral portions of the law. Others argue that we must follow the moral *and* the civil laws. But such a threefold law distinction does not hold because *all* the law given by Moses was moral, for it is collectively declared holy, righteous, and good (Rom 7:12). The New Testament views the law as a unified whole (see Jas 2:10).

Since the question of which portions of Scripture are still morally binding has such significant implications, I will provide further biblical support for the assertion that we are no longer under the Mosaic law.

1. *Galatians 3:19–25 says the law was our schoolmaster, given temporarily to lead us to Christ by demonstrating our sinfulness.* Furthermore, Paul says, "Now that this faith has come, we are no longer under a guardian" (v. 25). This clearly shows that the New Testament believer is no longer under the law; it has served its purpose by pointing people to Christ.

2. *Romans 7:4 says believers have died to the law and have been joined to Christ.* Romans 7:6 specifically says believers have been released from the law that they might serve in the

newness of the Spirit and not in the oldness of the letter. This specific language of release in the context of sanctification indicates that the believer is no longer under the Mosaic law. The way Romans 8 develops life in the Spirit confirms this interpretation, for the believer is said to live under the law of the Spirit (v. 2).

3. *Ephesians 2:15 specifically says Christ has abolished the law of commandments contained in ordinances.* The Mosaic law created alienation between Jews and gentiles, creating a "barrier" and a "dividing wall of hostility" (v. 14). In Christ, this ethnic alienation has been abolished because Christ has brought the two sides together by "setting aside in his flesh the law with its commands and regulations" (v. 15).

4. *In 1 Corinthians 9:20–21, Paul specifically says he is no longer under the law but would voluntarily put himself under the law to evangelize Jews.* In their outstanding book on how to read the Bible, Gordon Fee and Douglas Stuart give a helpful summary of the role of the Mosaic law for the New Testament believer: "All of the Old Testament law is still the word of God for us even though it is not the command of God to us."[7] By application, spiritual leaders who obligate people to obey the Mosaic laws without showing how those commands are reaffirmed in the New Testament are on faulty hermeneutical grounds.

INTERPRET ACCORDING TO NORMAL RULES OF LITERARY GENRE (TYPE OF LITERATURE)

While the Bible is unlike any other piece of literature, it should be read as literature. In other words, we are to interpret it based on the normal rules of literary genre. While most do not conscientiously apply "rules" to the different types of literature they read, we do it intuitively. For instance, we innately read and interpret the words of a poem differently from those of a historical account and differently from a political ad. Most hermeneutics textbooks have considerable discussion of the various literary genres found in Scripture, including historical narrative, law, poetry, wisdom, prophecy, gospels, letters, and apocalyptic.[8] Literary genre is a huge topic, so we will give a few hermeneutical principles on some genres found in Scripture.

Historical Narrative

Over 40 percent of the Bible is narrative, that is, history told through story. Much of the Old Testament, the Gospels, and Acts are narrative. All narrative, biblical or secular, is often best read by carefully noting the story's scene or setting (e.g., Ruth 1:1: "In the days when the judges ruled, there was a famine in the land"), conflict or problem (e.g., Ruth 1:5: "Both Mahlon and Kilion also died, and Naomi was left without her two sons and her husband"), dialogue, climax (e.g., Ruth 4:6: "At this, the guardian-redeemer said, 'Then I cannot redeem it because I might endanger my own estate. You redeem it yourself. I cannot do it'"), and resolution (e.g., Ruth 4:13: "So Boaz took Ruth and she became his wife . . . and she gave birth to a son"). It is beneficial to note repetition (e.g., compare Judg 17:6 and 21:25: "Everyone did what was right in his own eyes," ESV).

There are several important hermeneutical points to note about narrative.

First, *Old Testament narrative, in particular, recounts what happened but does not necessarily reflect what should have happened.* In other words, we cannot assume that the stories are examples to follow. As Fee and Stuart note, "Just because someone in a Bible story did something, it does not mean that a modern reader has either permission or obligation to do it too."[9] Old Testament narratives give trustworthy accounts of historical incidents, but the morality of those incidents is mixed. Many accounts are bad examples we should not follow (e.g., Jacob's deception of his brother and father in Gen 25 and 27, and Laban's deception of Jacob in Gen 29). Other stories are found in such a different cultural context than ours that it is challenging to know what moral or theological lesson modern readers should draw. For instance, was it morally inappropriate for Queen Vashti to refuse the king's request to show off her beauty to the drunken guests, reinforcing the belief that husbands should be "masters" in their own households (Esth 1:8–22)? Some evangelicals argue that Vashti was obligated to obey her husband even if his command was to appear before the guests naked. To do otherwise would be disobedience and disrespect, and it is "never right" for a wife to do either.[10] Other Scripture, however, would suggest Vashti had every right to deny her husband's request, but in Esther that point is ambiguous at best.

Furthermore, just because some narrative accounts record God blessing an individual, it does not follow that God approves of all of their actions. Instead, God sometimes accommodates himself to our limited understanding. For instance, Jacob, in another of his schemes, adopted a plan to increase the number of spotted goats being born by putting mottled (spotted) poles in the area where the livestock were breeding (Gen 30:37–43). The birth rates of spotted, speckled, and striped goats increased dramatically. But this appears to be a gracious concession by God to bless Jacob, not a "biblical" technique violating genetic science for modern shepherds to follow.

Second, *we should be reluctant to follow an Old Testament narrative example unless we can validate the principle elsewhere in Scripture.* For instance, while Gideon did discern God's will through the use of a fleece (Judg 6:36–40), nowhere else in Scripture do we find this sort of technique commanded or approved. It is by no means clear that God is commending the use of a "fleece" to modern believers for discerning his will.

It is essential to recognize that the overarching purpose of the Old Testament narrative is to demonstrate God's redemptive plan and how God chose, led, and preserved his covenant people through whom the Messiah would come. Thus, the specifics of many of those stories (such as in Esther) are not of primary importance. Some of the specifics are morally ambiguous.

Third, *Old Testament stories do have much to teach us.* The New Testament recounts them as such. For example, Paul notes that the Old Testament stories of the Israelites' idolatry, sexual immorality, grumbling, and God's judgment on those sins (see Num 16:11–35; 25:1–9) teach us important moral lessons. Paul writes that "these things happened to them [the Israelites] as an example, but they were written down for our instruction" (1 Cor 10:11 ESV; cf. Heb 11). Yet the key to drawing more lessons from the Old Testament narrative is to compare Scripture with Scripture. We must ask: (1) How do other biblical passages interpret this Old Testament story? (2) Does the story itself indicate God's perspective on the story? For instance, is there an element of divine judgment? (3) How do other biblical passages shed light on the actions of this story? For instance, numerous biblical passages affirm the necessity of honesty and the impropriety of dishonesty and deception (Exod 20:16; Prov 19:1; 2 Cor 4:2). For this reason, we know that God blessed Jacob despite his deception, not because of it. His dishonest actions are not an example to follow.

Destructive hermeneutical interpretations of historical narratives are common and costly. And as we've seen with allegory, you can "stretch" Old Testament stories to teach endless "truths" that aren't in the text and are at odds with other Scriptures. For instance, according to a recent report, the founding pastor of an Oregon megachurch engaged in sexual misconduct with a staff member.[11] Another local pastor was concerned about this rumor, conducted his own firsthand investigation, and met with the woman and one of the church elders. The investigation ultimately prompted some action. The accused pastor admitted to an "emotional affair" and was simply given some time off by the elder board. He then is said to have "returned to the pulpit without any official restoration or safeguarding." Reportedly the church elders claimed the account of Noah's sons covering their father's nakedness (Gen 9:20–23) as the biblical basis for their actions. Since the sons covered Noah's drunken nakedness, churches are apparently to cover up their pastor's sexual sins. This grotesque interpretation directly violates the apostle Paul's plain instructions in 1 Timothy 5:19–20 to publicly rebuke sinning elders, in order that others in the church would fear sinning.

Poetry

The entire book of Psalms, much of Proverbs, and many sections in the prophets are poetry. And we don't interpret poetry the way we interpret narrative. Let's note a few characteristics of biblical poetry.

First, *poetry uses many figures of speech that aren't intended to be understood literally.* For instance, God is described as a rock in Psalm 28:1. God obviously isn't a literal rock, but rocks are characterized by strength and stability, virtues that God embodies. Some of the most arresting figures of speech in the Psalms are personifications, attributing personal characteristics to inanimate objects to make a point. In Psalm 114:3–4, the psalmist declares, "The sea looked and fled, the Jordan turned back; the mountains leaped like rams, the hills like lambs." Seas don't literally run, and mountains don't actually leap. This is figurative language for dramatic effect. The context is the exodus, and the writer uses vivid language to stir the reader with the momentous significance of God's delivering the children of Israel from Egypt.

Second, *closely related to the previous point, Hebrew poetry uses highly emotive language for dramatic effect.* Duvall and Hays liken Old Testament poetry to magnificent paintings that

> appeal primarily to our emotions. Furthermore, they do not build complex grammatical arguments, but rather use images (like paintings) to convey their meanings. They paint colorful pictures with words to convey messages loaded with emotional impact. That doesn't mean that they ignore logic or write illogically. It simply means that they focus on emotional aspects more than on logical aspects.[12]

Hebrew poetry intends to engage the reader's will by engaging the heart. Recognizing this helps to solve some of the apparent contradictions between the Psalms and the Gospels. Jesus said we are to love our enemies (Matt 5:43–44), yet David said he hated and abhorred his abusive enemies (Ps 139:21–22). David was using poetry to convey his utter repudiation of abusive evil. David's words should not be taken literally and applied to Matthew 5:43–44 in a way that overrides the message of Jesus.

Third, *Hebrew poetry is characterized by parallelism.* Hebrew poets loved to communicate using phrases with similar or opposite meanings. This first category of Hebrew parallelism is *synonymous parallelism,* saying the same or nearly the same thing in different words and phrases. For instance, in Psalm 6:1 David prays, "Lord, do not rebuke me in your anger or discipline me in your wrath." Rebuking in his anger and disciplining in his wrath are similar, if not identical. Often, the psalmists will use *antithetical parallelism* (two phrases with opposite meanings) to convey their message: "Those who are evil will be destroyed, but those who hope in the Lord will inherit the land" (Ps 37:9). Evildoers and the godly will experience opposite fates. A less common but significant form of Hebrew parallelism is *climactic parallelism.* In this poetic device, the poet builds the message with each line (there is a progression). This seems to be the case in Psalm 1:1: "Blessed is the one who does not walk in step with the wicked or stand in the way that sinners take or sit in the company of mockers." Walk, stand, sit may well suggest a progression to deeper levels of evil.

Let's now give an example of how failing to understand Hebrew poetry can lead to harmful misreadings of Scripture. Psalm 91 gives an astounding list of blessings for those who put their trust in God, who make him their refuge and fortress. The psalmist declares that for this person:

> Surely he will save you
>> from the fowler's snare
>> and from the deadly pestilence.
> He will cover you with his feathers,
>> and under his wings you will find refuge;
>> his faithfulness will be your shield and rampart.
> You will not fear the terror of night,
>> nor the arrow that flies by day,
> nor the pestilence that stalks in the darkness,
>> nor the plague that destroys at midday.
> A thousand may fall at your side,
>> ten thousand at your right hand,
>> but it will not come near you.
> You will only observe with your eyes
>> and see the punishment of the wicked.
> If you say, "The LORD is my refuge,"
>> and you make the Most High your dwelling,
> no harm will overtake you,
>> no disaster will come near your tent.
> For he will command his angels concerning you
>> to guard you in all your ways. (Psalm 91:3–11)

This passage is used by many to affirm a "prosperity" gospel. If you have faith, you will not get sick, will always experience prosperity, and Satan will not be able to harm you. You will even be "immune from global disaster."[13] A literal reading of this text appears to support this assertion. What are abuse survivors to make of Psalm 91? Had God failed to deliver on his promises when they were terrorized and brutalized? I had just read this passage three years ago when we received an urgent message from our Ugandan director, notifying us that our beloved Mama Sylvie was missing. Sylvie was one of our Mending the Soul Congo regional directors. She never arrived home after a staff training. Celestia and I hardly slept that night, praying for her safety. The next morning, we received the tragic news that she had been murdered in an ambush by Muslim terrorists. If we take the language of Psalm 91 literally, God must have failed her, for she was captured by the fowler's snare (v. 3—she had apparently been tricked and trapped on the road). The arrow (weapon) that flies by day did strike her (v. 5). Earthly harm did overtake her (v. 10). Did Sylvie lack faith, or did God fail to keep his promises? Neither. This beautiful psalm is true and trustworthy but must be read for what it is—poetry crafted to evoke confidence in God in times of trouble. And it speaks emotionally from a big-picture perspective, impelling us to trust God with our eternal destiny. We must resist the temptation to apply the poetry of Psalm 91 in an overly literal manner. That is exactly what Satan did with this psalm when he used it to entice Jesus to throw himself down from the pinnacle of the temple, arguing that if Jesus did so the angels would "lift you up in their hands, so that you will not strike your foot against a stone" (Matt 4:5–6). It is worth noting that Satan's misreading of Psalm 91 is the only time this psalm is cited in the New Testament. Failing to recognize the nature of Hebrew poetry can be most destructive.

Bill Fullilove gives an additional helpful insight regarding the meaning of Psalm 91:

We must remember that poets talk in word pictures, with images meant to evoke, not just to instruct. And the general truth is that God does care for his people in specific and immediate ways, not just [in] a vaguely general sense. . . . If our frame of reference is limited to what occurs in this life, we will eventually be let down, but if our frame of reference is longer than this life, then we will see its truth. In that we recognize the foremost thing in our protection, protection from the devil's schemes that would destroy us forever.[14]

God had, in fact, protected Sylvie from the devil's destructive schemes. Sylvie's grieving husband Kasitro stood on this truth. In his first message to us after finding her body, he affirmed God's goodness and faithfulness. He declared, "God carried my beloved home. She is safe with Jesus. I will continue the work my Sylvie began. I will trust and serve Jesus until I die." Sylvie and Kasitro understood and applied well the poetic truths of Psalm 91—God is a sure refuge against all eternal dangers. Because he always cares for his children, we should fully entrust ourselves to him. Understanding the nature of poetry can keep us from misreading beautiful biblical promises.

The Book of Proverbs

The book of Proverbs is composed of a special kind of poetry reflected in its name. Proverbs are a form of wisdom literature common in the ancient Near East. It is essential to understand the nature of proverbs to interpret them correctly. Proverbs express truths about the nature of life in a pithy format. They describe how life normally works. As Old Testament scholar Tremper Longman notes, "Proverbs are not promises; they are generally true principles, all other things being equal."[15] But depending on varying circumstances, proverbs aren't true in every situation. Modern proverbs or maxims work the same way. Pairing some maxims reveals this. For instance, consider "many hands make light work" and "too many cooks spoil the broth." Both express true principles. Having ample help for a project most often helps the project succeed, but there are circumstances in which too many people, particularly with strong opinions, can impede progress. Both of these maxims are true, but they aren't true in every single circumstance.

Unless other Scripture declares otherwise, a proverb is not a foolproof formula or promise that admits no exceptions.[16] For instance, Proverbs 10:3 states, "The LORD does not let the righteous go hungry, but he thwarts the craving of the wicked." This proverb admits exceptions. Up to a million and a half Christian Armenians died of starvation in Turkey between 1915 and 1925. Some 200,000 Marionite Christians starved to death in Mt. Lebanon (Syria) between 1915 and 1918. Less than two decades later, up to five million Christian peasants living in modern Ukraine died of starvation between 1932 and 1933 (termed the *Holodomor*). We could multiply examples of the brutal exception to this proverb from world history. Proverbs 10:3 does not intend to teach a universal truth that applies to every situation without exception.

Sometimes we find exceptions to a proverb within Proverbs itself. We saw earlier that Proverbs 28:19 says those who work in the land will have abundant food, which is how life typically works, but there are exceptions. Such an exception to this general principle is found in Proverbs 13:23: "The fallow ground of the poor would yield much food, but it is swept away through injustice" (ESV). Injustice skews the way life often works, resulting in hardworking poor people going hungry anyway.

Let's now apply the hermeneutics of Proverbs to abuse. A self-identified biblical counseling website, in an article on abuse in the family, asserts that, based on Proverbs 15:1 ("A gentle answer turns away wrath, but a harsh word stirs up anger"), an abused wife must own and presumably repent of her role in provoking her abusive husband. They state:

> The biblical counselor should not stop at dealing with the externals of abuse, however. He should also kindly, yet courageously, deal with the root of the problem: the existing anger of the one person which increases to the point of abuse upon the provocation of the other. In other words, abuse is almost always a double-responsibility problem. Without the angry individual, it does not develop. *But also without the provocation of the other individual, abuse does not develop either. This can be said with some confidence biblically because "a gentler answer . . . turns away wrath"—makes it diminish instead of increase.* (emphasis mine)[17]

The author notes that "the biblical counselor has two people to counsel, not just one." But even if the abuser won't come to counseling, there is still hope because:

> Even if only the one being abused is present for counsel, they can be helped to understand their part in the abuse—provocation—and can let God's Spirit work in his or her life to become a part of the solution ("a gentle answer") rather than a part of the problem (a harsh word—"a word of pain").[18]

In other words, abuse victims are responsible for suffering abuse. They provoked it. It is partly their fault, so says God's Word. This conclusion, based on a complete misreading of Proverbs, is reprehensible. Abusers abuse because they have sinful, hardened hearts. Proverbs 15:1 expresses a general truth about how life works. Generally speaking, all things being equal, a gracious, gentle response does assuage an angry person. This typically works with your run-of-the-mill, non-abusive store clerk, neighbor, or spouse. But things aren't always equal. Abusers have their own unique, tragic characteristics. They abusively rage because something is broken inside of them, not because someone has sinfully "provoked" them. Scripture repeatedly attests to this truth. Saul became homicidally angry at David simply because women sang David's praises, not because David provoked him (1 Sam 18:7–9). Later on, when Jonathan graciously explained why David was not at the king's table, Saul again flew into a rage and attempted to kill him (1 Sam 20:26–33). Jonathan was not responsible for provoking his abusive father. King Asa became so "enraged" at Hanani that he threw him into prison, not because the seer sinfully provoked him but because Asa was abusive and rejected Hanani's godly words (2 Chr 16:10). Our Lord himself was praised by the people in Nazareth for the "gracious words that came from his lips." Still, moments later, those same people became "furious" and tried to murder him (Luke 4:22–29). Jesus is not to be condemned for "provoking" the people. In summary, Proverbs 15:1 articulates a general truth: a gentle answer in the proper context assuages anger. But this is not a watertight prediction that one should ever use to condemn domestic-violence victims.

Epistles

The New Testament epistles are among the most familiar portions of Scripture for most Christians, making it particularly important to understand their unique characteristics. Most of the New Testament (other than the Gospels, Acts, and Revelation) are epistles—that is, letters to individuals or churches. The structure of New Testament epistles or letters is virtually identical to that found in ancient Greco-Roman secular epistles (names of the writer and recipient, salutation or greeting, thanksgiving or prayer, body, closing/farewell), though not all New Testament epistles contain all of these elements.

The Occasional Nature of the Epistles

The single most important and challenging characteristic of the New Testament epistles for hermeneutics is that they are *occasional*, meaning that the writers were responding to specific situations (occasions) faced by their readers. Sometimes, we are unsure of the particular occasional situation (such as Paul's comment in 1 Cor 15:29 about baptizing for the dead), but doing historical background study, using Bible dictionaries and commentaries, will often shed helpful light on the occasional setting. The significance of the epistles' occasional settings cannot be overemphasized. Frequently Christians approach the epistles as if they were intended to be summaries of Christian doctrine or ethics manuals. Certainly, the New Testament epistles contain much theology and are replete with ethical material, but they were not written as theology or ethical textbooks per se. Rather, they are pastoral letters responding to specific situations and needs. Thus Paul was not necessarily attempting to give a specific ecclesiological (church) rule for all churches in all times and cultures when he commanded the woman at Corinth to wear a head covering in the assembly (1 Cor 11:4–7). His command is based on a specific situation involving Corinthian believers living in first-century Greco-Roman culture and had a precise cultural meaning, which would not necessarily be true in other cultures (i.e., that a married woman's uncovered head was dishonoring to her husband).

An additional challenge with recognizing and factoring in the occasional setting is our cultural preconditioning, which filters our reading of the text, tempting us to misread New Testament texts. For example, southern Christian slaveholders less than two centuries ago universally appealed to biblical statements commanding enslaved people to obey their masters (Eph 6:5–9; Col 3:22), even abusive masters (1 Pet 2:18–20), as approval of slavery for all cultures at all times. This interpretation harmonized with their cultural conditioning and advanced their own economic interests, but it destroyed millions of lives and horribly sullied the testimony of the church. Their preconditioning kept them from considering how the occasional setting of these Pauline and Petrine commands was a concession to the cultural conditions of the Roman imperial world. Furthermore, their cultural preconditioning kept them from recognizing the implications of other New Testament texts, such as equality in the body of Christ (Gal 3:28; Col 3:11–14).

The occasional nature of the Pauline epistles never threatens their divine inspiration or dampens their contemporary usefulness. However, it does mean that we must carefully factor in the occasional setting before seeking to interpret and apply the text to the twenty-first century.

In the next section of the book, we will apply the occasional setting of the epistles to several "poison" texts. One of those texts is 1 Timothy 5:19: "Do not entertain an accusation against an elder unless it is brought by two or three witnesses." This text is applied quite literally and restrictively by many churches when an elder is accused of sexual abuse. A friend told me about a situation he experienced as a young adult in which he observed the youth pastor engaging in sexual behavior with one of the high school girls. My friend was greatly disturbed and took his concerns to the executive pastor. The pastor said that this report was truly alarming, but since they were a church grounded on the authority of the Bible, his hands were tied. He cited 1 Timothy 5:19 and declared, "Unless another witness comes forward, there is literally nothing I can do. Scripture says I can't even consider this accusation." Tragically, this was not this predator pastor's only victim. This misreading of Scripture thwarted protection of the vulnerable. I will argue in chapter six that a recognition of the occasional nature of 1 Timothy 5:19 helps to preclude such a destructive interpretation and application.

The "Already" and "Not Yet" Perspective

We next introduce the second characteristic of the New Testament epistles with an illustration from a book by Pat Robertson, in which he responds to questions from his listeners. One woman stated that her husband had molested their daughter, but since then he had become a Christian. The mother wanted to know if she should share with other parents her husband's history of molesting their daughter "in the event that they [other parents] might unwittingly leave him with a child."[19] Robertson responds by saying, "Do not share this secret with anyone." He goes on to say that unless the husband has "ongoing, strong urges toward pedophilia," consider him a "new man" in Christ who has been set free from "past problems." In other words, while your husband did molest your daughter, now that he is a Christian he is a "new man." You, and parents of children he has access to, have nothing to worry about.

Robertson is apparently referencing Paul's statement in 2 Corinthians 5:17: "Therefore, if anyone is in Christ, the new creation has come: The old has gone, the new is here!" The King James Version of this verse, which may well have been what Robertson was referencing, is even more stark: "Therefore if any man be in Christ, he is a new creature: old things are passed away; behold, all things are become new." On the face of it, this verse does seem to make Robertson's point. The old has gone and the new is here! "All things are new!" This child molester is now a Christian. Everything has changed, and based on Paul's teaching this man is not a danger to minors. Or is he? Such a naive and destructive reading of this Pauline verse fails to account for a second major characteristic of the New Testament epistles.

Eschatology is the doctrine of last things—that is, the end of the present age and human history. Scripture teaches that two thousand years ago Christ our king came to earth. When he came, he "inaugurated" the kingdom of God on earth. He declared that the kingdom of God "has come" (Luke 11:20). However, Jesus's reign is not yet complete. That is, he will someday return again, bring about the final judgment against evil, make all things new, and establish shalom for all eternity (Rev 21:1–5). In other words, the *kingdom has been inaugurated but is not yet consummated.* This is often described as the "already and not yet."

Inaugurated eschatology helps us understand many statements in the epistles that initially appear contradictory, particularly statements about the believer's position in Christ. However, they make perfect sense through an "already" but "not yet" lens. For instance, the believer has already been seated in the heavenlies (Col 3:1, 3) but must continue to set his or her mind on the heavenlies (v. 2) until Christ returns—the not yet (v. 4). Believers have "already" died to sin (Rom 6:2–8), but they must not let sin reign in their lives—based on the "not yet" (Romans 6:11–13). Christ has "already" set believers free, but since believers are not yet perfect and glorified (the "not yet"), they must stand firm in their freedom and not subject themselves again to slavery (Gal 5:1). Believers are individuals who had been in darkness, and in Christ are now light (the "already," Eph 5:8a), but they must learn to walk as children of light (Eph 5:8b) because believers are not yet glorified. Because they are in Christ, believers have "already" put off the old self (Col 3:9–10), yet believers are still commanded to put off the old self (Eph 4:22–24) because they are "not yet" glorified.

So, coming back to the man who molested his daughter, assuming he truly trusted in Christ as his Lord and Savior, the "already" is that he is completely forgiven, has Christ's righteousness, and a new spiritual identity. The "not yet" is that he is not yet glorified and thus still has sinful urges and patterns that must be recognized and fought against until the day he dies. "New man" does not mean his pre-Christ urges, perversions, and patterns have simply vanished. Such a naive reading of 2 Corinthians 5:17 is unbiblical and dangerous.

SUMMARY

We have covered a lot of ground in this and the previous chapter. We saw that two essential prerequisites to sound biblical interpretation are reliance on the Holy Spirit and a humble, receptive posture. We went on to identify six hermeneutical principles:

1. Clarify the context.
2. Let Scripture interpret Scripture.
3. Look for the plain, literal meaning.
4. Identify the most likely meaning of the author.
5. Recognize the limits and function of the Old Testament law.
6. Interpret according to normal rules of literary genre.

In the next part of the book, we will apply these hermeneutical principles to common "poison" passages, starting with Scripture addressing marriage.

Part 2

THE HARMFUL USE
OF SCRIPTURE

Chapter 4

PASSAGES ON MARRIAGE

The home remains the most dangerous place for women.
—UNITED NATIONS, "GLOBAL STUDY ON HOMICIDE," 2019

Adam and his wife were both naked, and they felt no shame.
—GENESIS 2:25

It was one of those invitations you don't turn down. A friend on the Phoenix city council had set up this unique meeting. I had been asked to share our abuse organization's mission and resources with the directors of the largest domestic-violence shelters in Maricopa County. I was encouraged by the turnout. Each person listened carefully, attentively tracking the entire presentation. Toward the end, I could feel hot emotion swelling in the room. One woman seemed ready to burst. As I paused for questions, she almost leaped out of her chair and blurted out, "What does Mending the Soul believe about the biblical commands for wives to submit to their husbands?" Most of the women in the room nodded, making it clear they had the same urgent question. This theologically oriented question took me aback, one I expected from my seminary students, not secular social workers.

However, after many more years serving survivors, I'm no longer surprised at the urgency of this question. Every one of these directors had extensive, bitter experiences with biblical phrases like "wives should submit" used as spiritual battering rams to justify domestic violence. Celestia and I have over fifty years of combined experience in the abuse field. We are convinced that "wives should submit to their husbands" and the closely related "the head of the woman is man" are among the most poisonously misused verses in all of Scripture. Hence, in this chapter we will look in some depth at Ephesians 5:24 ("wives should submit"), Ephesians 5:23 and 1 Corinthians 11:3 (the husband is the "head"), and a final key marital text—Malachi 2:16 (God "hates" divorce).

1. EPHESIANS 5:24

"Now as the church submits to Christ, so also wives should submit to their husbands in everything."

We could share countless tragic examples of perverse applications of Ephesians 5:24, as abusive Christian men almost universally cite it.[1] Please note that some readers may find portions of this chapter somewhat difficult or triggering to read. Ruth Tucker provides one of the starkest examples of the destructive abuse of Ephesians 5:24. Even though she was a highly accomplished author and seminary professor, life inside her home was sheer terror and powerlessness. She describes almost twenty years of marital torment with chronic physical, verbal, sexual, and spiritual abuse before she and her son fled. She recounts that her husband, a seminary graduate and pastor, demanded utter blind obedience. He bullied, berated, and abused

Ruth for simply voting differently than he did or for not changing her lecture notes to agree with his views. She reflects on the factors that influence wife battering and states:

> I'm certain a psychiatrist could write an entire volume on my ex-husband. But from my vantage point, his perspective on male supremacy and female submission was front and center. He repeatedly quoted Scripture to defend his headship and to enforce my unconditional obligation to submit—from "the kitchen to the bedroom" . . . His rule was absolute and final—most notably during his violent moods. Black-and-white Bible, black-and-blue wife.[2]

Tucker's problem is not with the Bible but with "black and white" (rigid) distortions of its teachings. While the factors behind domestic violence are complex, research on abusers shows that Tucker's ex-husband's faulty belief system is quite typical. Lundy Bancroft, one of the world's leading experts on domestically abusive men, notes that some of the most common erroneous beliefs of abusive men (religious or not) are a sense of superiority, the right to control family members, and entitlement (he is above the rules others must live by).[3] It should be easy to see how such a skewed mindset can be further fueled and cemented by a power-based, male-headship theology.[4]

The Role of Power

To understand the toxic potential of Ephesians 5:24, we must briefly clarify the fundamental role power plays in abuse, particularly abuse against women. Abuse of every form involves the misuse of power (physical, verbal, sexual, economic, spiritual, etc.) to take advantage of another. Ultimately, human potency or power is a gift from God, who gave humans the right to "rule" over all of creation

(Gen 1:26–28). But in a fallen world, sinners will use their power in sinful, destructive ways. Scripture itself repeatedly makes this link between abuse and power. The writer of Ecclesiastes woefully observes, "I saw the tears of the oppressed—and they have no comforter; *power was on the side of their oppressors*" (Eccl 4:1, emphasis added). The prophet Micah describes abusers who "plan iniquity" and "plot evil . . . because it is *in their power to do it*" (Mic 2:1, emphasis added). Domestically, the Scripture declares that men will be tempted to misuse their power against their wives. In Genesis 3:16, immediately after the fall, God turns to the woman and warns her that "your desire will be for your husband, and he will rule over you." While some over the years have taken this verse as a divine mandate for men to rule their wives, that interpretation ignores the context of the verse (hermeneutical rule number one). In the context, God is stating the negative fallout of human sin, including pain in childbirth (tragic physical effects of the fall), women's unhealthy desire for their husbands (tragic emotional and relational effects of the fall), and husbands' tendency to dominate harshly (tragic relational effects of the fall). The Hebrew word used here for desire is only used two other times in the Old Testament, once in Genesis 4:7 of sin desiring Cain, and once in Song of Solomon 7:10 of a lover's desire for her beloved. This rare Hebrew word for desire has a range of meanings, but most likely here it refers to a romantic desire that is unhealthy, what we today might call *codependency* (trying to get from a man what you can ultimately only get from God). Men, on the other hand, will be tempted in the post-fall world to dominate women. Human history bears tragic testimony to the accuracy of this divine prediction. While women are just as sinful as men and quite capable of abusing others, men are far more likely than women to misuse their power to perpetrate physical or sexual abuse due to biological differences resulting in men having greater physical power and aggression.[5]

Power-Heavy Understandings of Male/Female Roles

Unfortunately, many evangelical leaders, typically labeled as *complementarian*, put tremendous emphasis on high-authority male headship and all-encompassing female submission, making these dominant themes in all teachings on marriage. *Complementarian* refers to the belief that men and women are spiritually equal but have different, complementary roles, with the husband being the authority in the home. For instance, one counseling professor argues that the wife's submission to her husband "is to be her lifestyle at all times, in all places, and in everything." Not submitting is "rebellion against God himself."[6] Another counseling professor argues that "our difficulties with authority and submission come from our sinful pride."[7] Sadly, the author appears oblivious to the "difficulties with authority and submission" created by the widespread abuse of male authority. Another influential pastor and theologian goes so far as to say that marriage is defined by all-encompassing male headship, for without the husband's headship, "there is no marriage."[8] This author goes on to say that male headship means leading a wife with a "firm hand," not based on what she says she needs but on what the husband thinks she needs.[9] Elsewhere, in a chapter on rape, this author vehemently defends power-based male headship and authority. He suggests that Scripture does not condemn what society would call marital rape based on the husband's all-encompassing authority.[10] He states:

> However we try, the sexual act cannot be made into an egalitarian pleasuring party. A man penetrates, conquers, colonizes, plants. A woman receives, surrenders, accepts. This is, of course offensive to all egalitarians, and so our culture has rebelled against the [biblical] concept of authority and submission in marriage.[11]

This latter application of male authority to marriage is revolting in its crudity and brutality. Such headship teaching promotes and justifies domestic abuse. While this author is more extreme than most, many other evangelical writers' descriptions of "godly" submission can unquestionably facilitate abuse.[12] For instance, consider the following descriptions of appropriate male headship. It is said to mean that:

- The husband should "rule over" and "control" his wife and children.[13]
- The husband oversees his wife's finances, including food and clothing purchases.[14]
- The husband has been given by God "lordship, the authorization to subdue and rule" in all of life, including marital and domestic life.[15]
- It is a blessing for a Christian wife to be married to a "strong, forceful, bossy man." This "command man" doesn't want her "involved in any project that prevents her from serving him. . . . She is on call every minute of her day. Her man wants to know where she is, what she is doing, and why she is doing it. He corrects her without thought. For better or worse, his nature is to control."[16]

Consider the following descriptions and illustrations of biblical submission. It is said to mean that a godly wife:

1. Evidences godly submission when she disagrees with her husband's requests and is silent, or better yet, responds with a single word: "sure."[17]
2. Must get her husband's permission to go to someone to get advice. Without her husband's consent, she may not even go to her pastor or pastor's wife.[18]

3. Will not try to change her husband but will quietly adapt and submit to him even if he is a tyrant who "militaristically" dictates what she wears and does every day, even if he neglects his family and spends the bulk of the family income on his hobbies while the family goes without.[19]

4. Understands that submission is "no resistance," so a wife should simply accept her husband without attempting to change him. This is illustrated by a wife who learned to accept her alcoholic husband, who came home in the middle of the night reeking of alcohol and perfume, and does not challenge or confront him but offers to make him his favorite meal.[20]

5. Is positively exemplified by Sarah in Genesis 12 when she submitted to her husband Abraham's directive to lie to Pharaoh by saying she was Abraham's sister, making herself vulnerable to being raped.[21]

6. Graciously consents and submits to her husband's proclamation that their children don't need to wear a seat belt while traveling in the car, which may result in their being thrown from the back seat when he suddenly hits the brakes.[22]

7. Is demonstrated when a husband is evil toward his wife and she responds not by practicing "tough love" but by "patiently enduring," "submitting and suffering for righteousness," and responding kindly by filling the car with gas, making his favorite meal, initiating lovemaking, and confessing her sins.[23]

Such submission-models facilitate abuse, and in many of the illustrations that is precisely what was facilitated. Most of the authors of these quotes are very influential evangelical leaders, and most of the books containing these quotes have sold well, with some having sold hundreds of thousands of copies. It is critically important to look at Ephesians 5:24, the passage most frequently cited by these and other conservative authors who argue for all-encompassing male authority in the home.

At the outset, I will make my conclusions clear. I contend that *the husband's position or role is more about responsibility than power over. Furthermore, Scripture places strict limits on a husband's "authority."*

Understanding Ephesians 5:24: "Wives Should Submit" in "Everything"

Let's tie this discussion to Ephesians 5:24, the most sweeping New Testament marital-submission command. While a wife's marital submission is addressed in five other New Testament passages,[24] most of the principles we survey here apply to those. Let's begin by citing the passage:

> [21]Submit to one another out of reverence for Christ.
>
> [22]Wives, submit yourselves to your own husbands as you do to the Lord. [23]For the husband is the head of the wife as Christ is the head of the church, his body, of which he is the Savior. [24]Now as the church submits to Christ, so also wives should submit to their husbands in everything.
>
> [25]Husbands, love your wives, just as Christ loved the church and gave himself up for her [26]to make her holy, cleansing her by the washing with water through the word, [27]and to present her to himself as a radiant church, without stain or wrinkle or any other blemish, but holy and blameless. [28]In this same way, husbands ought to love their wives as their own bodies. He who loves his wife loves himself. [29]After all, no one ever hated their own body, but they feed and care for their body just as Christ does the church—[30]for we are members of his body. [31]"For this reason a man will leave his father and mother and be united to

his wife, and the two will become one flesh." [32]This is a profound mystery—but I am talking about Christ and the church. [33]However, each one of you also must love his wife as he loves himself, and the wife must respect her husband.

So how do we understand "wives should submit" in "everything?" Here are several key principles from this passage.

"Wives Should Submit" Is Given in the Context of Mutual Submission

Verse 21 begins this family-guidelines section (what scholars call the "household code"), which commands husbands and wives to submit to each other.[25] In other words, submission is not unilateral based on gender. It is *mutual.* Yes, wives are to submit to their husbands, but husbands are also commanded to submit to their wives. Much ink has been spilled on the relationship between the mutual submission enjoined in Ephesians 5:21 and the subsequent submission commands given to wives. Complementarian writers reject mutual marital submission by arguing that husbands are never explicitly commanded in Scripture to submit to their wives.[26] But Ephesians 5:21 gives such a command, being clearly addressed to husbands *and* wives. Other functional, mutual-submission-type commands in the Pauline epistles apply to husbands and others in authority. All believers (including those with greater power) are to defer to others (including those with less power) by putting others needs above one's own (Phil 2:3–4), serving one another in love (Gal 5:13), and "bearing with one another in love" (Eph 4:2). Furthermore, there is another very relevant Pauline marital text, 1 Corinthians 7:4, which is often overlooked in discussions of male authority in marriage. It explicitly addresses husbands, limiting their marital "authority" by giving it to their wives (and does the same to their wives). Here, in the context of marital sexual intimacy, Paul says the "wife does not have authority over her own body but yields it to her husband. In the same way, the husband does not have authority over his own body but yields it to his wife." Paul is affirming a mutual, reciprocal yielding to one's spouse. This is mutual submission. Additionally, in this text, the husband's "authority" is severely limited, for he is said not to have unilateral authority over his own body. Instead, the wife has authority over her husband's body and vice versa.

Coming back to Ephesians 5:21, complementarians such as Wayne Grudem argue that this text does not affirm mutual submission by asserting that "submit to one another" does not encompass both partners in the marriage. It is restricted to those with less power. It means "to be in submission to others in the church who are in positions of authority over you."[27] But this is not what the text says. This is reading into the text what is not there (*eisegesis*). Grudem also appeals to the reciprocal "one another" pronoun used here (*allēlōn*), arguing that it is not always reciprocal but often means "some to others," eliminating a mutual submission of husbands and wives. He uses Galatians 6:2 ("bear one another's burdens," ESV) to illustrate this alleged restricted usage, but it does not prove his point. All believers are to bear the burdens of other believers to the extent they can. The "submit to one another" command in Ephesians 5:21 does not apply only to "some" believers. *Allēlōn* generally indicates complete, not partial, reciprocity. To restrict this reciprocity would undermine and distort many biblical texts. For instance, believers are commanded not to speak evil against "one another" or to grumble against "one another" (Jas 4:11; 5:9). Surely this does not mean that only some believers need to avoid this behavior. Other passages positively use *allēlōn* to describe a wholesale reciprocal relationship. All believers (not just some) are to bear with and forgive "one another" (Col 3:13 ESV), to live in harmony with "one another" (Rom 15:5 ESV), and to love "one another" (1 Thess 4:9 ESV). Similarly, husbands and wives are to mutually, reciprocally submit to one another.

In arguing for mutual submission in Ephesians 5:21, I am not denying the New Testament affirms somewhat differing roles for husbands and wives, with husbands having some leadership role that the wife is to respect and positively respond to. New Testament submission is not devoid of all authority, but the authority is significantly qualified. Thus, in marriage, there is a mutual submission and a "voluntarily yielding in love" submission a wife gives her husband. We see this multifaceted view of submission elsewhere in early Christian literature.[28] In summary, the mutual submission enjoined in Ephesians 5:21 qualifies the authority denoted in the wife's submission in Ephesians 5:22, 24, since the husband is also to yield to his wife.

"Wives Should Submit" Is Given in the Context of the Lordship of Christ

Throughout the "family guidelines" in Ephesians 5:21–6:9, in which Paul instructs one group to submit to another group, Paul repeatedly clarifies that God/Christ alone is the ultimate authority. We submit to one another "out of reverence for Christ" (Eph 5:21). While the husband is the head of the wife, "Christ is the head" of the entire church (5:23). Enslaved Christians are ultimately "slaves of Christ" (6:6). Children are to obey their parents "in the Lord" (6:1). Earthly enslaved people and their earthly enslavers have the same "Master" in heaven (6:9). In light of Paul's emphasis on family members being under the lordship of Christ, it is quite troubling that much evangelical marriage literature places great focus on submission to earthly authorities, particularly husbands and parents, while ignoring two critical realities. First, due to human depravity, those with greater power will often abuse their power, and hence obedience to earthly authorities will often conflict with obedience to Christ. Second, all earthly authorities are penultimate; Christ alone is the sovereign Lord of every believer. Any discussion of the nature and parameters of submission must begin with affirming the lordship of Christ. Christ himself anticipated the challenge of conflicting loyalties, mainly due to familial ties. He warned his would-be followers, "If anyone comes to me and does not hate father and mother, wife and children, brothers and sisters—yes, even their own life—such a person cannot be my disciple" (Luke 14:26; cf. Matt 10:34–39).[29] This powerful statement of Christ's lordship superseded all familial relationships in a Jewish culture that placed a premium on kinship loyalties.[30] The importance of Christ's lordship over all other loyalties and relationships applies to wives and husbands. In other words, no earthly love or authority, neither a husband nor a wife, should supersede our love for and obedience to Christ. A husband's authority does not extend over his wife's spiritual relationship with Jesus her Lord.

The New Testament household codes, particularly the Pauline codes, apply this very principle. While in Greco-Roman society, the husband had tremendous power and authority over his family, including determining the family's religion and spiritual life, Paul makes it crystal clear that the husband is not the ultimate lord (*kyrios*); Christ is. A strong case can be made that the household codes in Colossians and Ephesians serve to clarify the nature of Christ's lordship over his church. In Colossians, for instance, the household code comes immediately after the command to do all in the name of the Lord Jesus (Col 3:17). Christ alone is the ultimate Lord of life and Lord of the household. This concept in and of itself governs a husband's authority over his family.

When we compare the Pauline household codes to first-century secular household codes, we see several notable differences that restrict the husband's authority. In the secular Greco-Roman codes, husbands are given complete authority over the rest of the household. This authority notably included final religious authority. For example, the influential first-century Greek moral philosopher

Plutarch wrote a famous treatise on marriage titled, "Advice to Bride and Groom." His instruction to wives highlights the all-encompassing spiritual authority of husbands: "A wife ought not to make friends of her own, but to enjoy her husband's friends in common with him. The gods are the first and most important friends. Wherefore it is becoming for a wife to worship and to know only the gods that her husband believes in, and to shut the front door tight upon all queer rituals and outlandish superstitions."[31]

The tremendous authority Plutarch gives to husbands is contrasted by the apostle Paul, who asserts that Christ is the supreme authority of both husbands and wives. Plutarch furthermore argues that a virtuous wife should have no feeling of her own but should take on her husband's; should graciously accept her husband having a mistress; should only be visible in her husband's company; when he is away she should hide herself at home; and should do her talking to or through her husband.[32] Nowhere in the Pauline household codes do we see this type of one-sided patriarchal focus.[33] In short, the command for wives to submit "in everything" is limited and governed by the lordship of Christ. A wife's unrivaled loyalty and obedience must be to Christ alone.

"Wives Should Submit" Is Given in the Context of Male Sacrificial Service

It is tragically ironic that Paul's command of submission to wives in Ephesians 5:24 has often been used against wives to condone or justify harsh and abusive behavior by husbands and unqualified submission by wives. Yet the focus in this paragraph (quantitatively and qualitatively) is overwhelmingly on husbands. In Ephesians 5:21–33, Paul uses a mere 47 words to admonish wives, but 143 words to admonish husbands.[34] More importantly, Paul raises the bar for husbands as high as possible by commanding them to love their wives sacrificially, as Christ loved the church and gave himself for her. This is undoubtedly the most demanding command given to husbands in the Bible. Yet Paul does not leave the reader with a sweeping and lofty "imitate Christ" injunction. He elaborates on several specifics of Christ's costly sacrifice for the church. In 5:28–29, he again admonishes husbands to love their wives as Christ loved the church and elaborates on the application. Paul weaves a rich metaphor into this command by instructing husbands to love their wives as their own bodies, tenderly nourishing and cherishing them just as Christ tenderly cares for and nurtures his body, the church. Paul then finishes this paragraph by noting the mysterious sacred "one flesh" intimacy of marriage, which shows Christ's union with the church (vv. 31–32). If Ephesians 5:24 is understood in its context, selfish mistreatment of wives by husbands is utterly precluded. This passage makes such selfish manipulations by dominating husbands a slanderous assault on Christ, for marriage is to be a most winsome picture to the world of Christ's love and care for his bride. *This passage focuses on the husband's service, not his power.*

"Wives Should Submit" Is a Call for Voluntary Submission, Not Obedience

This dramatically contrasts with first-century Greco-Roman household codes, in which the husband was given the right and even the responsibility to *make* his wife submit. Never in Scripture is the husband given such authority. Husbands are not commanded to "rule" their wives but to nurture them, cherish them, and not be bitter against them. The command "to submit" is given directly to wives. It indicates a voluntary surrender to her faithful and ultimate authority, Christ (Col 3:18, "as is fitting in the Lord").[35] Again, we see that the husband's authority is limited in extent.

While "submit" (*hypotassō*) has a range of meanings, it generally denotes a willingness to yield to, defer, or follow another invested with some type of authority. But we must be careful to recognize that *hypotassō* does not denote unbridled power when used by humans.

Many commentators have observed that *hypotassō* indicates submission, not obedience. Obedience is what Paul asks enslaved people and children to give their parents and masters, but this is not what he asks of wives.[36] So, instead of asking wives to obey their husbands as an enslaved person obeys a more powerful master, he asks wives, as equals, to yield to their husbands voluntarily. This usage of *hypotassō* for wives is probably similar to other uses of *hypotassō* in the New Testament and the early Christian literature, indicating voluntary yielding to another in love. For instance, in 1 Corinthians 16:16, the Corinthians are urged to submit (yield in love) to Stephanas's household. Several decades later, a similar command is given to this same church, "Let each man be subject to his neighbor" (1 Clem. 38.1). This is not to suggest that there is no authority inherent in *hypotassō*, but it conveys a softened authority that is best understood in terms of voluntarily yielding to another in love.

Biblical Parameters of Submission

I will now propose six specific limits to a husband's authority over his wife. In other words, a wife must not surrender to her husband's leadership or authority when the following principles apply.

First, *a wife must not submit to her husband when obedience to him would violate a biblical principle (not just a direct biblical statement).* All but the most extreme fundamentalists agree that a wife should not obey her husband if it involves violating a direct command of Scripture. But many moral issues that wives face today are not directly addressed in Scripture (internet pornography, in vitro fertilization, gambling, cosmetic surgery, abortion, sexual fetishes, etc.). If we accept the doctrine of the sufficiency of Scripture, then we must not restrict a woman's right to refuse to submit to her husband to those instances in which she can cite a direct biblical statement that contradicts her husband's command. For example, Celestia has spent almost twenty years as a professional counselor. She has worked with numerous Christian wives who struggled with a husband's decree that she participate in anal sex, have unwanted cosmetic surgery (particularly breast implants), or shave her pubic hair. None of these activities are addressed directly in Scripture. Yet many, if not most Christian ethicists, argue that these behaviors violate biblical principles regarding sexuality, marriage, and the proper care of the body. Often, a wife may not be able to point to a specific biblical text to justify her objection to her husband's command but can only appeal to her sense of the broad teachings of Scripture, which she believes are applicable to the issue at hand.[37]

Second, *a wife must not submit to her husband when obedience to him would compromise her relationship with Christ.* We have noted that Christ, not a husband, is a Christian wife's supreme Lord. She is Christ's bride first and foremost. For instance, religious authorities commanded the early Christian apostles to quit teaching about Christ. Their response is instructive: "We must obey God rather than men" (Acts 5:29 ESV). Modern Christian wives must recognize that their first allegiance is to Christ. Their husband is neither their priest nor their lord. A wife is responsible for nurturing her own spiritual life and that of her family. Hence, a husband cannot dictate his wife's relationship with Christ. In practical terms, a wife should not obey her husband if he tells her not to go to church or a Bible study, forbids her from going to a counselor, pastor, or Christian advisor, or prohibits her from spending time with a trusted friend.[38]

Third, *a wife must not submit to her husband when obedience to him would violate her conscience.* Sometimes, a husband orders his wife to do something she cannot identify as patently unbiblical, yet the behavior is internally objectionable. That is, it would violate her conscience. Again, based on the fact that Christ is her Lord and on Paul's teaching that we must always act in faith before Christ and not violate our conscience (Rom 14:22–23), a wife should not obey a husband if doing so will violate her conscience.[39] This principle is beneficial when a husband requests his wife to participate in sexual practices that she finds objectionable.

Fourth, *a wife must not submit to her husband when obedience to him would compromise her children's care, nurture, and protection.* God calls adults to prioritize protecting and caring for the vulnerable, particularly children (Isa 1:17; Jer 22:3). Care for the vulnerable, including children, is described as the purest form of religion (Jas 1:27). In Scripture, both fathers and mothers have a responsibility to care for their children physically and spiritually (Deut 6:4–7; Prov 31:10–31). Children are commanded to obey their fathers *and* their mothers (Prov 1:8; Eph 6:1). Physically abusive as well as harsh and verbally abusive parenting creates significant long-term damage. We should note that children innately develop their sense of God's character from their experience with their earthly father. So children whose fathers are abusive or harsh develop distorted views of their heavenly Father. If a husband is harsh, verbally abusive, or uses excessive forms of punishment (including physical abuse), a wife has a moral obligation to protect their children regardless of her husband's requests or demands.

Years ago, in pastoral ministry, I worked with a man who had lost his marriage due to his compulsive sexual sin. He was one of the most obsessive and self-destructive addicts with whom I have ever worked, despite his charm and knowledge of Scripture. As we worked on his personal history to ascertain patterns and roots of his sinful behavior, he described a childhood incident that had been highly influential in his development. When he was five, he stole a small object from his neighbor. When questioned about this, he lied and said he knew nothing about the missing item. Before long, his parents discovered his deception. His father, an official in their small town, was quite embarrassed that his son had lied and hurt his reputation. The following day, the father wrote "liar" in red lipstick across his son's forehead, made the son go outside, and locked the door behind him, forcing him to spend the entire day publicly exposed with this vice emblazoned on his forehead. This father's harsh, humiliating punishment proved destructive for this boy. Apparently the boy's mother did not have the courage or believe she had the right to intervene and protect her son from this harsh, harmful discipline.[40]

Fifth, *a wife must not submit to her husband when obedience to him would enable (facilitate) her husband's sin.* Not only should wives avoid obeying a husband's command to sin, but they should also avoid following any directive that facilitates a husband's sin. The holiness of God requires that we not enable others to sin with greater ease. One of the best biblical examples of this concept is Abigail, whose foolish husband Nabal refused to aid David and his men (1 Sam 25:2–13).[41] While the text does not explicitly say that he forbade Abigail from assisting David, it is implied since Abigail gave generous supplies to David's men but kept her actions from her husband (1 Sam 25:19). David was deeply impressed with Abigail's character, and after Nabal died he asked her to become his wife (1 Sam 25:39–42). In our culture, this principle of not submitting when obedience would facilitate sin is applicable when a wife disobeys an alcoholic husband who asks her to purchase him more alcohol, or when this same husband commands her not to tell their pastor about his drinking problem.

It also applies to the woman who asked me how she should respond to her husband, who ordered her to always walk several steps behind him in public. This command was part of a broad pattern of demeaning behavior toward her and others. It also reflected a pattern of pride that caused him to reject his church elders' attempts to confront his behavior. I advised her *not* to obey her husband's command since it would only facilitate his sin and demean her.

Sixth, *a wife must not submit to physical, sexual, or emotional abuse.*[42] While many, if not most, complementarian writers have recently acknowledged that biblical submission does not entail submitting to abuse, there is still significant confusion on how the church in general, and wives in particular, are to respond to abuse. Enduring avoidable abuse, including from one's authorities, is *not* commended biblically. Scripture affirms the wisdom and propriety of fleeing an abuser. "The prudent sees danger and hides himself, but the simple go on and suffer for it" (Prov 22:3 ESV). There are numerous biblical accounts of godly individuals who avoided physical abuse from their authorities (civic and religious) whenever possible. For instance, David (1 Sam 18:11; 19:10; 23:14), Elijah (1 Kgs 19), Jesus (John 7:1; 8:59), and Paul (Acts 9:22–25; 14:5; 17:8–10) all fled from avoidable assaults by kings, priests, and other authorities. David fled from Saul for several years, yet he respected Saul's authority (1 Sam 24:4–6; 26:8–11) and was incredibly blessed by God.

Not only is it entirely biblical for a wife to flee or otherwise refuse to submit to abuse, but not submitting to an abusive husband is also best for the husband. Wives are to do good to their husbands (Prov 31:12), and one of the best ways wives of abusive husbands can do this is by challenging the abusive behavior through fleeing, filing assault charges, contacting church authorities, or otherwise stimulating real accountability and painful consequences for the abusive behavior. Refusing to submit to abuse, and instead taking action not to allow it to continue, is suitable for the husband because (1) this is one of the best ways to break through the abuser's distorted thinking and stimulate repentance, and (2) it decreases the temporal and eternal consequences that accrue the longer a husband abuses.[43]

2. EPHESIANS 5:23 AND
1 CORINTHIANS 11:3

"The husband is the head of the wife." (Eph 5:23)
"The head of a wife is her husband." (1 Cor 11:3 ESV)

It was a fascinating and chilling story. Our thirteen-year-old daughter Abby had just returned from her first missionary trip. She had spent the summer in Central America with a well-known mission organization specializing in youth mission trips. Before the teams of teens went to their assigned countries, they all attended a ten-day "boot camp" at the organization's headquarters. The teens engaged in team-building exercises, work projects, and Bible classes from dawn to dusk. One of the classes was on male-female relationships. The teacher presented a very gender-hierarchical model of marriage. Over dinner, some of the boys made immediate, malignant application of the lesson. In all seriousness, they declared that "girls have to do what they [the boys] tell them to do because God made them [the males] the 'head.'" I was dumbfounded and appalled at how quickly these boys had taken a biblical phrase and twisted it to suit their fleshly desires. After "wives should submit" in "everything," the other biblical phrase most frequently misused against women in general and wives in particular is "the husband is the head of the wife." As this simple story illustrates, we fallen humans have a frightening capacity to distort biblical teaching. If one wants to justify abusive male dominance, 1 Corinthians 11:3 and Ephesians 5:23 can be distorted to serve as influential proof texts.

Headship in Ephesians 5: Turning *Kephalē* on Its Head

Let's start with Ephesians 5:23 since we have just looked at that passage. Paul states, "The husband is the head of the wife as Christ is the head of the church, his body, of which he is the Savior." Much debate has been on the meaning of the Greek word *kephalē*, translated as "head." Egalitarians (those who believe there are no gender-based role distinctions in the home or church) generally argue that *kephalē* does not denote authority, citing ancient texts where the word refers to a "source" or "origin" (as the source of a river). However, virtually none of these texts are from the first century. Other egalitarians argue that *kephalē* can mean preeminence or most honored, but those uses are not as expected or clear. My own study of *kephalē* convinces me that it often involves some form of authority.[44] This is evidenced in Ephesians 5:22–24 where the husband's headship is the basis for the wife's submission. However, we must recognize Paul's emphasis. It is not on the husband's power but on his sacrifice. The husband is the head "as Christ is the head of the church," "of which he is the Savior." Christ exercised his "headship" over the church not through power and authority but through surrender and sacrifice. Michelle Lee-Barnewall's historical research on the use of "head-body" in ancient Greco-Roman sources sheds much additional light on this concept. She shows that the customary usage of the "head-body" metaphor affirmed that "the head" was the most honored one for whom "the body" should always be sacrificed. "The head, as ruler, was not called to be the one who loves but rather was more deserving of being loved." The "head's duty was to ensure its preservation" even at the expense of the body.[45] Thus, Paul's teaching on "head-body" in marriage is very radical. It reflects a countercultural kingdom ethic, which turns *kephalē* (head) on its head.

1 Corinthians 11:3: A Radical Transformation of Headship

First Corinthians 11:3 is the other biblical text that allegedly teaches male headship. We read, "I want you to understand that the head of every man is Christ, the head of a wife is her husband, and the head of Christ is God" (ESV). This is an exceedingly helpful text for understanding male headship because we are given a specific model—the Father's headship over the Son. While it is common for complementarians to argue for the eternal subordination of the Son to the Father, many of us are strongly convinced Jesus was only "under the Father's headship" during his earthly incarnation.[46] I believe that is the context here. One of the most helpful texts for understanding the Father/Son relationship is John 5:18–24.[47] The Father's headship over the Son radically transforms what headship means in marriage.

The Nature of the Father's Headship

What kind of authority do we see the Father exercising over the Son? Is it the type of power-intensive, top-down, hierarchical authority that many Christian writers assert? This is hardly the case. There is authority in the Father/Son's incarnational relationship—the Son does what the Father commands (John 15:10), does the Father's will (6:38), and does nothing on his own authority (8:28–29). However, upon further investigation, we see that even these statements do not denote a power-intensive, rigidly hierarchical type of authority structure, for the Father shares authority with the Son and their work is amazingly mutual and interconnected.[48] For instance, while the Son does carry out the Father's commands, the Father, in turn, gives the Son *all* authority in heaven and on earth (Matt 28:18; cf. John 17:2). While all things that the Son has come from the Father, the Father gives all to the Son so that all that is the Father's is the Son's (John 3:35; 16:15; 17:10). Christ did teach his disciples to pray for the Father's kingdom to come (Matt 6:9–10). At the same time, the Father placed the Son on David's throne so that the Son's kingdom would never end (Luke 1:32–33).

Furthermore, after the Son's obedience on the cross, the Father exalted him to the highest position of authority and honor. The Father will someday compel every created being to worship the Son and affirm his lordship (Phil 2:8–11). Male authority being patterned after the Father/Son significantly qualifies the husband's headship, deemphasizing its authority and instead emphasizing mutuality and empowerment. So, in marriage, a husband is to use his headship to lift and empower his wife so that they might work together as one.

The Activities of Headship

The tasks or activities of headship involves initiation, protection, provision, and honoring and empowering in the unbroken context of oneness and love. Celestia refers to this headship as "an authority of love, not an authority of power." The Father and Son's roles are not entirely reversible. Though they work in union with each other and enjoy rich, mutual, and overlapping activity in many of their works, during the incarnation the Father initiates, protects, and provides for the Son in ways the Son does not for the Father. The Son, then, joyfully responds to the Father's initiation, protection, and provision, which is where submission comes in. We might describe the surrendered response of a wife to her husband as "receiving well" his initiations of support, protection, and care. Let's briefly break down the essence of male headship seen in the Trinity.

Initiation of Love

The Father is the ultimate creator of everything, and Christ is the agent of creation (1 Cor 8:6). The Father is the one who planned and initiated redemption by sending Christ to secure our salvation (John 8:42; 10:36). The Father plans and initiates various redemptive acts.[49] Husbands are to use their headship to initiate lovingly for the sake of their family. While all too often husbands are sinfully aggressive, using their physical and social power to dominate their wives, in our culture husbands usually go to the other extreme by becoming harmfully passive.[50] This may be connected with the common masculine need to be in control and correct. When men are unsure of the best course of action, they often do nothing, leaving their wives and children to care for themselves.

Protection and Provision

In Scripture, the Father's protection of the Son is a strong theme, particularly in messianic psalms such as Psalms 2 and 110. We also see the Father's provision for the Son in terms of giving him a position of honor. For instance, in Psalm 110:1, a text cited frequently in the New Testament, God promises to give Christ a position of honor and to defeat his enemies (making them his footstool). In Psalm 2, in the context of rebellious human rulers, the Father empowers the Son and warns earthly rebels to honor the Son or face destruction. Following this example of the protective headship of God the Father, a husband should use all of his resources (including his physical strength and stamina, which is most often considerably more significant than his wife's) to protect and provide for her. While this certainly means protecting one's wife from any hostile physical threats, in the Western world this is much less frequent than the myriad of more subtle but essential expressions of protection and provision.

Honoring and Empowering

Our human experience teaches us that those in positions of "headship" or "authority" receive the greatest honor and enjoy the greatest power. *The Trinity teaches us otherwise.* Jesus scandalized the Jewish leaders in John 5:23 by declaring that the Father had given all judgment to the Son so "that all may honor the Son just as they honor the Father." John says that the Father gives the Son authority to judge, with the strategic purpose that the Son would be honored to the same extent that he, the Father, is honored.[51] Therefore, husbands exercise incarnational headship when they deliberately strategize to lift up their wives, empower them, and see that they receive honor. God threatens not to answer a man's prayer if he does not learn how to honor his wife (1 Pet 3:7).

Rightly understood, the husband's being the head of the wife utterly precludes male abuse of power and turns male power into sacrificial responsibility. Proper (biblical) male headship will be modeled after the Father-Son relationship. This is characterized by love and mutuality demonstrated in the husband protecting, providing for, honoring, and empowering his wife as the Father did for the Son.

3. MALACHI 2.16

"'I hate divorce,' says the Lord, the God of Israel." (NASB)

In the introduction, Cheryl recounted growing up in a church where the wife was responsible for preserving the marriage regardless of the cost because "God hates divorce." While she was in a particularly legalistic church, this biblical phrase has historically been one of the most common obstacles for abused Christian women to flee their abusive husbands. Less than a month ago, a woman who had endured years of torment by an abusive husband cited this text to me as the reason she couldn't leave her husband. I've had countless survivors tell me their pastors used this text to admonish them to stay in their abusive marriages at the expense of great physical and psychological harm. So, let's look at this text.

What God Truly Hates

One of the initial challenges encountered in interpreting Malachi 2:16 is that it is a difficult verse in Hebrew to translate, leading to somewhat different readings in various translations. In the NIV, it reads, "'The man who hates and divorces his wife,' says the Lord, the God of Israel, 'does violence to the one he should protect.'" The ESV reads, "'The man who does not love his wife but divorces her,' says the Lord, the God of Israel, 'covers his garment with violence.'" The NASB (2020) reads, "'I hate divorce,' says the Lord, the God of Israel, 'and him who covers his garment with violence.'" Regardless of these differing readings, the big picture of this verse is clear. God hates divorce. But this statement is only half of what God hates. God also hates domestic violence (literal or metaphorical) against wives. In other words, God hates abuse. Malachi 2:16 is a verse that, seen in its context, should encourage abused wives. It condemns abusive men, not their victims.

Let's get a bit more specific. Malachi 2:16 says there are two things God hates—divorce and the man who covers his "garment" with "violence." This could mean that God hates divorce as much as he hates such a detestable sin as violent physical assault that sheds blood (Prov 6:16–17; Jer 22:1–5; Mic 3:1–4). Or (more likely) the prophet is showing that divorce under circumstances such as this (hypocritical religious men abandoning their Jewish wives for foreign women, Mal 2:11; cf. Ezra 9:1–2) was metaphorically an act of violence toward wives and children and detested by God who also hates and harshly judges those who shed innocent blood. Either way, the point is clear that divorce under these circumstances is as hated by God as a violent assault. He detests both.

We should note Malachi's play on words here, for cover (Hebrew *kasa*), is used earlier in verse 13 of these immoral men "covering" the altar with their tears; instead, God says he sees them "covering" their garments with blood. Malachi may also be hinting at the fact that though they splashed the altar and their robes with the actual physical blood of sacrificial lambs, all God saw was the metaphorical blood they shed through their abusive treatment of their wives. God did not listen to these immoral men because they had viciously annihilated a sacred covenant. Each one had abandoned their marriage "companion" and "wife by covenant" (v. 14 ESV). The women being abandoned by divorce were the victims. Malachi expresses God's compassion for these wives and anger at their cruel husbands.

Divorce and Abuse

In ancient Israel, an abused woman did not have the legal right to initiate divorce proceedings against an abusive husband. So, how do we apply biblical teaching on divorce in a modern context? Is abuse grounds for divorce? Many evangelical leaders are dogmatic in rejecting divorce for abuse as a biblical option. It is often argued that if one has a high view of Scripture, only sexual sin and possibly desertion by an unbelieving spouse are grounds for divorce. But there are notable examples of Protestant Reformation and Puritan theologians who saw abuse as grounds for divorce and remarriage. The late J. I. Packer argued that most Puritans reasoned that all conditions that nullified the marriage relationship in practice, including intolerable conditions, were grounds for divorce and remarriage.[52]

Currently, influential conservative scholars such as Wayne Grudem, the founder of Council on Biblical Manhood and Womanhood, John Frame, and Russell Moore argue that Scripture does allow for divorce in cases of abuse.[53] Those who believe abuse gives grounds for divorce and remarriage generally draw this from 1 Corinthians 7:10–16.[54] I strongly affirm that this latter text does give abuse victims grounds to divorce and remarry.

Let's start with Matthew 19:3–9. Most evangelical leaders agree that this text clearly affirms divorce and remarriage if one's spouse commits sexual sin. Matthew 19:9 states: "I tell you that anyone who divorces his wife, except for sexual immorality, and marries another woman commits adultery." The Greek word used here for "sexual immorality" is *porneia*. This noun encompasses the broadest range of sexual sins and would refer to any type of forbidden sexual activity.

Elsewhere I have argued that, biblically, *porneia* encompasses more than physical sexual intercourse and could include contemporary practices such as chronic usage of pornography, attendance at strip clubs, and cybersex.[55] We should also note that Jesus's exception clause governs divorce and remarriage; if one has grounds for divorce, one has grounds for remarriage. So, in terms of abuse, *if an abusive spouse is engaging in sexual sin, the nonoffending spouse has biblical grounds for divorce and remarriage.*

Desertion by an unbelieving spouse is the other condition widely accepted by evangelical scholars as grounds for divorce and remarriage. This is found in 1 Corinthians 7:10–16. Here, Paul alludes to Jesus's teachings on divorce (Matt 5:31–32; 19:9) and says married Christians should not divorce their unbelieving partners simply because they don't share their faith (1 Cor 7:10, 12–13). If Christians do leave their spouses, seemingly for "irreconcilable differences," they should remain unmarried or be reconciled (v. 11) since, based on Jesus's teachings, they do not have biblical grounds for divorce or remarriage. Paul goes on, however, to add to biblical instructions on divorce, for in verse 12, he writes, "I [say], not the Lord." *This doesn't mean that this is merely his opinion but that he was consciously adding to Jesus's teachings.* As an apostle, Paul wrote with unique divine authority (cf. Eph 2:20). When Paul occasionally gives a nonauthoritative opinion, as he does later in this very chapter, he makes that clear ("now about virgins: I have no command from the Lord, but I give a judgment," 1 Cor 7:25). So, in 1 Corinthians 7:12 Paul consciously broadens biblical teaching on divorce.

First, Paul allows for marital separation. Though he doesn't spell it out, most likely the separation would result from irreconcilable differences that prohibit the couple from living together in harmony (1 Cor 7:11). In this case, divorce is not permissible. A different scenario is addressed in verse 15, where Paul deals with the possibility of the unbelieving spouse leaving their Christian mate. If the unbelieving spouse is determined to leave, the believing spouse should let them go ("If the unbeliever leaves, let it be so"). The Greek verb used here for leave (*chōrizō*) is used in biblical and ancient secular Greek to refer to divorce (Matt 19:6; Mark 10:9), and that is the most logical meaning here. In this event, Paul says, "The brother or the sister is not bound in such circumstances; God has called us to live in peace" (1 Cor 7:15). The Greek verb used here for "bound" (*douloō*) is a strong term used elsewhere for "enslavement" (Acts 7:6;

Rom 6:22; Titus 2:3), and in this context refers to being bound by the marriage covenant.

Interestingly, Paul gives a reason the deserted believer is released from the marriage covenant—God calls us to "peace" (1 Cor 7:15). The spouse who deserts their partner has violated their sacred commitment to their spouse and created destructive disharmony. This is not God's desire. Since the unbelieving spouse has already decided to leave, the believer's freedom is more than the freedom to let them go, since they have already gone. Instead, Paul says the believer is free to remarry (i.e., they are not enslaved to their marriage covenant since the unbeliever's desertion has dissolved it). It makes sense for Paul to use the strong verb "enslave" since earlier in the passage he indicates that a Christian is bound to the marriage covenant (vv. 10–11) and has no right to divorce just because their spouse is not a Christian. Paul is now indicating the instance in *which the believer is freed from the marriage covenant—that is, desertion by one's spouse.*

Paul reiterates the freedom of an abandoned spouse to remarry later in the chapter. He does not command remarriage here due to the distress and persecution that the Corinthians were experiencing (vv. 26, 29); Paul instead advocates singleness (vv. 28b, 32–35). At the same time, he says that if they have been released from a wife (v. 27), it isn't sinful if they remarry. The noun used for "release" in verse 27 (*lysis*) can mean "divorce," and in this context makes the most sense.[56] Paul earlier (v. 15) spoke of the case of an unbelieving spouse divorcing a Christian and advised the Christian to let them go. In verses 17–26 Paul warns individuals to remain in the state in which they were called. In verse 27, he returns to the theme he left in verses 15–16—namely, the issue of a Christian whose marital status has just changed due to divorce by their spouse. To this individual, Paul says they are free to marry (again).

Yet what about the man or woman abandoned by a spouse who is a professing believer? I am convinced that Paul's instructions here would still be applicable, and the one abandoned would have grounds to remarry. My primary argument for this is the occasional nature of Paul's letters, something we discussed in chapter 3. Paul is giving pastoral guidelines to a congregation of first-generation believers in Corinth. He is addressing the actual situations they are facing. Paul's first visit to Corinth was in AD 50 or 51, and he wrote this epistle from Ephesus just a few years later. So it makes sense that in this small group of new believers that many of them would have unbelieving spouses. Apparently some of those spouses were quite unhappy at their partner's conversion to the Christian faith and had abandoned their Christian spouse. It seems no professing Christians in this congregation had abandoned their spouses, so Paul doesn't address that situation. I see nothing in Paul's line of argument that wouldn't apply to a believer abandoned by a professing believer.

Interestingly, many theologians, notably Reformed theologians, reach the identical practical conclusion by applying the church-discipline guidelines of Matthew 18:15–17. Here Jesus instructs us to confront a brother or sister who sins against us. If they do not respond, we take someone with us and try it again. We must take them before the church if they still don't repent. If, at that point, they refuse to respond, Jesus says, "Let him be to you as a Gentile and a tax collector" (v. 17 ESV). Thus many Reformed theologians argue that when this process of church discipline is applied to the abandoning spouse who refuses to respond, they are to be treated as an unbeliever. The guidelines of 1 Corinthians 7 release the one abandoned by their spouse despite an (empty) profession of faith.

What about the husband or wife whose spouse hasn't abandoned them but stays and abuses them? Could abuse be considered a form of abandonment? Conceptually, I believe it certainly can be. While the Greek word *chōrizō* used in 1 Corinthians 7:15 of desertion most often refers to literal physical distancing (cf. Acts 18:1 of Paul departing from Athens), it is also used metaphorically. *Chōrizō* is used for nonphysical distancing, which relationally or otherwise radically separates someone from another person or thing. It is used of Jesus being separated from sinners (Heb 7:26) and of believers not being separated from the love of God (Rom 8:35). Abuse profoundly separates. It shatters a relationship, one's heart and soul, and ultimately the marriage covenant. Russell Moore's comments here are very insightful:

> An abusive spouse, in fact, has abandoned the marriage. Abuse is much worse than abandonment, involving the use of something holy (marriage) for satanic ends. Abuse of a spouse or a child is exactly what God condemns everywhere in the Bible—the leveraging of power to hurt the vulnerable (Psalm 9:18; Isaiah 3:14–15; Ezekiel 18:12; Amos 2:7; Mark 9:42; etc.). While abuse is worse than abandonment, it is no less than abandonment.[57]

Wayne Grudem makes a slightly different argument based on a word study of "and such things" in 1 Corinthians 7:15, but he draws similar conclusions. He argues that this phrase means "in this and other similarly destructive situations," such as spousal physical abuse, child abuse, extreme, prolonged verbal and relational cruelty, and credible threats of harm. In these instances the spouse is released from the marriage covenant.[58]

A final point needs to be made regarding applying 1 Corinthians 7:15 to abuse and desertion. While Paul explicitly addresses an occasionally generated situation in Corinth where some pagan spouses were the ones doing the abandoning, this is not markedly different from that of an abused spouse who is forced to flee for safety. Many of the Puritans made this exact argument. The influential Puritan pastor and theologian William Perkins, in discussing divorce in 1 Corinthians 7:15, states, "For to depart from one and drive away one by threats are the same."[59] One could argue, as Wayne Grudem does in a discussion of abused spouses being forced to flee, that "in some ways, such abuse is worse than desertion because it involves repeated demonstrations of actual malice, not simply indifference."[60]

In conclusion, God hates the abuse of power by those entrusted to love. Divorcing because one is being abused does involve sin—the sin of the abuser, not the victim.

In the next chapter, we will address Scripture passages related to children.

Chapter 5

PASSAGES ON CHILDREN

The old should be treated with due respect.
Children should be treated with gentleness.
—AFRICAN PROVERB

What you do to children matters. And
they might never forget.
—TONI MORRISON, *GOD HELP THE CHILD*

He took a little child whom he placed among them.
Taking the child in his arms, he said to them,
"Whoever welcomes one of these little children in
my name welcomes me; and whoever welcomes me
does not welcome me but the one who sent me."
—MARK 9:36-37

Scripture repeatedly affirms that children should be loved, protected, and deeply valued. They are one of the greatest blessings given by God. Jesus made many radical statements about children in an ancient Greco-Roman world in which children had virtually no legal rights. Roman fathers wielded the power of life and death over their children. Unwanted female and disabled children, in particular, were routinely put to death or abandoned to be killed by wild animals or snatched up by brothel owners. First-century Jewish culture did value children but prioritized adults. When Jesus's disciples rebuked parents for bothering him by bringing their children to him, Jesus implicitly chided his disciples by calling the children to himself and declaring the kingdom of God belongs to "such as these" (Luke 18:15–17). Jesus said receiving a child in his name is akin to receiving him (Mark 9:36–37). He welcomed, affectionately touched, and blessed children (Matt 19:14). Jesus honored them and proclaimed they were to be treated with great care (Matt 10:42; 21:16). Furthermore, Jesus pronounced terrible judgment on anyone who harms children (Matt 18:5–10). It is most troubling when those who claim to love and follow Jesus abuse children. It is most horrifying when this is done while quoting Scripture. So, we will now look at the Scripture passage most often used to defend child abuse. Please note that some readers may find portions of this chapter difficult or triggering to read.

1. PROVERBS 23:13–14

"Do not withhold discipline from a child; if you strike him with a rod, he will not die. If you strike him with the rod, you will save his soul from Sheol." (ESV)

The headline read, "Son had 36 bruises. Mom quoted the Bible as defense."[1] The accompanying photo of the boy's grotesque bruises was genuinely sickening. Reportedly, this mother, a Burmese immigrant named Khin Par Thaing, viciously beat her son with a coat hanger, leaving thirty-six large, deep bruises across the boy's back, thigh, arm, and cheek. Thaing didn't deny beating him but justified it based on Proverbs 23:13–14. She was quoted as saying, "I was worried for my son's salvation with God after he dies. . . . I decided to punish my son . . . to help him learn how to behave as God would want him to."

Thaing cited Indiana's Religious Freedom law as a defense against the child-abuse charges. Asian immigrants are not the only ones using Scripture to justify beating disobedient children. A quick internet search reveals numerous accounts of American parents, pastors, and Christian reform schools accused and convicted of beating children. They repeatedly cite Proverbs to justify harsh corporal punishment. For instance, the late fundamentalist Baptist pastor Lester Roloff founded several reform schools for boys and girls. Almost all were eventually closed due to lawsuits, abuse allegations, and criminal convictions. Tragically, it appears that many of the homes restructured, renamed, and continued to use Scripture to justify child abuse. During a court hearing, which led to his prosecution for the mistreatment of sixteen girls in his homes, Roloff notoriously stated, "Better a pink bottom than a black soul."[2] Again, abuse was implicitly justified with Proverbs 23:13–14.

Child Discipline and Spanking in Proverbs

Does this Scripture actually promote child abuse? What are we to make of this and similar texts such as Proverbs 13:24, "Whoever spares the rod hates their children, but the one who loves their children is careful to discipline them," and Proverbs 22:15, "Folly is bound up in the heart of a child, but the rod of discipline will drive it far away"?

Today, many evangelicals reject any form of corporal punishment as biblical. William Webb has been particularly influential in this regard. He argues that Proverbs does indeed advocate for injurious corporal punishment of children; thus, we need to "go beyond the Bible biblically" by identifying the "unrealized ethic of Scripture." We supposedly do this based on the ethical trajectory where Scripture seems to lead, revealed in the redemptive movement from ancient (pagan) Near Eastern culture to the Old Testament, the New Testament, and ultimately beyond the Bible. In other words, we are to look past the specific instructions of Scripture to pursue the ultimate application of Scripture.[3] Webb sees redemptive movement from the ancient world to Scripture through less harsh, softer forms of punishment—a movement toward greater kindness, gentleness, honor, and dignity for the punished person. Using this "trajectory" hermeneutic, Webb argues that Christians should abolish corporal punishment altogether.

Webb's work is quite helpful in identifying the dramatic difference between ancient Near Eastern and Old Testament teaching on women, enslaved people, and discipline. He correctly notes how much more gracious, humane, and protective the Old Testament is compared to secular ancient Near Eastern law codes from the same period. Webb rightly notes that there are some very challenging Old Testament texts. However, he fails to identify changes or movements between Old and New Testament teaching on child discipline. While I appreciate and obviously share Webb's passion to eradicate child abuse, I believe his understanding of discipline in Proverbs is flawed and impugns Scripture. His hermeneutic is exceptionally complicated (he proposes eighteen cultural/transcultural criteria[4]) and highly subjective, lacking clear hermeneutical controls.[5] Instead, I am convinced that Proverbs has much helpful teaching on discipline and does not countenance abuse.

We must step back and get the bigger picture before making sense of discipline texts in Proverbs. Otherwise, these texts will appear harsh, even cruel. Actually, the author of Proverbs is driven by compassion. The book's goal is stated at the beginning of the first chapter. These sayings are given "for gaining wisdom" (Prov 1:2).

From start to finish, the author wants his son (and the reader) to gain wisdom so that he will experience rich blessings from God and avoid needless suffering and ultimate destruction. Much like the litany of blessings attributed to Scripture in Psalm 119, Proverbs ascribes so many blessings to wisdom that one can hardly count them.

Wisdom brings security (Prov 1:33), success (2:7), peace and prosperity (3:1), health and nourishment (3:8), blessing (3:13, 18), riches and honor (3:16), and much, much more. Walking in wisdom protects from catastrophic dangers—calamity and disaster (1:26–27), destruction (1:32), and death (7:27; 9:18). The author desperately wants his son to experience blessing and avoid harm, yet realizes there are many threats to wisdom—destructive peer pressure (1:11–18), seductive temptations (7:5–27), and worst of all, our innate foolishness (22:15). In the service of his compassionate objectives, the author advises child discipline.

Proverbs Forbids Abusive Child Discipline

I will give six arguments to show that Proverbs does not sanction child abuse and does not make corporal punishment the primary form of discipline.

First, *the logic of Proverbs 23:13 precludes severe corporal punishment ("they will not die").* Children *do* die from beatings. Annually, an estimated ninety-four thousand American children are physically abused, resulting in five children dying (on average) every single day. The actual death rate may be several times higher than this.[6] Homicide is a leading cause of death among children, and for murdered children ten years or younger the perpetrator is most often an abusive parent or caregiver.[7] The writer of Proverbs cannot be advocating severe, injurious beating of children because the discipline he advocates does not physically endanger the child. The author of Proverbs expressly states that the child given biblically sanctioned discipline "will not die," indicating he or she will not be physically endangered. This simple point is quite significant. We must not hear in the corporal-punishment language of Proverbs what is not actually there. Such misperception can have tragic consequences. For instance, there have been at least three cases of Christian parents being convicted for fatally abusing their children, in which the parents possessed and reportedly applied/misapplied teachings from the popular book *To Train Up a Child* by Michael and Debi Pearl.[8] The Pearls strongly admonish parents to spank their children, from six months old to adolescence. The book's teachings that repeated blows from a quarter inch rubber hose, withholding food ("a little fasting is good training"), and having disobedient children hosed off outdoors with a garden hose appeared to have been influential in the fatal abuse of three children.[9] Despite the Pearl's assurances that a quarter-inch piece of plastic tubing (one of their favorite instruments of discipline) will not damage tissue or bones, it most certainly can, and that is precisely what contributed to Lydia Schatz and Sean Paddock's deaths. Injurious beatings are not biblical discipline but abuse.

Second, *Proverbs gives various types of child discipline that do not include corporal punishment.* First, we should note that the English word *discipline* found in the Old Testament (*musar* in Hebrew) has a broad scope of meanings, ranging from instruction (Prov 1:2; 4:13) to warning (Job 20:3) to corporal punishment (Prov 13:24; 22:15).[10] Old Testament scholar Paul Wegner convincingly argues that Proverbs reveals six different levels of child discipline: (1) encouraging proper behavior (1:8–9; 4:7–8); (2) informing of improper behavior (1:10–15; 3:21–22); (3) explaining the negative consequences of sin (1:18–19); (4) gently exhorting (4:1–2, 14–16); (5) gently rebuking (3:12); (6) corporal punishment that does not cause physical harm (19:18; 23:13–14).[11]

Wegner demonstrates that the author of Proverbs gives two additional forms of discipline that are *only* to be used on adults by civil authorities. The first of these is corporal punishment, which causes physical harm (Prov 20:30: "Blows and wounds scrub away evil, and beatings purge the inmost being"). This form of corporal punishment is to be administered only by royal or civil authorities (Deut 25:3).

The second form of adult discipline alluded to in Proverbs is capital punishment (death). This form of discipline is also *only* authorized for civil authorities, not parents (Gen 9:6; Rom 13:4).[12] It may well be that the admonition to use corporal punishment on your child lest they die (Prov 19:18) is referring to the possibility of capital punishment if that child continues on a rebellious, sinful path (Deut 21:18–21). In summary, discipline for children and adults in Proverbs is carefully nuanced and is much more than corporal punishment.

Third, *corporal punishment is not the primary form of child discipline.* Of the six types of parental discipline in Proverbs set forth by Wegner, only one (type [6]; see above) involves corporal punishment. This is the most crucial point. Models of child discipline such as that espoused by the Pearls, who assert that godly parents must whip a child's bare skin until they are "totally broken,"[13] are abusive and utterly unbiblical. For many conservative Christians, corporal punishment is the default method of child discipline. These parents spank their children for every infraction. This is simply not what Proverbs teaches. Instead, parents must employ various methods to guide their children away from unhealthy, foolish choices so that they learn to walk in wisdom. We noted previously that Proverbs admonishes five forms of discipline before corporal punishment: (1) encouraging proper behavior (1:8–9; 4:7–8); (2) informing of improper behavior (1:10–15; 3:21–22); (3) explaining the negative consequences of sin (1:18–19); (4) gently exhorting (4:1–2, 14–16); (5) gently rebuking (3:12). Corrective discipline can also involve natural and logical consequences. The latter can include corporal punishment, but it is only one form of discipline out of many. Wegner argues that the levels of discipline found in Proverbs suggest an ascending level of painful consequences; parents should use the least amount of power necessary to curb negative, harmful behavior.[14] Something is seriously amiss when a parent frequently relies on spankings to discipline.

Fourth, *Proverbs does not promote corporal punishment as the ultimate form of discipline.* While Proverbs countenances corporal punishment, it acknowledges its limited value. While fools' mouths "invite a beating" (Prov 18:6), this is not the best or ultimate method of curbing foolishness and inculcating wisdom. For a teachable person, a rebuke is most effective. Proverbs 17:10 notes that a "rebuke goes deeper into a man [or child] of understanding than a hundred blows into a fool" (ESV).

Fifth, *Proverbs condemns verbal abuse and unbridled anger.* Biblical child discipline always involves a gracious, self-controlled posture reflected in gentle words and actions focused on building up the child. Abusive child discipline almost always involves parental loss of control and unbridled anger. Most often it includes verbal abuse. These behaviors are thoroughly condemned throughout Proverbs. Wise people turn away from anger and carefully restrain their words (Prov 17:27; 29:8). Anger produces strife and leads to many sins (15:1; 29:22; 30:33). People who use rash, harsh words are declared sinful fools (29:9; cf. 14:16–17). Parents who use rash, harsh words are using their tongues like "swords" to pierce and destroy their children (12:18), for the tongue has "the power of life and death" (18:21). An angry parent is in no condition to discipline a child, particularly through the use of corporal punishment. Biblical discipline involves merciful words that give life and promote healing (12:25; 16:24). Wise, gracious words are an essential part of positive discipline, for they "promote instruction" (16:21).

Finally, *biblical discipline is motivated by love and grace.* Beyond the book of Proverbs, Scripture's description of child discipline precludes abusive child discipline. Parents are to emulate the way God parents and disciplines his children. He is utterly motivated by love (Heb 12:5–11). God cherishes his wayward children and grieves over their sinfulness (Matt 23:37). He experiences pain when his children suffer, even when they suffer from their own sinful choices (Isa 63:9). God is loving and compassionate toward his sinful children, and slow to anger; he doesn't repay us according to our iniquities but shows us tender compassion (Ps 103:8–13). Our heavenly Father gently leads his wayward lambs (Isa 40:11). God longs not to punish but forgive and bless his children; he graciously seeks us out when we forsake him (Luke 15).

Godly human parents are to be gentle and to lovingly care for their children (1 Thess 2:7). For those who cause children to stumble, it would be better to be dropped into the sea with an enormous millstone tied around one's neck than to experience God's wrath against those who harm his children (Matt 18:1–6). Since God knows the devastating, life-altering effects of child abuse, he severely warns anyone who would seek to harm a child.[15] Finally, we should note the relevance of Paul's admonitions to parents. In a discussion of parental child discipline, Paul instructs fathers not to "exasperate" their children (Eph 6:4). Provoking children to anger will break their spirits and discourage them (Col 3:21). These admonitions utterly preclude abusive child discipline. Andrew Lincoln gives a helpful explanation of this admonition in Ephesians 6:4:

> Fathers are made responsible for ensuring that they do not provoke anger in their children. This involves avoiding attitudes, words, and actions which would drive a child to angry exasperation or resentment and thus rules out excessively severe discipline, unreasonably harsh demands, abuse of authority, arbitrariness, unfairness, constant nagging and condemnation, subjecting

a child to humiliation, and all forms of gross insensitivity to a child's needs and sensibilities.[16]

In summary, while Proverbs allows for non-abusive corporal child discipline, this is not given as a primary form of discipline. And Proverbs, along with the rest of Scripture, prohibits abusive child discipline.

2. EPHESIANS 6:1–2

"Children, obey your parents in the Lord. . . . 'Honor your father and mother.'"

Jennifer articulates the painful dilemma that children of abusive parents experience. She recounts:

I grew up in a Christian family. We faithfully attended [church]. . . . My mom homeschooled us and led children's worship. My dad had a PhD and taught adult Sunday school. In public, he was intelligent and composed. In private, he could go from studying Louis Berkhof [a famous theologian] to beating his daughter in a heartbeat.

In our family, I was taught to honor my father and mother, forgive others, and not gossip, but homes warped by abuse have their own language. "Forgive" meant pretend you're happy, even when you're covered in bruises. "Honor your father" meant obey him, even when you're terrified he might kill you. And we were repeatedly warned not to "gossip," which meant telling anyone the truth.

As I matured, I was torn between my desire to please God and my need to escape my father. I agonized over the fifth commandment—"Honor your father and your mother" (Ex. 20:12)—and felt like a fake Christian for hating my dad's behavior. . . . For years, I wrestled with PTSD from over 20 years of abuse. . . . How could I honor a man who is dishonorable? Surely, God doesn't want me to obey an evil person, or submit to a dangerous man?[17]

What are we to make of honoring and obeying parents who are dishonorable and unsafe? At the most extreme end of the spectrum, how do you honor an evil parent? Let's begin by noting the importance of letting Scripture tell us what honoring parents does and doesn't mean. Often, parents do what Jennifer's parents did—in word and deed they teach their children what honoring them means. Their distorted messages can brainwash their children into feeling guilty for not following the abuser's perverted definitions of "honor."

Are Adult Children Commanded to Obey Parents?

Ephesians 6:1–2 is one of the most frequently cited texts on this subject. The context of these verses is a household code where Paul gives guidelines to various household members (husbands, wives, children, parents, slaves, and masters). Paul's admonitions in this passage are directed at children still in the parent's household. (The word used here for "children" is *teknon*, and though it can refer to adult children, it very often refers to preadult children, as it does here and elsewhere in the New Testament.[18]) When Paul says, "children obey your parents," he is not referring to adult children. What is the scope of a child's obedience? Colossians 3:20 says children are to obey their parents "in everything." As we saw with the submission of wives in Ephesians 5:24, "everything" cannot mean "every single thing." Ephesians 6:1, a parallel account of the Colossian household code, clarifies the scope of the child's obedience. It is to be "in the Lord." As one commentator said, "Ephesians requires obedience to parents, provided this is in the Lord, that is, consistent with Christian commitment."[19]

What Is the Scope of Parents' Authority?

Scripture does not give parents unqualified authority over their children. A child must obey only when such obedience does not compromise obedience to Christ. Abusive parents typically demand total loyalty and slavish obedience, even of their adult children. But this is an utterly illegitimate demand. Ultimate authority is reserved for God alone. Obedience to God always governs and limits a child's obedience to their parents. Jesus, who affirmed the command to honor parents (Luke 18:20), clarifies this qualification. Consider how shocking it would have been to Jesus's hearers, in a first-century Jewish culture in which even adult children were expected to obey their earthly fathers as long as they were alive, to hear Jesus say, "Anyone who loves their father or mother more than me is not worthy of me" (Matt 10:37). Elsewhere Jesus says, "If anyone comes to me and does not hate father and mother, wife and children, brothers and sisters . . . such a person cannot be my disciple" (Luke 14:26). In other words, one's relationship with Jesus trumps the most cherished family relationships and parental authority.

A final, very relevant text for clarifying what obedience to parents looks like for preadult children is Luke 2:41–51. Jesus went to the temple when he was twelve without telling his parents. When his mother finally found him and scolded him for the anxiety he had caused, Jesus gently scolded her for not realizing he would be focused on his heavenly Father's business. What is most fascinating is that immediately after recounting this event, Luke says Jesus returned with his parents to Jerusalem "and was obedient to them" (Luke 2:51). In other words, biblical obedience for a child is strictly limited by obedience to God. It may involve respectfully confronting parents with truth and failing to conform to their unbiblical expectations.

Honoring Parents

Closely related to obeying parents is honoring them. In Ephesians 6:2, Paul goes on to command children to honor their father and mother (a conflation of Exod 20:12 and Deut 5:16). While Paul's focus on "honoring" in Ephesians 6:2 is obedience, this concept biblically is broader. The Hebrew verb used in Exodus 20:12 for honor is *kavad*, which means "to give weight to, to prioritize." But this doesn't tell us precisely what honor means. Let's flesh this out for adult children. Honoring parents means the following five things.

Providing Necessary Financial Support

In Hebrew culture, honoring parents is particularly understood to refer to adult children providing material care for their aging parents. The New Testament affirms this. Jesus condemned the Pharisees for using clever legalistic maneuvers to avoid giving funds to their needy parents (putting their money under "corban"), thus violating the command to "honor" their parents (Mark 7:9–13; cf. 1 Tim 5:3–4, 8). Providing material support to parents is very case specific. In our culture (unlike ancient Jewish culture), many parents have financial means in their old age and are not dependent on their children for material support. However, in other cases, aged parents need material care, and their children must prayerfully consider how they can assist them.

Sometimes, God may lead them to bring their elderly parents into their homes to care for them at the end of life. Yet having an abusive parent in the adult child's home may not be wise, and God will reveal different ways the parent can be given material support. The fundamental principle is to find ways to offer appropriate material care for elderly parents who need such assistance. In this way, we honor parents regardless of whether they have been honorable. For children of abusive parents, this is a beautiful act of grace and honors God.

Being Respectful

Scripture has much to say about honoring or respecting others (these terms are virtually synonymous). It is essential to note that biblically there are two kinds of respect: *assigned and achieved*. The position gives assigned respect. The latter (achieved respect) is earned through respectful and honorable character and behavior. Assigned respect is owed to those in a position that Scripture says we are to honor, including the elderly (Lev 19:32), parents (Deut 5:16), governmental authorities (1 Pet 2:17), spiritual leaders (1 Tim 5:17), and others who have a unique role in one's life that God commands us to honor, such as family members (Eph 5:33; 1 Tim 6:1; 1 Pet 3:7). We are to give honor to those to whom assigned honor is due (Rom 13:7), whether or not that person's actions are honorable. It is instructive that Peter and Paul, who both lived under ruthless, pagan Roman authorities who would ultimately put them to death, tell us to honor civil authorities. That is, we speak respectfully. We honor their position. In our culture, we do this in our judicial system by standing when a judge enters the courtroom and referring to them as "your honor." The judge may or may not be honorable, but he sits in an honorable position of authority. We are to honor their position. What does being respectful mean for those who are abusive and yet are in a position that we are to honor?

We find an excellent example from the life of Paul recorded in Acts 23:1–5. Paul stood before the Sanhedrin—first-century Palestine's supreme religious authority. Paul began his defense by declaring that he lived with a clear conscience. Upon hearing those words, Ananias, the high priest, commanded that Paul be struck in the mouth. Paul immediately responded by harshly rebuking the high priest, declaring, "God will strike you, you whitewashed wall! You sit there to judge me according to the law, yet you violate the law by commanding that I be struck!" Those who witnessed Paul's rebuke scolded him, saying, "How dare you insult God's high priest!" Paul's response to them is very instructive, for Paul says he didn't realize Ananias was the high priest. (For many years, Paul had been on his three missionary journeys, rarely in Jerusalem, and apparently did not recognize the high priest by sight.) Paul immediately apologizes and references Exodus 22:28, which prohibits speaking evil (in this context, speaking harshly or disrespectfully) about the ruler of the people. Paul does not apologize for telling the truth. It was true that he had a clear conscience, and it was accurate that Ananias had hypocritically violated Jewish law. However, Paul did apologize for speaking disrespectfully to this Jewish leader. Thus, adult children of abusive parents honor their parents by being respectful, particularly in their words toward their parents. They should not curse their parents (Deut 27:16) or speak to them harshly.

Speaking the Truth

Honoring parents does not mean we cannot speak the truth about a parent's abuse. God is a God of truth and calls us to speak the truth (Eph 4:25). He is the one who pronounces woe (judgment) on those who acquit the guilty and who call evil good; see Isaiah 5:20, 23 (the context is those guilty of physical, verbal, and economic abuse). Calling abuse perpetrated by one's parents sinful and evil is not inherently dishonoring to them. It honors the God of truth to call abuse what he calls it. God hates abuse and unrepentant abusers (Pss 5:6; 11:5). He is the one who says it would be better for a child abuser to have a millstone tied around his neck and be dropped in the sea than to face what God will do to that abuser (Matt 18:5–6). At the same time, God loves evildoers and does not desire them to face eternal judgment—he takes no delight in the death of the wicked. He desires that they repent and find life (Ezek 18:23). Respectfully confronting abusive parents with the truth about their abuse and pleading with them to confess their sins and turn to Jesus is a biblical way of honoring them. This is a beautiful way to speak "the truth in love" (Eph 4:15). Adult children of abusive parents also have the right and responsibility to warn others who might be at risk of being abused by those abusive parents. Godly individuals in Scripture often called out the evil of their parents and grandparents and warned others not to follow their destructive example (2 Chr 30:7; Ezra 9:7; Neh 9:16–17). Honoring parents requires speaking and living out the truth.

Let's now relate speaking the truth to the second type of biblical respect or honor, called *achieved honor*. This involves respecting someone not for their position of authority but for their character. We honor them because they are honorable. God calls believers to "win the respect" of others (1 Thess 4:12). Moses told the people to find wise, respectable men to put in leadership (Deut 1:13). Cornelius the Roman centurion was respected by the Jews because of his character; he was "a righteous and God-fearing man" (Acts 10:22). While this is much easier said than done, we must not confuse these two types of honor. We can and should respect even abusive authorities, including parents, for their position. But we must not call honorable what is not. If a parent acts dishonorably, they are dishonorable. We must not distort reality and call what is black, white. Achieved honor is to be reserved for the honorable. Proverbs 26:1 says, "Honor is not fitting for a fool." Proverbs 26:8 says that giving honor to dishonorable people will backfire and cause harm. It is likened to tying a stone to a sling. The stone will come back and hit you in the face! Children of abusive parents must not be cowered, shamed, or tricked into labeling their parents' abusive actions and ungodly character as anything less than what they are.

Setting Healthy Boundaries

Larry was from a large, close Italian family. He had three brothers and two sisters living near their parents on the east coast. Larry had left his hometown when he went to college on the West Coast.

Larry married Kay, his soulmate whom he met shortly after graduating from the church singles group. In a few years, they had two daughters and increasingly missed being near family. Kay's divorced parents lived in the Midwest, but she didn't have a close relationship with them. So when a sales position opened for Larry to transfer to his hometown, he jumped at it. Larry was delighted to be back home with family and childhood friends. But several months into this relocation, they were blindsided with a bombshell. One evening, after coming home from her grandparents, their six-year-old daughter Brittany tearfully stated she didn't want to go to their house again. After several hours of patient, nerve-wracking conversation, Brittany confided that her grandfather had been touching her "private parts" when she napped or took a bath. Thankfully, Larry and Kay had been well-trained in responding to abuse disclosure in their church. They reported the disclosure to the authorities. As soon as Child Protective Services gave them clearance, they told their family of the revelation and said the grandfather would no longer have any access to the girls, including over the upcoming holidays. Larry's mother and siblings were initially supportive, saying they didn't understand what had happened but respected Larry and Kay's boundaries. However, the family members completely reversed themselves in less than a week. Larry's mother and siblings accused him of destroying their family. With great self-righteousness, they declared that Larry was violating a cardinal biblical command to honor his father.

Furthermore, they rejected Larry and Kay's offer of having the family, minus the grandfather, come to their house on Christmas evening. Larry was shocked at their declaration: "From now on, we will not come to any family event you won't allow Dad to attend. We will not stand by and allow you to dishonor our father. True Christians don't do that." Unless one has faced this situation, it is hard to appreciate how much confusion and guilt parents who enact protective boundaries often experience. So it is essential to affirm that honoring parents does not preclude setting boundaries to protect the vulnerable and to limit destructive behavior. As we will see in more detail in part 3, protecting the vulnerable is an overwhelming biblical mandate. Those who care for children have a nonnegotiable responsibility to protect them. Civil, spiritual, and familial leaders are called to seek justice, defend the oppressed, take up the cause of the fatherless, and plead the case of the widow (Isa 1:17). They are to "speak up for those who cannot speak for themselves" and to "defend the rights of the poor and needy" (Prov 31:8–9). Such protection must be as robust and bold as the threats: "Defend the weak and the fatherless; uphold the cause of the poor and the oppressed. Rescue the weak and the needy; deliver them from the hand of the wicked" (Ps 82:3–4). Protecting the vulnerable from abusers is not optional. Failure to do so brings divine judgment (Jer 5:28–29; Obad 10–12). In summary, we honor God by protecting children. Stated inversely, we do not honor our parents by dishonoring God and dishonoring the children he has entrusted to us.

Setting boundaries with unhealthy or abusive parents is also appropriate to protect oneself. While Scripture does call us to be willing to suffer abuse for the gospel (Matt 24:9; Acts 5:40–41), it does not promote indiscriminate suffering. Scripture gives us numerous examples of godly individuals who set specific, often rigid boundaries to avoid abuse. Jesus repeatedly avoided physical assault and sought safety by hiding (John 8:59), by maintaining physical separation from his abusers (Matt 12:14–15; John 11:53–54), and by eluding them (John 10:31, 39). Though ultimately Paul laid down his life for Jesus, over many years he fled from abusers whenever possible (Acts 9:22–25; 14:5–6; 17:8–10). David and Jonathan give us specific examples of setting firm boundaries with unhealthy parents. Abusive King Saul was Jonathan's biological father and David's functional father, since David lived in Saul's household. Up to this point in the biblical record, David and Jonathan are repeatedly described as godly, yet they refuse to passively accept Saul's abuse or his ungodly statements. David, in particular, set extreme boundaries and fled from Saul for several years for his own protection (1 Sam 20–27). We do not dishonor parents by setting limits to protect our children and ourselves. We can honor abusive parents when challenging their ungodly behavior. Thus, I appreciate how Jennifer Greenberg closes her article on honoring an evil father. She writes:

> Honoring ungodly people means calling them to repent of their sin, encouraging them to do what is right, and preventing them from doing further evil. An honorable response to sin is confronting it, refusing to enable it, and reporting crimes to law enforcement.
>
> In the spirit of the law, I honored my father by refusing to succumb to the damage his sin inflicted. I honored my father by reporting his abuses. I honored my father by breaking the cycle and being a godly parent to my children. I honor my father daily by not letting him near my daughters.[20]

Allowing Parents' Sins and Failures to Drive Us to Jesus

Those who experience soul-shattering betrayal, especially from parents or spouses, must focus on the truth that only God is utterly reliable. When humans, especially family members, crush us in their abuse or betrayals, by God's grace this can drive us into the arms of our heavenly Father. The whole of Psalm 27 is beneficial in this context. It is a psalm of confidence in which David expresses deep intimacy with God in the face of painful threats and mistreatment. In grappling with the pain of untrustworthy and dangerous humans, he experienced heightened intimacy with God, ultimately the only one we can fully trust. Concerning family, David declares, "My father and mother have forsaken me, but the LORD will take me in" (Ps 27:10 ESV). It may well be that David isn't speaking of literal but emotional abandonment, which is suggested by his father Jesse failing to even introduce David as one of his sons to the prophet Samuel, and by David's oldest brother's verbal abuse and contempt (1 Sam 16:6–11; 17:28–29). David learned to let parental and filial abandonment drive him to deeper intimacy with God.

Amber is a joyful wife, mom, and musician. Her warm smile is engaging and infectious, belying a very painful childhood. Amber recounts growing up terrified that her peers would discover her father was serving a life sentence for murder. His abandonment of his family and the terrible crimes he committed filled Amber with lies and shame. But instead of giving in to bitterness or despair, Amber allowed the pain of her father's sinful abuse to drive her to Jesus. She articulates this in a song she wrote titled, "Where I'm From." It reflects the fruit of acknowledging the truth of her father's destructive choices, seeing the image of God in her father, recognizing the blessings she experienced from her deceased mother, and extending the grace to her father that she had experienced from Jesus. She answers the critical question, "Amber, where are you from?" by boldly and honestly declaring:

> I'm from my dad, Doug Hunter, a man with a heavy
>   heart.
> Whose words were as desperate as beggar cries,
> And as sharp as darts.
> I'm from his house of cards that we'd shoot down
>   with rubber bands.
> I'm from the depth of his sorrow; I'm from his artistic
>   hands.
>
> You ask me where I'm from; I'm from the heart
>   of God.
> You ask me why I've come; I've come to love.

I'm from that bitter day when I found out he was
    locked up in a cage.
'Cause he bowed down to darkness and became its
    slave when he shot down a man in a fit of rage.
I'm from heartbroken tears; I'm from walls of shame.
I'm from a lonely place of confusion and anger,
    disguises and blame.

You ask me where I'm from; I'm from the mercy of
    my God.
You ask me why I've come; I've come to love.

I'm from a woman named Trudy; I came out of
    her womb.
I'm from her turtleneck sweaters and her vanilla
    perfume.
I'm from the warmth of her smile and her dark
    brown hair.
I'm from her humble heart and all her love and care.

You ask me where I'm from; I'm from the grace
    of God.
You ask me why I've come; I've come to love.

I'm from the one called Jesus. I'm from his
    perfect life.
I'm from the nails in his hands. I'm from his sacrifice.

He gave sight to the blind and crushed the captive's
    chains.
He loves unconditionally, and he's taught me to do
    the same.

You ask me where I'm from; I'm from the faithfulness
    of God.
You ask me why I've come; I've come to love.
You ask me why I'm here today; I'm here to love.[21]

Celestia and I marvel at Amber's deep intimacy with Jesus. It
is a beautiful, redemptive example to others who live with the deep
pain of abusive parents.

In the next chapter, we will move beyond biological family to
spiritual family. We will look at key passages regarding the church.

Chapter 6

PASSAGES ON THE CHURCH

If I want to find an abuser, I go to church!
—A DIVORCE ATTORNEY

All the believers were one in heart and mind. No one
claimed that any of their possessions was their own, but they
shared everything they had. With great power the apostles
continued to testify to the resurrection of the Lord Jesus.
And God's grace was so powerfully at work in them all.
—ACTS 4:32-33

Karen and Jordan went to south Asia as missionaries in the
summer of 2014. They had attended seminary to prepare for
full-time Christian ministry. Shortly after marrying they began
attending a megachurch in Texas. They joined the church, which
included signing a "covenant membership" agreement. The church
supported their goal of going to the mission field with SIM, a large
mission agency. Less than a year after arriving in Asia, Karen sensed
that something was wrong. After catching Jordan in a flagrant lie,
she began pressing him for the deeper truth. She eventually received
what she called a "pseudoconfession" and "pseudorepentance." He

admitted to viewing adult porn and masturbating a few times while they were on the mission field.[1] While Jordan gave the same "confession" to the mission agency and their church leaders, Karen sensed she still wasn't getting the whole truth. Almost three weeks later it came with seismic force. Jordan admitted to viewing child pornography for almost ten years. He acknowledged a sexual preference for prepubescent children four years and older, though he reportedly admitted to viewing infant children and masturbating to "thoughts of children in his care."[2] Karen reported his confession to SIM leaders, and they promptly flew Jordan back to the US, did their own investigation, and terminated him. Several weeks later, Karen returned to Dallas and sought the assistance of The Village Church leaders. She had decided to have her "fraudulent" marriage annulled and asked her pastors to help her and Jordan split their finances fairly. She reports that the elders refused to assist them because they felt doing so seemed like a step toward divorce. She then states, "When I asked why the elders felt my choices about finances were in the scope of their authority, they said that in the context of separation or divorce 'every aspect of your marriage is under the authority of the elders of the church.'"[3] She recounts that after she explained the extensive counsel she was receiving from the mission agency, her mentors, family members, and her Christian counselor, affirming her decision to annul her marriage, one of her pastors said that only they, the church leaders, were her spiritual authorities and "you need to wait to see what *we* decide you should do" (emphasis mine).[4]

Shortly after this, Karen formally withdrew her church membership. Shockingly, three months later the elders sent an email to six thousand church members, explaining that Karen was now under church discipline for pursuing a marriage annulment and for disregarding pastoral counsel. They also refused to accept her resignation from church membership. While condemning Karen, that same email praised her pedophiliac husband for his submission to the elders.

Karen quickly went public with a response to the church's email, correcting "deliberate misrepresentations" for the sake of "other past, present, and future victims of spiritual abuse by [their church] and similar churches."[5]

The church's email drew widespread, heated public censure. Soon, the church reversed itself, issuing an apology, acknowledging they had failed Karen, releasing her from church membership, and affirming that she had biblical grounds for annulment/divorce. Karen graciously accepted their apology.[6] While we can be thankful that in this instance, church elders acknowledged they had harmfully misused their power, it raises a pressing question: What is the extent of church leaders' authority over church members? As many spiritual leaders claim, *do* they have authority over every aspect of members' lives? If our pastor asks us to jump, is the godly response to meekly ask "how high," as Cheryl's youth pastor taught her? Is it true, as best-selling author John Bevere claims, that we "should not take upon ourselves the pressure to discern beforehand whether [our spiritual] leaders are right or not"; we just need to obey them?[7] Does Scripture really teach that God shows our spiritual leaders things he doesn't show us and that failing to obey our spiritual leaders in everything is to rebel against God himself?[8] Given the fact that the evangelical church is currently inundated with high-profile spiritual-abuse scandals, these are very timely questions. Let's turn to look at four Scripture passages that abusive church leaders often use to justify their actions.

1. HEBREWS 13:17

"Obey your leaders and submit to them." (ESV)

Hebrews 13:17 is a pivotal text on the authority of church leaders. The writer commands the readers to "have confidence in your leaders and submit to their authority" (NIV). The Greek verb used here for leaders (*hēgeomai*) refers to those who are "in a supervisory capacity, leaders, guides."[9] The guiding role of church leaders is emphasized throughout this passage, particularly in verse 7, which uses the same Greek word for church "leaders" and calls the readers to "remember your leaders, who spoke the word of God to you. Consider the outcome of their way of life and imitate their faith." Church leaders influence (lead, guide) their congregations through the example of their godly lives and faithful teaching of Scripture. This is very different from the power-based authority model many espouse.

The Nature of Church Leadership

The following two verses further clarify the nature of biblical church leadership. Immediately after telling his readers to consider their leaders' faith and biblical teaching, he proclaims that Christ is "the same yesterday and today and forever" (Heb 13:8). While this might seem like a departure from the topic at hand, it actually serves as a link to the next verse, which warns the readers not to be led astray by false, unbiblical teachings. The point is this— while godly church leaders play an important role in the church, those leaders are still human, finite, and fallible. Only Jesus is unchanging and utterly trustworthy. And God's Word contains Jesus's authoritative voice.

To the extent that church leaders point their flock to Jesus and his Word, they have influence and authority. But their authority is limited and contingent. As A. J. Coetsee notes from this passage, "[Church] leaders do not have any authority in themselves; the Word of God is their authority . . . church members should submit to their leaders because they preach the authoritative Word of God."[10]

Further strengthening this assertion that church leaders' authority is found in Scripture, and is not inherent to their position as elders or pastors, are the specific commands found in verse 17. The readers are instructed to "have confidence in your leaders and submit to their authority." Neither of the verbs used here are the submission terms used in the household codes. The first comes from a Greek word (*peithō*), which most often refers to being won over as a result of persuasion (Luke 16:31; Acts 18:4; 2 Cor 5:11). The second imperative translated "submit" (*hypeikō*) is used only here in the New Testament and means "to yield, give way." In other words, we are to allow our church leaders to persuade us from Scripture, and when they do so we are to yield to that teaching. We are to obey it. "These two imperatives should never be understood to promote blind obedience."[11] Church leaders have no biblical warrant to demand obedience simply because they are church leaders.

Jesus, Paul, and Spiritual Authority

We must allow Scripture to interpret Scripture by making two other final observations about the nature and scope of spiritual authority from Jesus and Paul. Paul, who had apostolic authority (which was much greater than the authority of a local church pastor), rarely used his apostolic authority to compel obedience. Nor did he spiritually "lord it over" the flock (2 Cor 1:24; cf. 1 Pet 5:3). Rather, Paul repeatedly appealed to his own exemplary lifestyle and his love for them as their spiritual father to get his listeners to behave in a particular manner. He graciously sought to persuade by appealing, not demanding.[12] Paul says he could have used his apostolic authority to compel their obedience, but that was not his method (1 Thess 2:6–7). Modern pastors should follow Paul's example.

On the flip side of the spiritual-authority coin, we find the Pharisees and Sadducees. They leveraged their authority in a heavy-handed manner. People were not allowed to have a contrary spiritual conviction or to disagree with them; the Jewish laypeople were to simply and slavishly obey their teachings and commands. To do otherwise invited shame, censure, and even expulsion from the community of faith (John 9:1–35; cf. 3 John 10). How did Jesus respond to these men, his own spiritual authorities? When their teachings accorded with Scripture, he commended them and told others to obey (Matt 23:3a). But when he believed their lifestyles or teachings were unbiblical, he called them out in the staunchest terms (Matt 6:1–17; 23:3b–36; Luke 20:46–47). Jesus boldly challenged, defied, and refused to be bullied into obeying his authorities' unbiblical rules and dictates (Matt 9:9–13; 12:1–8; Mark 3:1–6). Ultimately, Jesus took his marching orders from his heavenly Father (John 5:16–17; 8:12–29). So must we.

I'll allow Diane Langberg, one of the country's most respected evangelical abuse experts, to give the final word on obedience to church leaders. She notes that all human power is derivative. It comes from Christ, our only Lord, who has all power and authority (Matt 28:18). She admonishes us:

> Do not trust in a successful leader, ministry, or growing numbers. Do not trust in fame or accolades. Do not trust in books sold or great knowledge acquired. Those things are not Jesus Christ. He did none of those things. Leaders, do not measure yourselves by such standards but by the character of our Lord. Followers, do not follow any leader with all the above trappings who bears little or no likeness to Christ. There is only one Lord, and he is neither a human leader nor a human system.[13]

2. PSALM 105:15

"Do not touch my anointed ones."

This text is the ultimate get-out-of-jail-free card for abusive leaders. Pentecostals frequently cite it to preclude any criticism. Benny

Hinn says we "must not raise a voice [of criticism] against a man of God even if he is wicked." Doing this brings divine judgment, sickness, and even death.[14] Pentecostals aren't the only ones to use "do not touch [God's] anointed" to make themselves untouchable. In the Introduction, Cheryl recounted how her fundamentalist pastor had done the same thing. How do we understand this biblical warning?

The Context

This poisonous reading is a glaring example of violating the context of a passage. Psalm 105:15 and 1 Chronicles 16:22 are virtually identical texts with identical contexts. Who are these texts describing? Hint: it isn't modern-day pastors. In ancient Israel, divinely chosen leaders, particularly kings, and prophets, were literally anointed with oil to symbolize their being set apart for sacred service (1 Sam 10:1; Pss 89:20; 105:15). The New Testament never describes church leaders as "God's anointed." Instead, *all* believers are said to "have an anointing from the Holy One"—that is, the indwelling Holy Spirit (1 John 2:20, 27; cf. 2 Cor 1:21–22).

Furthermore, the specific command not to touch God's anointed has nothing to do with criticizing spiritual leaders. It refers to physically harming Old Testament kings and prophets. This command is given in the context of Israel's journey of deliverance from Egyptian bondage to the occupation of the promised land of Canaan. When pagan kings sought to attack and annihilate Israel and her anointed leaders, God supernaturally protected her. He brought judgment on her adversaries who attempted to harmfully "touch" her (Pss 105:14, 28–36; 136:10–20). This is the context of "do not touch" God's "anointed."

Other Relevant Passages

Two other critically relevant Old Testament texts confirm this interpretation of "do not touch" God's "anointed." While David was fleeing from King Saul, David had two specific opportunities to kill him. Once, when Saul went into a cave to relieve himself (1 Sam 24) and once at night when Saul and his troops had fallen into a deep sleep (1 Sam 26). In both instances, David declared that he would not harm God's "anointed"—that is, physically attack and kill Saul (1 Sam 24:6, 10; 26:9, 11, 23). But David had no qualms about proclaiming the truth and criticizing Saul. He pronounced him wicked (1 Sam 24:13; cf. 26:18–20). Legitimately criticizing spiritual leaders' teachings and actions is thoroughly biblical (Matt 23; 3 John 10). It has nothing to do with "not touching" God's "anointed."

In conclusion, contemporary church leaders who seek to evade accountability by citing Psalm 105:15 or 1 Chronicles 16:22 distort Scripture. They are not anointed Jewish kings. Criticizing is not "touching." Legitimate criticism will not provoke divine punishment. However, arrogant false teaching and spiritual abuse do invoke God's judgment (Jude 8–16).

3. PROVERBS 6:19

God hates the "one who sows discord among brothers." (ESV)

Kate grew up on the church doorsteps. Don, her father, was a deacon in their large community church. Her mother sang in the choir and taught Sunday School. Her family was revered throughout the congregation. But no one knew that Don had been molesting Kate for the past five years. When Kate's younger sister hit adolescence, Don shifted his sordid attention to her. Kate simply couldn't contain the family secret any longer. She confided the abuse to her youth pastor, who was initially skeptical until Kate showed him some notes her father had written, confessing to the abuse, promising to stop (which he hadn't), and warning Kate not to tell anyone, lest their family and the church be destroyed.

Sadly, Kate's youth pastor affirmed the "wisdom" of her father's warning. He cautioned her that she must not tell anyone else about the abuse because that would create great dissension in the church and harm its gospel witness. After all, God hates the "one who sows discord among brothers" (Prov 6:19 ESV; cf. Rom 16:17). So, the direction given to Kate, seemingly supported by Scripture, was that nothing was worth harming the unity of the church, even if it meant covering up abuse.

Such misapplication of Scripture to cover up unhealthy, unethical, and even abusive behavior is typical. For instance, many high-profile Christian leaders, such as pastors Mark Driscoll and James McDonald, have been heavily criticized for reportedly abusing their power by punishing parishioners who "create dissension" and harm the ministry by giving any criticism, particularly about the senior pastor.[15]

Similarly, when employees at Ravi Zacharias International Ministries (RZIM) raised questions about Zacharias's troubling behavior, including solo international travels with his female massage therapist, they were reportedly reprimanded and told "derogative remarks of any kind . . . must cease immediately as they do not glorify the Lord"; they harm relationships and the ministry.[16] Though the board of RZIM had reportedly received allegations of sexually inappropriate behavior for over fifteen years, it appears they repeatedly and summarily dismissed them. It wasn't until after Zacharias died in 2020 that the board was pressured into authorizing an independent investigation, which found extensive evidence that Zacharias had engaged in sexual misconduct and likely sexual abuse of dozens of women over many years and had aggressively used hundreds of thousands of RZIM funds to cover it up. These revelations eventually led to the unraveling of RZIM. Does Scripture require silence at all costs to preserve unity?

The Context

This is a classic example of the importance of paying attention to context and the full teaching of Scripture (Scripture interpreting Scripture). Let's begin by noting the context of Proverbs 6:19. The writer lists seven things God hates (6:16–19), culminating in "a person who stirs up conflict in the community" (Prov 6:19). The first glaring observation is that of the previous six things God hates, most involve some form of abuse ("a lying tongue," "hands that shed innocent blood," "a heart that devises wicked schemes," "feet that are quick to rush into evil"). *This text does not pit unity over abuse but highlights God's hatred of abuse.* Furthermore, the immediately preceding verses clarify the conflict-instigating troublemakers whom God hates. This is not a generic precipitator of community conflict but "a villain, who goes about with a corrupt mouth, who winks maliciously with his eye, signals with his feet and motions with his fingers, who plots evil with deceit in his heart—he always stirs up conflict" (Prov 6:12–14). The conflict instigators whom God hates are evil and abusive. We can now see how perverse it is to use Proverbs 6:19 to shut down credible abuse allegations. Church leaders, including Kate's youth pastor, must hate what God hates. God hates it when churches ignore abuse allegations and silence victims by labeling what they share as "gossip."

Other Relevant Passages

Before we proceed, I want to affirm the importance of unity in the faith community. Jesus prayed that his followers would experience unity and intimacy as he did with the Father (John 17:20–23). The apostle Paul urged church members not to allow divisions but to strive for unity (1 Cor 1:10; Phil 2:1–4). The psalmist declares, "How good and pleasant it is when God's people live together in unity!" (Ps 133:1). Scripture identifies numerous threats to unity, such as dishonesty (Prov 16:28), selfish ambition (Phil 2:2–3), greed

(Prov 28:25), foolish theological speculation (2 Tim 2:23), pride (Prov 13:10), jealousy (1 Cor 3:3), and a hot temper (Prov 15:18; 29:22). So if any of these are the causes of disunity, by all means the one creating disunity must repent and take corrective action. But in other instances, "disunity" is not the result of a sinful or foolish "divisive report." Instead, it may result from a godly person speaking the truth about a sinful leader or an unhealthy environment. While unity is God's ideal, it is sometimes unattainable because this world is not ideal. We live in a fallen world with competing powers and mutually exclusive loyalties. Jesus himself declared, "Do not suppose that I have come to bring peace to the earth. I did not come to bring peace, but a sword" (Matt 10:34). The context of this jarring statement is the importance of loyalty to Jesus above all other loyalties, even to family. Sometimes fidelity to Jesus will not create peace but dissension. Unfortunately, unhealthy churches often demand loyalty to the system or to the charismatic leader above all else.[17] But if the system or the leader acts in ways that do not honor Jesus, speaking the truth about that reality, even if it causes dissension, is godly and necessary.

There are countless examples in Scripture of godly individuals creating conflict by shining the spotlight of truth on the unhealthy, ungodly behavior of spiritual leaders. Jesus spent much of his public ministry calling out the Pharisees' erroneous theology and ungodly practices. This created intense, chronic conflict (Matt 12:1–14; 21:1–46). Similarly, when the apostles proclaimed God's truth, it sometimes created riotous dissension (Acts 6:12; 13:50; 14:2). The Jewish leaders' ungodliness ultimately created disunity. Repeatedly, the Hebrew prophets caused great dissension in the Jewish community by calling out the sins and errors of the community and the leaders. The prophet Jeremiah's lengthy public ministry was marked by conflict with his day's spiritual and political leaders. He repeatedly exposed their sins, particularly injustice, abuse, and oppression of the vulnerable. He declared they stood under divine judgment for these gross sins (Jer 2:23; 7:5–6; 9:3–9). The leaders, in return, insisted that everything was just fine and that Jeremiah should shut up (Jer 11:21; 26:1–11). But God condemned Judah's leaders for refusing to acknowledge their moral sickness created by their failure to address abuse and oppression. He declared: "They [the leaders] dress the wound of my people as though it were not serious. 'Peace, peace,' they say, when there is no peace" (Jer 8:11). Abuse and oppression by spiritual leaders are grievous evils that must be identified and condemned, even if doing so causes turmoil. Peace at any price facilitates evil and impedes healing.

Gossip

Let's conclude this section by addressing the closely related issue of gossip. Tremendous confusion exists regarding what exactly constitutes gossip. Scripture uniformly condemns gossip (Prov 16:28; Rom 1:30), but what exactly is it? Is it simply giving a "negative report" about someone? Bullying pastors love to accuse anyone who criticizes them of being a sinful, divisive gossip. Even seeking help by sharing personal accounts of being abused is sometimes labeled "gossip." Rebecca Davis gives numerous examples in her excellent discussion of abuse and gossip. She recounts the experience of one woman who was silent about her abuse for twenty-three years, only to be shamed for "gossiping" when she finally did seek help by disclosing.[18] So, let's begin by carefully defining this term. Genuine gossip involves sharing unverified negative information and/or sharing with an unhealthy motive. The Greek word group used for gossip in the New Testament includes the word for a "rumormonger or talebearer" (e.g., Rom 1:29) and that which one of these persons spreads—that is, "derogatory information about someone that is offered in a tone of confidentiality" (e.g., 2 Cor 12:20).[19] In other words, gossip most often involves a report of uncertain or dubious accuracy. We've all experienced the sting of unjust rumors lobbed against us. They are unfair and destructive. So gossip involves the content of the message. But it may also be defined by a sinful motivation for giving the negative report—a self-righteous desire to feel superior to the one being criticized, a mean-spirited gloating over another's moral failures, an idolatrous need for attention from others, etc. Such unhealthy motivations are implied in Proverbs 18:8: "The words of a gossip are like choice morsels; they go down to the inmost parts." Gossip is juicy. Gossip flows from a sinful heart.

But are all adverse reports gossip? Absolutely not. The same apostle Paul, who condemned gossip by placing it in a list of moral vices along with envy, murder, strife, deceit, and malice (Rom 1:29), gave a very negative report about a man named Alexander. He told Timothy, "Alexander the metalworker did me a great deal of harm. . . . You too should be on your guard against him" (2 Tim 4:14–15). This negative report was accurate (Paul had the facts) and came from a healthy motivation (Timothy's protection). It was a very negative report, but it wasn't gossip. Similarly, the writer of 3 John gives a brutally candid report of a church leader named Diotrephes. The author declares that Diotrephes was arrogantly refusing to receive traveling ministers and was abusing his power by throwing people who disagreed with him out of the church. The author comments on Diotrephes's sinful attitude and actions (vv. 9–10), noting that he was self-serving and arrogant (he "loves to be first"), lied and slandered (he spread "malicious nonsense"), and abused his power ("he even refuses to welcome other believers. He also stops those who want to do so and puts them out of the church"). Not only does the author give a very negative written report about Diotrephes, but he also promises to declare these criticisms publicly if he can visit the church (v. 10; cf. Gal 2:11–14).

These biblical examples are highly relevant to modern abuse allegations. Sharing a verified or credible report of harmful or

141

abusive behavior is not gossip when it is done to protect others. This might include sharing a negative report on behalf of someone unable to advocate for themselves. Proverbs 31:9 says that those with a position of influence and a voice (it is written to King Lemuel) are to be a voice for the voiceless: "Speak up and judge fairly; defend the rights of the poor and needy." Sharing a concern about a church leader to protect the vulnerable and promote church health is the opposite of gossip. It is godly and necessary.

4. 1 TIMOTHY 5:19

"Do not admit a charge against an elder except on the evidence of two or three witnesses." (ESV)

We saw earlier that a strict reading of this text is often used against abuse survivors who are unable to provide witnesses to corroborate their abuse. This text is commonly understood to mean that one cannot consider even the most serious allegation against a pastor without corroborating witnesses. For example, one pastor argues from this verse that:

> Timothy, and the Ephesian church by extension, is commanded to not ever welcome or even crack the door to any accusation against an elder. If someone comes with an accusation against one who has already been vetted and ordained to serve the church of Jesus Christ as an overseer/elder/pastor, you slam the door in their face. Don't entertain the idea. Don't hear them out. Don't even consider it. They come knocking and you send them packing.[20]

Sadly, here's how it often goes: The frightened teenager reports her elder father has been molesting her. *Send her packing! Don't listen to a word she is saying! Don't give her concerns and allegations a single second of reflection. If she can't marshal witnesses, she should shut her mouth.*

Are these responses valid applications of 1 Timothy 5:19? No! They are toxic perversions of biblical teaching. Such flawed responses are tragic examples of how strict, Pharisaical interpretations of Scripture fixate on the minutia of a passage and miss the biblical big picture. This is precisely what Jesus accused the harsh Pharisees of, straining "out a gnat" and swallowing "a camel" by missing "the more important matters of the law—justice, mercy and faithfulness" (Matt 23:23–24), all the while crushing the vulnerable with their rigid interpretations (Matt 23:4).

The Mosaic Law Backdrop

Let's look more specifically at 1 Timothy 5:19. For starters, let's note that it draws on a teaching found in the law of Moses—one should not be convicted of a crime based on a single accusation (Deut 17:6; 19:15). This makes perfect sense as a general principle. Ironically, as Old Testament theologian Christopher Wright notes, the purpose of having a plurality of witnesses "is clearly the protection of the accused, especially the protection of the weaker individual from the vindictiveness of a more powerful opponent."[21] How tragically ironic when this legislation is used not to protect the vulnerable but to harm them. Condemnation of oppression of the vulnerable by the powerful is a dominant theme in the Old Testament.[22] Repeatedly, the law of Moses legislates protection for the poor and marginalized (often identified as widows, orphans, and foreigners) to safeguard them against the more powerful who sought to defraud them.[23] This supports Wright's understanding of the "plurality of witness" legislation. However, this multiple-witness requirement is a general principle.

Mosaic law allowed for specific exceptions. For instance, after giving this general two-witness requirement in Deuteronomy 19:15, Moses immediately addresses a particular exception to the general rule.[24] In the case of an accusation by a "malicious witness" without any other witnesses, the judge is to interview the two parties and conduct a thorough investigation, and based on those interviews he is to make a definitive ruling. If the judge determined that the one making the accusation had lied, the accuser was to receive the penalty that the one they falsely accused would have received for the alleged crime. Notice that in this specific situation the judge was to make a definitive ruling without any corroborating witnesses. Some conditions are of such a nature that additional witnesses cannot be secured, and the Mosaic law makes provisions for those unique exceptions.

The Impropriety of Applying 1 Timothy 5:19 to Abuse Accusations

Sexual abuse is undoubtedly one of those exceptional cases where even the Mosaic law makes exceptions to the multiple-witness requirement. As Scott McKnight and Laura Barringer note, sexual abuse is almost always perpetrated in secret with no other witness. For this reason, they argue that 1 Timothy 5:19 "rarely works for sexual abuse allegations against church leaders. Using Matthew 18 and 1 Timothy 5 in such cases is profoundly *un*biblical and profoundly harmful to victims of sexual harassment and abuse."[25] The Mosaic law supports this assertion. Deuteronomy 22:25 gives legislation concerning an engaged or married woman who is raped in a private setting (the countryside), with no witnesses to hear her cries for help. In such a situation, the judges must receive, weigh, and act on her testimony.[26] If the judges determined that she was telling the truth and was raped, the rapist was to be given capital punishment, and she was to be deemed guiltless (specifically as blameless as a murder victim). Notice that the judges were to make a verdict in cases of sexual-assault allegations despite having no other corroborating witnesses.

In summary, the general rule is that civil or spiritual leaders should be given due process and not be tried and declared guilty based on a single person's accusation. However, there are exceptions to this principle, particularly for abuse. Such exceptions should and must be made in the case of alleged abuse by a church leader. Failing to listen to abuse allegations against a church leader because there are no other witnesses is astoundingly foolish and harmful.

Matthew 18:15–20 gives general guidelines for dealing with relational conflict caused by another's sinful actions:

> If your brother or sister sins, go and point out their fault, just between the two of you. If they listen to you, you have won them over. But if they will not listen, take one or two others along, so that "every matter may be established by the testimony of two or three witnesses." If they still refuse to listen, tell it to the church. (Matt 18:15–17)

As with 1 Timothy 5:19, this is a most helpful general principle for dealing with sin in the church. Unfortunately, churches sometimes uncritically insist that it is followed to the letter, even in cases of abuse. Often, abusers will cry "foul" if their victims go to ecclesiastical or civil authorities before coming to them.[27] The impropriety and psychological harm of abuse victims having to go privately (making them even more vulnerable to being abused) to the very one who weaponized their power against them should be obvious. A survey of Scripture also shows this demand violates the tenor of hundreds of Scripture passages. As we will develop in the book's final section, Scripture dogmatically prioritizes the well-being and protection of the vulnerable.

Protecting the vulnerable from abuse summarizes what God

requires of his people, particularly spiritual leaders (Isa 1:17). God expects human leaders to "defend the weak and the fatherless; uphold the cause of the poor and the oppressed" (Ps 82:3; cf. Ps 72:4). Instructing abuse victims to go privately to the more powerful one who allegedly abused them is a ludicrous application of a general principle never intended to apply to every situation. This very chapter of Matthew suggests the guidelines in verses 15–20 about going privately to one who sins is a general principle. Later in this chapter (vv. 28–31), Jesus tells a parable about an unforgiving servant who abuses (chokes) and unjustly imprisons a man who owes him a small amount of money. When their fellow servants saw this, instead of going to the abusive man, they went straight to the master and reported the abusive behavior. Strictly speaking, they violated Jesus's previous instructions about going privately to the one who sinned. Jesus doesn't comment on, let alone condemn, their procedure. He places the focus and blame squarely on the unforgiving abuser.

The Occasional Setting

Finally, in considering how to apply 1 Timothy 5:19 to abuse victims, we should consider the occasional nature of the New Testament epistles. We don't have enough data to know what kind of accusations against elders were most likely being experienced at the time of writing of this epistle. Still, I would suggest that whatever the general multiple-witness requirement was, it was suitable for this situation. William Mounce suggests, based in part on the same use of the word used here to refer to an accusation in Titus 1:6, that Paul is addressing the situation of formal charges being brought against an elder for extravagance or insubordination.[28] Raymond Collins suggests that it might have been a similar situation addressed a few years later in 1 Clement, in which some of the younger men had rebelled and wrongly deposed the church leadership.[29] In these situations, the general principle of multiple witnesses provides helpful protection against false accusations. Abuse allegations against an elder are different and should be dealt with differently. Churches should and must receive and weigh abuse allegations against church leaders. Abuse victims should not be required to confront their abusers privately.

Now that we have looked at essential passages regarding the church, in the next chapter we will focus on texts directed explicitly at or related to abuse victims.

Chapter 7

PASSAGES ON ABUSE VICTIMS

It's something everybody wants—for someone to see the
hurt done to them and set it down like it matters.
—SUE MONK KIDD, *THE SECRET LIFE OF BEES*

The LORD builds up Jerusalem;
    he gathers the exiles of Israel.
He heals the brokenhearted
    and binds up their wounds. . . .
The LORD sustains the humble
    but casts the wicked to the ground.
—PSALM 147:2–3, 6

In this chapter, we will examine four of the most common biblical passages that are weaponized against abuse survivors. We will begin with Matthew 5:39.

Celestia and I have heard thousands of abuse stories. Each one is tragic in its own way. Cheryl's was one of the saddest—not because of the details of the abuse but because of its effect. Her reading of Scripture almost destroyed her and drove her away from Jesus.

1. MATTHEW 5:39

"But I tell you, do not resist an evil person. If anyone slaps you on the right cheek, turn to them the other cheek also."

About Matthew 5:39, Cheryl states:

As an innocent girl, I tried to live up to the teachings of Jesus the Savior. And I went on turning my cheek, trying to be the nice, sweet, polite girl my mother had brought me up to be. I strived to obey and respect all and sundry, particularly the elders in the family, even though they did not care, forgot to care, and were outright abusive.

And according to the Savior, I was not supposed to retaliate. So, I just allowed my perpetrators to be released of any responsibility, accountability, repentance, and atonement. They were free of guilt or remorse as they did not grasp that they had done wrong because I behaved nicely, pleased them, and did what they wanted. I was a people pleaser, even when they trampled on my needs and feelings. I went on turning the other cheek.

Cheryl concluded that Matthew 5 instructs survivors to passively accept abuse and not hold abusers accountable. She believed "tolerating abuse would make me a saint and lead me to heaven."[1] Paradoxically, tolerating abuse almost destroyed Cheryl. She eventually decided that the only way to save her life was to let go of her commitment to Jesus and Scripture.

Survivors are not the only ones who believe Scripture teaches that abuse is to be passively endured. Some professional caregivers also believe this is what Scripture demands. One such example is a medical doctor named Alex Lickerman, who describes the message in Matthew 5:39 as harmful and even immoral.[2] Cheryl's tragic story illustrates the fact that not only can other people weaponize Scripture against survivors, but sometimes survivors are poisoned without outside help.

Observations About Matthew 5:38–42

The paragraph in Matthew 5 is an admittedly tricky passage that deserves our attention. Let's make three observations, beginning with context.

First, *Jesus's commands in this paragraph are given in a very specific context: nonretaliation and love of enemy.* Jesus issues five commands in this paragraph: "Do not resist an evil person"; "Turn to them the other cheek"; "If anyone wants to sue you and take your shirt, hand over your coat as well"; "If anyone forces you to go one mile, go with them two miles"; "Give to the one who asks you, and do not turn away from the one who wants to borrow from you." The stated context for these commands is found in verse 38—a prohibition against getting revenge against one's enemies. The following paragraph (vv. 43–48) closely relates to this and focuses on loving one's enemies. Loving one's enemies is particularly relevant to going the extra "mile," giving your "coat," and giving "to the one who asks." These themes (nonretaliation and enemy love) are so closely related that we might consider them two sides of the same coin. Stated negatively, we are not to get revenge against our enemies. Stated positively, we are to love our enemies.

Furthermore, these two themes are part of a bigger section (Matt 5:21–48) in which Jesus says six times, "You have heard that it was said . . . but I say to you" (e.g., Matt 5:38–39 ESV). In other words, Jesus responds to Jewish misconceptions of biblical teaching and gives his clarification and corrections. In this "turn the other cheek" section, Jesus is responding to the common misconception that the Old Testament "eye for eye, tooth for tooth" teaching (Exod 21:24; Deut 19:21) allowed for personal revenge against one's enemies.

The paragraph that follows (Matt 5:43–48) corrects the misguided belief that we should love our neighbors and hate our enemies. Jesus instead instructs us to love our enemies. We must place Jesus's teaching in the context of nonretaliation and love of enemies. *He is not giving unrestricted guidelines for responding to abusers.* Instead, Jesus is giving guidelines for loving our enemies when our natural human instincts are to take revenge and hurt them for hurting us.

Second, *Jesus uses hyperbolic (exaggerated) language to emphasize an important point.* In the Gospels, Jesus frequently uses hyperbolic (exaggerated) language that is not intended to be taken literally. Duvall and Hays note in their excellent hermeneutics textbook that Jesus often used exaggeration to "connect powerfully with his listeners and drive home his point. Exaggeration occurs when a truth is overstated for the sake of effects to such an extent that a literal fulfillment is either impossible or completely ridiculous."[3] Hyperbole does not communicate literal (factual) truth. Rather, it expresses "emotional truth."[4] I would add that hyperbole can also be identified when a literal fulfillment would violate other biblical passages.

Sometimes biblical hyperbole is obvious, as in Psalm 18:42: "I beat them [my enemies] as fine as windblown dust; I trampled them like mud in the streets." David could not and did not literally crush his enemies into tiny, dust-sized particles. This is exaggerated language used to powerfully convey a point—he utterly defeated his enemies. Jesus indisputably uses hyperbole. A literal reading of Matthew 5:29–30 ("If your right eye causes you to stumble, gouge it out," "If your right hand causes you to stumble, cut it off") is nonsensical and would violate the tenor of other Scriptures. Obviously, if you poke out your right eye, you can still struggle with greed and can lust with just one eye. And it is not literally possible when giving to the poor to "not let your left hand know what your right hand is doing" (Matt 6:3). If, in Luke 14:26, Jesus literally meant that anyone who does not "hate father and mother, wife and children, brothers and sisters" cannot "be my disciple," he would be asking us to violate repeated biblical commands to love others and honor our parents—commands Jesus himself affirms elsewhere.

As we can see, each of these commands by Jesus is hyperbolic and intended to convey succinct emotional truths. (1) No price is too great to have victory over sin; do whatever you need to do to mitigate against temptation. (2) Do not give to people in need to gain approval from others. (3) Our loyalty to and love for Jesus must be supreme; he must come first over our most cherished human relationships (cf. Matt 10:37). (4) We should love our enemies in costly ways by "going the extra mile" and not retaliating, etc. The command *"Do not resist an evil person" cannot be a blanket prohibition against resisting evil people.* We must recognize the hyperbolic language Jesus is using in this passage.

Third, *other Scripture confirms that "do not resist an evil person" does not mean passive acceptance of evil.* Scripture commands us to fight against evildoers. Godly leaders "defend the afflicted," "crush the oppressor" (Ps 72:4), and "rescue those being led away to death" (Prov 24:11). God's people, when fighting against evildoers, are not to seek revenge by dishing out "evil for evil" but instead are to "overcome evil with good" (Rom 12:17, 21). Jesus is clear. We are not to retaliate, and this is Jesus's point in Matthew 5:39. But this does not mean we cannot and should not stand up against evildoers.

Jesus himself resisted evil people and did not passively accept the Pharisees's wicked practices and corrupt teachings. Instead, he confronted, publicly exposed, and shamed them (Matt 10:16–17; see Matt 23). On one occasion, he went so far as to overturn greedy money changers' tables in the temple and drive them out with whips (John 2:14–17). It is worth noting that the same Greek word used here in Matthew 5:39 for resist (*anthistēmi*) is used elsewhere in the New Testament in a positive sense. Believers are commanded to actively resist the devil, the ultimate evil one (Jas 4:7). Paul said he withstood (resisted) Peter face-to-face when Peter shamed gentile believers and compromised the gospel of grace (Gal 2:11). Lest someone try to assert that Jesus allows us to resist abuse and other forms of evil perpetrated against *others* but not against *ourselves*, we should note the numerous examples in Scripture of godly individuals doing just that. We saw earlier multiple examples of David, Jonathan, Jesus, and Paul not passively accepting abuse but actively thwarting it. When Paul discovered that forty men had taken a vow to kill him, he orchestrated a detailed plan to derail his abusers' murderous plot (Acts 23:12–24). In the Old Testament, godly Nehemiah led the people in rebuilding the wall of Jerusalem to protect them from enemy attacks. They were to carry their trowel in "one hand and [hold] a weapon in the other" (Neh 4:17). Abuse victims have every biblical right to confront their abusers and protect themselves, but not to seek revenge. This is what Jesus meant by "do not resist an evil person."

"Turn" the "Other Cheek" Is Also Hyperbolic

While many commentators attempt to interpret this saying, found in the second half of Matthew 5:39, with concrete literalness—even conjecturing precise body posture after one turns a right versus a left cheek and what that might signify, etc.—this misses Jesus's point and the context. First, we should note that in ancient Jewish culture, a slap on the cheek was not a physical assault but a shameful public insult. These slaps on the cheek were typically given to one's social inferiors. Instead of retaliating when we are insulted, Jesus commands us to turn our other cheek to the one shaming us and not respond in kind. There are other instances of face slapping in Scripture, revealing that Jesus is using exaggeration here to make a point about retaliation. He is not speaking literally. For example, Jesus and Paul protested when they were slapped and did *not* turn the other cheek (John 18:23; Acts 23:3). In another incident, Paul shamed the Corinthians for allowing false apostles to exploit, take advantage of, and slap them in the face (2 Cor 11:20). Again, we see that passivity in the face of abuse is not being advocated or praised.

Pastor Dan Lacich's explanation of "turn . . . the other cheek" is a beneficial clarification and application of this passage for abuse survivors. He states:

> What Jesus is speaking about here is not letting someone pummel you into a pile of broken bones. Rather He is talking about taking an insult. A backhanded slap is just that. It is an insult that challenges you to retaliate. It is an attempt to shame you and get you to either back down in utter humiliation or lash out and escalate the conflict.
>
> To turn the other cheek is neither humiliating nor retaliation. It is rather a response of strength that says, "I will not seek revenge because I am stronger than that." It also says, I will not respond in shame because I have dignity in Christ. My dignity is not found in if I can hit you back and hurt you. My dignity is found in Christ, and I will respond in just the way He would respond.[5]

In summary, Jesus's commands to turn the other cheek and not to resist evildoers are not a call to passive acceptance of abuse. Instead, they call abuse survivors to respond to abuse with Christlike character by loving their enemies and not seeking revenge.

2. 1 CORINTHIANS 13:7

"Love bears all things, believes all things, hopes all things, endures all things." (ESV)

Paul's eloquent description of love can be easily misconstrued to mean that abuse victims must endure any and all forms of destructive maltreatment. For instance, one pastor argues, without any qualification, that *enduring all things* means "we are willing to stand in there and take some abuse in the name of seeing each other through to the end."[6] Furthermore, he argues that "believing all things" means "we give others the benefit of the doubt. It means that we expect the best." He then insists we must "repent of this terrible sin" of failing to "believe all things" about others. Instead, we should always "trust that others have our best purposes in mind" and are "looking out for us."[7] Unfortunately, like many others, this commentator has failed to account for Paul's hyperbolic language.

Some Things Shouldn't Be Endured

Some things shouldn't be believed, born, or endured. Not everyone is looking out for our best interests. Some people genuinely want to harm us, and telling ourselves otherwise would be distorting reality and inviting unnecessary harm. In this passage, Paul uses exaggerated, emotional language to describe the power and costliness of agape love. This is similar to what we saw in Matthew 5:38–42. It is a severe mistake to construe the language of 1 Corinthians 13:7 in strictly literal terms. Paul himself often cautions his readers to discriminate and not believe everything about everyone. Some people are not to be believed based on their character and teachings. Thus, Paul commands his readers to "let no one deceive you with empty words" (Eph 5:6; cf. 2 Thess 2:3). We must not trust everyone in every context. Paul cautioned Timothy to "be on your guard against" Alexander, the metalworker, for he was an untrustworthy person who had done Paul "a great deal of harm" (2 Tim 4:14–15). This is our instruction too: there will be people we can trust and those we cannot trust.

It is noteworthy that the same Greek verb Paul uses positively of love "bearing" (*stegō*) all things in 1 Corinthians 13:7 is used in 1 Thessalonians 3:1 of Paul not being willing to continue "to bear" being away from the beloved Thessalonians. So he sent Timothy as his representative to nurture their faith. In other words, love dictates that some negative situations must not be endured. Other biblical texts affirm this principle. In Revelation 2:20 God condemns the church at Thyatira for "bearing" (enduring) what shouldn't be endured—namely, Jezebel, a false teacher who led God's people into sexual immorality. On the other hand, the Ephesian church was commended for its "patient endurance" in the faith while refusing to "bear with those who are evil" (Rev 2:2 ESV). Some things and people are not to be endured (tolerated). God does call us to endure hardship and persecution (2 Tim 4:5; cf. 1 Cor 4:12), but this does not apply to the vast majority of abuse suffered in North America. Enduring sexual harassment, domestic violence, or schoolyard bullying is hardly ever necessary for spreading the gospel in our culture. In other parts of the world and other settings, agape love will, at times, require enduring abuse. Even then, the Holy Spirit must guide in applying what agape love requires one to bear.

On one occasion, Paul was willing to be beaten for the gospel, refusing to use his legal rights as a Roman citizen to avoid a beating. This led to the Philippian jailer's entire household coming to faith (Acts 16:22–39). But on another occasion, Paul fled and avoided being attacked and potentially killed by his adversaries (Acts 9:23–25). Once, when Paul and Barnabas were preaching the gospel in the town of Iconium, they discovered their adversaries were planning to "mistreat them and stone them," so they fled and escaped being abused (Acts 14:1–6). But in the next town they fled to (Lystra), these same opponents caught them, stoned Paul, and left him to die. This time, after regaining consciousness, instead of fleeing Paul went right back into Lystra to continue his gospel ministry, risking further attacks (Acts 14:19–22). The demands of love are quite context specific and must be Spirit directed.

Let's pull this together. Agape love is costly. Loving others requires bearing all manner of costly sacrifices. It involves believing and having faith that no person is beyond change and redemption, including abusers. Agape love is not naive or ignorant of the dynamics of evildoers. Nor does it simply tolerate evil or indiscriminately suffer abuse.

3. PROVERBS 19:11

"It is to one's glory to overlook an offense."

Tim's lay counselor quoted this verse after Tim recounted his painful childhood being raised by a tyrannical, alcoholic father. Tim had tremendous childhood pain and felt very conflicted in his relationship with his unbelieving father, who refused to own his chronic destructive behavior. Furthermore, Tim's father continued in the present to bully and berate Tim every time they were together. The counselor advised Tim that as sad as his childhood was, he needed to let go of his father's past and present hurtful actions. He explained that "overlooking an offense" means completely putting it out of sight. You forget it. Refuse to bring it up. Move on. He assured Tim that a godly person would "overlook an offense" and that God would bless and honor him if he did this with his father. Does Proverbs 19:11 require abuse survivors to simply overlook their abuser's destructive actions?

The Context

Let's apply sound hermeneutical principles from part 1, starting with the immediate context, for it significantly limits the scope of this verse. This verse does not address global offenses. Note the first half of the verse: "A person's wisdom yields patience." In other words, in our impulsiveness or impatience, we may inordinately fixate on wrongs done to us. A wise person doesn't act or speak without thinking first. They refuse to harbor grudges or keep a laundry list of inappropriate or hurtful actions. They are patient. "Offenses" is not a specific term but a general reference to actions that frustrate, anger, or hurt us. There are countless "offenses" that can accumulate in a day—a snide comment from an insecure coworker, a loud honk and obscene gesture from an impatient driver, a rude in-law who must always have the last word, an arrogant supervisor who fixates on the slightest mistake, a spouse who lacks gratitude. A wise person learns to exercise patience toward such common, daily offenses. This is a sound general principle for life.

The Genre

We must remember the genre of Proverbs is wisdom literature. Wisdom literature offers general principles that are not intended to cover every situation. Other Scripture passages teach us that some offenses must not be overlooked. These offenses involve serious moral deficiency for the offender and severe consequences for the offended. For instance, Proverbs 27:5–6 says, "Better is open rebuke than hidden love. Wounds from a friend can be trusted, but an enemy multiplies kisses." In other words, love requires us not to overlook some offenses but to confront them. "*Rebuke*" and "wounds from a friend" suggest a bold confrontation for grave sin. Leviticus 19:17 gives a similar warning in even starker terms. It states: "Do not hate a fellow Israelite in your heart. Rebuke your neighbor frankly so you will not share in their guilt." Again, the language here of "guilt" suggests grave sin, not trivial offenses. In the context of someone we are close to—a friend, family member, or neighbor—overlooking their offensive sins is metaphorically hating them.

Let Scripture Interpret Scripture

We can easily confirm this principle of not overlooking serious offenses by noting its affirmation in the New Testament. On numerous occasions, Jesus, Paul, and John refused to ignore others' sins and instead confronted people's "offenses," particularly when those offenses caused grave harm to others (Luke 20:45–47; 2 Tim 4:14–15; 3 John 9–11).

In summary, godly character requires us to overlook minor offenses. These trivial, daily hurts should be born patiently. In contrast, serious sins must, whenever possible, be confronted. Overlooking serious sin offenses does not reflect love or Christian virtue, regardless of what a well-meaning but misguided authority figure or counselor might tell us.

4. 1 PETER 2:18 AND 3:1

"Slaves, in reverent fear of God submit yourselves to your masters, not only to those who are good and considerate, but also to those who are harsh. . . . Wives, in the same way submit yourselves to your own husbands so that, if any of them do not believe the word, they may be won over without words by the behavior of their wives."

Eileen Gray and her children suffered years of physical and emotional abuse from her husband, David, a Christian school teacher. She said she reached her breaking point after a particularly severe episode in which David physically abused one of the children, raving that the girl "needed to experience more pain." The daughter was reportedly so distraught after this traumatic incident that she began pulling her hair out. Eileen also indicated that the children reported David had assaulted, kicked, tried to suffocate, and wanted to kill them. When Eileen realized the gravity of the children's suffering, she went to her church leaders at Grace Community Church (GCC) for help. At this point, Eileen had taken her children and separated from her abusive husband. She recounts that the associate pastor instructed her not to leave her husband. He said that even if the husband was not repentant, Eileen should model for the children how to "suffer for Jesus" by enduring her husband's abuse.[8] Eileen did not yield to the counsel, and ultimately senior Pastor John MacArthur announced to the church that Eileen was being placed under church discipline and should be treated as an unbeliever for refusing to reconcile with her abusive husband. Shortly after Eileen left David, she discovered that he had also been sexually abusing the children. Though David was convicted and given a twenty-one-year sentence for physically and sexually abusing their children, GCC leaders reportedly continued to insist that Eileen had no biblical grounds for leaving.

Telling abuse victims to stay and "suffer for Jesus" and "suffer like Jesus" is most often supported by 1 Peter 2:18–3:6. This was the case with the GCC pastor who advised Eileen to stay and risk suffering more abuse. This "biblical" guidance for abused wives is given to future counselors at the GCC's seminary, Masters Seminary. John Street is the chair of the graduate program of biblical counseling and an elder at GCC. In lectures on counseling abused wives, he says abused wives should not leave to avoid abuse. Instead, they should, by their passive obedience "without a word," win over their husbands. He references 1 Peter and states:

> We learn his [God's] faithfulness through all those hardships. . . .
> In most abuse counseling you don't hear that, because most abuse
> counselors will be very quick to get that person to escape and not
> teach them God's faithfulness or the importance of their faithfulness in living out Christianity even in the midst of severe affliction.[9]

Does God call abused wives and children to voluntarily endure "severe affliction"? Unfortunately, GCC and the Master's Seminary staff are not the only ones telling wives to submit to abuse based on 1 Peter 2–3.[10] As Eileen Gray tragically illustrates, the stakes are high for correctly interpreting 1 Peter 2–3.

The million-dollar question is, *How should this text be applied today?*[11] Let's begin by acknowledging that Peter does instruct abused slaves to submit quietly to their maltreatment. And it appears he is giving similar advice to wives of ungodly pagan husbands. However, the key to understanding Peter's instructions to abuse victims is found in the occasional setting of this letter. Peter was writing to a particular audience with particular and identifiable needs. One cannot accurately apply this passage to modern abuse victims and ignore what occasioned these admonitions.

Let's look at the context and make several important observations.

First, *Peter writes to a congregation being persecuted for their faith and on the cusp of widespread persecution.* First Peter was likely written around AD 62–64, shortly before the persecution enacted by Emperor Nero. It appears the recipients were experiencing local persecution shortly before the intense persecution initiated by Nero in the summer of AD 64. While some Christians were already suffering painful persecution (1 Pet 1:6; 4:12), others had not yet experienced it but were facing a future threat (3:14, 17). The persecution appears to have been limited in scope but had the potential for rapid expansion, mainly through slander and misunderstandings by unbelieving pagans (2:12; 3:16; 4:4, 14). Peter's Christian readers stood on the verge of dangerous large-scale persecution because widespread prejudice and malice were liable to erupt at any time and grow into widespread violence. This threat of increased violent persecution leads us to the following principle regarding abuse and suffering in 1 Peter.

Second, then, *Peter instructs the Christian church to submit passively to the Roman authorities to protect their community.* The specific offense of these early Christians that provoked Roman persecution is reflected in pagan writings of this period. For the Romans, religious life and the social order of the community were inextricably linked. Hence, new religions that did not honor the old traditions and social practices were seen as a treasonous threat to the social order and, as such, were deserving of hatred and punishment.[12] Pagan authorities feeling threatened by the Christians' failure to follow social customs is the background to Peter's admonitions regarding passive submission to "the authorities" (1 Pet 2:13–3:7). Specifically, this setting is suggested by Peter's affirmation that even pagan civil authorities are ordained of God (2:13–14) and that by doing good, including showing proper respect to everyone and honoring the king, one can sometimes silence the slander of unbelievers (2:15, 17). Peter urges these believers to let their upright behavior be their response to the pagan slander. They were not to resist abusive authorities, for such resistance would have confirmed Roman fears that the new Christian faith harmed the social order.[13]

Third, *Peter's instructions to enslaved people to passively accept abuse reflects the utter powerlessness of first-century slaves.* In 2:18–20 Peter admonishes enslaved people who are beaten by their morally corrupt masters to patiently and passively endure their "unjust suffering." This is expressly suffering from physical beatings.[14] Scripture emphatically condemns physical abuse as a great evil (Prov 6:17; Isa 10:1–2; Ezek 45:8–9), which should be confronted (Isa 1:17; Jer 22:3–4; Ezek 22:2), but the first-century Roman social order prevented slaves from challenging abuse they received from their masters.[15] The fact that in verse 18 Peter addresses household slaves (*oiketēs*) is significant, for household slaves, by their proximity to their masters, were often more susceptible to physical and sexual abuse by the master and other family members.[16]

Also, enslaved people were not considered fully human in ancient

Roman society. They were the chattel property of the owner. One of the Greek words for slave, *andrapodon*, comes from two Greek words that refer to *man* and *foot*. It denotes a "man-footed creature." Slaves were considered dumb animals who must be ruled by fear and pain. As the first-century Roman philosopher Seneca stated, "[We] maltreat them [slaves], not as if they were humans, but as if they were beasts of burden."[17] Slaves had no legal rights and no recourse when mistreated.

Furthermore, under the Roman "power of the father" law (*patria potestas*), the household master had virtually unlimited, tyrannical power over his slaves.[18] This included the power of life and death. Masters often employed professional torturers who were particularly adept at inducing pain and creating fear. In legal proceedings, enslaved people were required to be tortured during questioning because they were considered inherently untrustworthy.

Crucifixion was the execution method reserved for slaves, regardless of whether they had committed serious crimes or any crimes.[19] Since 33–40 percent of the Roman population was enslaved, the Romans were quite anxious to keep all of them under tight control. This was done through fear and intimidation. Severe physical punishment, even for accidents, was believed essential to maintaining social order. The early second-century Roman magistrate Pliny warned that enslaved people must be constantly afraid, for "no master can feel safe because he is kind and considerate."[20] Roman historian K. Bradley notes that "any slave who offended his owner could expect not only punishment but severe punishment, the penalty often exceeding the transgression, especially in cases of sheer accidents." Consequently, the "threat of punishment" always hung over slaves.[21]

What, then, could Christian slaves (who had no legal rights) and Christian citizens (who stood on the cusp of widespread persecution) do when experiencing abuse? Their safest response was to simply let their godly behavior challenge unjust treatment and unjust slander, which is precisely what Peter repeatedly prescribes (1 Pet 2:12, 19–20; 3:16). Peter's admonition that the abused submit passively and entrust themselves to God would be appropriate for abuse victims in many non-Western settings, such as current fundamentalistic Muslim cultures governed by strict Islamic law (Sharia). In these settings, abused women, in particular, have few legal rights or protections, so a passive response might well be the safest response. In other cultural settings, particularly in the West, various options for challenging the evil of physical abuse would be available and quite appropriate for abused believers.

Fourth, *Peter's admonitions to Christian wives to quietly submit reflect the relative powerlessness of first-century women.* While a first-century wife did have some legal rights in the Roman Empire, she was under the rule of her husband (*patria potestas*). Christian women married to pagan husbands were in a particularly difficult situation. According to Roman social mores, a wife was to take her husband's religion. It was considered shameful and rebellious for a wife to do otherwise. This was a grave offense to the social order and reflected appalling disloyalty to the master of the house. While wives were certainly higher on the social ladder than slaves, in terms of loyalty it was imperative in Roman culture that wives and slaves remain obedient to the house's master or face severe consequences.[22] Thus, Christian women married to pagan husbands were, by virtue of being Christians, disloyal to the master of the house (their earthly lords). In doing so, much like slaves, they were much more likely to be abused by their husbands. (This fact might help us understand why Peter makes a positive reference to Sarah being submissive and calling Abraham lord or sir in 1 Pet 3:6.)[23] Wife-beating was common in ancient Roman society. It was actually considered appropriate and even necessary for husbands to beat their wives for disobedience or other inappropriate behavior.[24] After all, the husband was responsible for disciplining those in his household, since a properly ordered family was believed to contribute to the good of the entire community. This helps explain why wife-beating was generally acceptable behavior and was rarely subject to legal punishment.

Caryn Reeder, an expert on abuse in the ancient biblical world, states that in ancient Roman society, "there are, so far as I know, no cases in which physical violence alone is the reason for a legal complaint" against a husband.[25] Wife-beating was so common and socially accepted that even brilliant Christian leaders such as Augustine took it for granted and advised wives that the best way to avoid being severely beaten by their husbands was to be utterly submissive and obedient. Augustine, citing the example of his own mother Monica, who was married to a quick-tempered, "violent" pagan, argued that wives whose faces were "disfigured" by their husbands' beatings had only themselves to blame for using their tongues to inflame their husbands' anger.[26] Monica's example taught Augustine that an immoral or angry husband "should not be opposed" in any way, by word or deed. Her silence was her best, if not only, protection against a beating. Given the powerlessness and vulnerability of Christian wives married to pagans and the social pressure for husbands to beat their wives into submission, Peter's admonition of passive silence is a wise and appropriate strategy. But as Caryn Reeder notes regarding Peter's instructions to Christian wives:

> If we are going to claim this text as authoritative Scripture and take its message seriously, we must also take its context seriously. This context does limit the applicability; it is not a message to wives everywhere, at all times. It is certainly not applicable to wives in the United States, where there are laws against domestic violence and recourse for abused women, and, moreover, where Christianity is not identified as a subversive threat to household

or national security. . . . To tell Christian wives in the United States that, on the basis of 1 Peter 3:1–6, they must submit to abusive husbands is a misuse of biblical authority.[27]

Christian Abuse Victims and the Giving of Blessing

Christian abuse victims have a unique goal: to give a blessing (1 Pet 2:11–12; 3:8–9). While the occasional context of 1 Peter 1–2 does limit its application to modern Western abuse victims, there is much in the passage that is fully applicable, particularly the outlook of an abuse victim. While any abuse is a terrible evil to be condemned, *Peter gives abuse victims in any era a unique goal—namely, that they seek to bless their abusers. But this does not preclude modern abuse victims from assertively responding to their abusers and seeking to stop the abuse.* Peter states that a mistreated believer (in this case, one slandered) should maintain excellent behavior so that the persecutors might observe their good deeds and "glorify God on the day he visits us" (2:12). The vast majority of commentators rightly assert that Peter is referring to unbelievers being converted by witnessing the good works of slandered believers. This radical, counterintuitive response to verbal abuse is ultimately based on Jesus's command for believers to love their enemies and bless those who curse them (Matt 5:44; Luke 6:28). In 1 Peter 3:8–9 Peter strongly reiterates this theme of mistreated believers seeking to be a source of blessing upon those who mistreat them. In 3:9, summing up the warnings he has just given, Peter reminds these believers that they should not return evil for evil or insult for insult but instead give a blessing. The irony here is that God has called believers to inherit a blessing, but this blessing partly comes from believers being a blessing to the very ones who want to harm them.

Abuse victims can be a blessing by not personally seeking revenge against their abuser (1 Pet 3:9; cf. Rom 12:14, 17–21) and by praying for the abuser (Matt 5:44). But if the social order permits it, there are other ways to bless one's abuser that are often overlooked. Boldly confronting the sin of abuse (Luke 17:3), physically separating from an abuser (1 Sam 19:12–30:31), notifying ecclesiastical (1 Cor 5:1–13; 1 Tim 5:19–20) and civic authorities (Acts 23:12–22; Rom 13:1–4) of the abuse are all biblically sanctioned safeguards for abuse victims. Each of these responses can contribute to the abuser being convicted of their sin, repenting, and receiving divine blessing instead of divine judgment. Carol Adams argues that ministers, as well as wives, should not allow abusive husbands to escape negative consequences for their behavior. Her rationale is that "men batter because it works, producing the desired results without penalty."[28] Hence, abused wives, as well as their ministers, can extend grace to abusive husbands by implementing negative consequences for the abuse and not allow the abuse to work. It is notable that secular social-science literature on the treatment of abusive men strongly notes the need for abused wives, as well as the broader community, to confront abusive behavior and create costly consequences if abusive men are ever going to recognize the destructive nature of their abuse and change.

Abused Christians and the Example of Jesus

All abused Christians have a powerful example to guide them: Jesus (1 Pet 2:21–25). In the context of unjust physical abuse, Peter says these believers have been called *for this purpose.* The believers to whom Peter wrote were called for the purpose of abusive suffering, and Christ, our example, suffered the most extreme abuse with quiet resignation. Does it not follow that a modern Western abused wife (or child) should passively accept all abuse, knowing that it will ultimately be redemptive? No. Again, we must remember that Peter wrote to a specific ancient audience in a very particular setting. God always desires to redeem suffering and to bring good out of it (Rom 8:28; Jas 1:2–4; 1 Pet 1:6–7). Believers of all ages can be comforted by knowing that our good, all-powerful God works sovereignly in our lives. He allows suffering for good purposes. He delights in redeeming suffering, particularly abuse (Gen 50:20). Jesus's example is a most powerful one for abuse survivors, but we must not crystalize its application. Peter gave Jesus's example of passive suffering to powerless, abused slaves whose suffering was unavoidable. Let's now expand on the nature of Jesus's example for abuse victims.

First, how Christ serves as an example for abuse victims must be carefully nuanced. Believers cannot follow Christ's example in every way since his suffering was unique.[29] He suffered *for* sin, whereas abuse victims suffer *because* of sin (they are sinned against). Furthermore, Peter does not teach that all abuse is redemptive. The only kind of abuse that Peter recognizes as redemptive (i.e., as having transformative spiritual value) is that which (1) is unavoidable and (2) is based on the victim's godly character.

Let's further clarify how Christ serves as an example for abused believers. Peter uses the example of Christ to strengthen his argument that believers are called to endure unjust suffering in a godly manner, for he quotes from Isaiah 53:9 at 1 Peter 2:22 ("he committed no sin, and no deceit was found in his mouth") to highlight the fact that when Christ suffered, he was innocent and pleasing to God, despite the condemnation and injury he received from his abusers. The basis for Christ's suffering being redemptive was not his silence but his innocence and his godliness. In this case, the former evidenced the latter. Silence in and of itself can make even a fool appear virtuous (Prov 17:28). What made Christ's silence virtuous and imitable for abused believers was his refusal to use his speech to revile or threaten his abusers. Again, *the point here for abuse victims is not that they must accept their abuse with passive silence but that they must follow Christ's example of responding to abuse in a godly manner.*

We do not want to allow our abusers' evil to stimulate us to respond in kind. We must "repay no one evil for evil" (Rom 12:17 ESV).

An additional aspect of Christ's example needs to be noted. Christ's suffering was redemptive because it was unavoidable. Peter strongly infers the necessity of Christ's suffering by stating that Christ bore our sins in his body (1 Pet 2:24). This language, drawn from Isaiah 53:5, 12, pictures the suffering servant as the sacrificial sin bearer. Christ accepted abuse with godly resignation because it was the only way he could secure human salvation. He was necessarily wounded so that sinners might be healed. If there had been a way to save humans other than the abuse of the cross, he would indeed have taken it ("Father, if you are willing, take this cup from me," Luke 22:42). Scripture does not sanctify avoidable suffering. Christ repeatedly avoided physical assault, most often from the Jewish leaders (his authorities) by hiding (John 8:59), by maintaining physical separation from his abusers (Matt 12:14–15; John 11:53–54), and by eluding them (John 10:31, 39). Jesus did not teach his disciples to accept abuse (evil); instead, he taught them to pray that God would deliver them from it (Matt 6:13). Conversely, seeking avoidable suffering and expecting it to be a means of gaining favor with God lay behind the heresy of Paul's opponents in Colossae. These false teachers promoted rigid rules that demanded the "harsh treatment of the body" to gain favor with God (Col 2:20–23).[30] Thus, *modern Western abuse victims should follow Christ's example by fleeing their abusers and escaping avoidable suffering.*[31]

At this juncture, we can note a related principle that flows from 1 Peter 2:23. This verse states that Christ "continued entrusting himself to him who judges justly" (ESV). By way of application, this text suggests that *victims of domestic violence must come to accept God's view of their worth and character, not that of their abuser.* This is much easier to articulate than to do. Husbands who repeatedly beat their wives have a pathological need to belittle and control them.

These men justify their hideous sin by rationalizing that their wives *deserve* to be beaten.[32] Victims of domestic violence must come to understand that their abusive husbands' (or wives') declaration of their worthlessness is no more reliable than the judgments of Christ's accusers regarding his character. Christ looked to the Father, not to his abusers, to assess and vindicate him (1 Pet 2:23).

I will summarize this section with a personal story to illustrate the relationship between passivity, unavoidable suffering, and personal protection. A few years ago, Celestia and I led a training team of Africans and Americans to the Democratic Republic of the Congo to facilitate several trauma-healing intensives. Although we have led dozens of conferences in East Africa, this was one of the most memorable and impactful. The first conference was held at a beautiful denominational retreat center in the city of Butembo. We didn't realize it at the time, but approximately thirty years previously, this was the sight of a horrendous massacre in which five hundred men were rounded up and slaughtered. One of the few survivors of that massacre, now a pastor, attended the conference. After hearing teachings about God's desire for all of his children to avoid unnecessary suffering—be it from abusive spouses, murderous rebel bands, or corrupt officials—he stood and shared his personal story. He testified that when the rebels came, he fled, barely escaping the fate that awaited hundreds of his peers. He vulnerably shared his struggles with survivor's guilt because of surviving what his friends ended up perishing from. We were thankful he could publicly share his feelings for the first time and find some resolution for the shame he had hidden for so long.

Throughout our two weeks with the participants, we heard many testimonies of God miraculously redeeming the evil these precious brothers and sisters had suffered. God was actively bringing good out of evil. We were reminded of Paul's words in Colossians 1:24, where he writes, "I rejoice in what I am suffering for you, and

I fill up in my flesh what is still lacking in regard to Christ's afflictions, for the sake of his body, which is the church." Obviously, Paul was not saying that in terms of human salvation, Christ's sufferings on the cross were incomplete (John 19:30; Heb 10:14). Rather, he is speaking of the application of Christ's sacrifice. To build and serve Jesus's church requires suffering. Paul penned these words from prison. He could have avoided suffering by not sharing the gospel and thus not offending hostile unbelievers. But because he was willing to suffer for the gospel's sake, he experienced great joy. However, on other occasions, he avoided persecution when it was avoidable.

I identified with this biblical text. Quite unexpectedly, during this same conference, I became seriously ill from a combination of malaria and typhus. By nightfall, I was unconscious and went to the hospital early the next morning. I was put on life-saving intravenous medication and slowly recovered enough to continue teaching a few days later. I felt joy, despite my physical misery, knowing that my tiny suffering—compared to the daily Congolese sufferings—was serving a beautiful, eternal purpose—something bigger than what I could see. God never wastes suffering that is surrendered to him. If we can't avoid it, we must entrust ourselves to God, patiently enduring, knowing that God can use our adversities to showcase his works and power (John 9:3). This was Peter's message to first-century persecuted Christians. It is God's message for us today.

Now that we have surveyed some key biblical passages about abuse victims, we will turn to key passages about the Christian life.

Chapter 8

PASSAGES ON SPIRITUAL LIFE

Everyone thinks forgiveness is a lovely idea
until he has something to forgive.
—C. S. LEWIS, *MERE CHRISTIANITY*

He looked around at them in anger and, deeply distressed
at their stubborn hearts, said to the man, "Stretch out your
hand." He stretched it out, and his hand was completely
restored. Then the Pharisees went out and began to
plot with the Herodians how they might kill Jesus.
—MARK 3:5-6

Mark, a hospice chaplain, is one of my closest friends. I've known and deeply respected him and his family for decades. But I was utterly unprepared for his call. I knew that recently Anna, their teenage daughter, disclosed that an older cousin had raped her on a camping trip the previous year. Mark and I discussed how he should respond to this crisis. He promptly reported the assault to law enforcement and initiated counseling for his daughter. Even though she was getting help, she was still very traumatized. She didn't think she could testify in court, particularly after learning her cousin's wealthy family had hired an extremely aggressive defense attorney. Her therapist was concerned about what a trial might do to her mental health. Even though multiple victims over eight years alleged that he had abused or attempted to abuse them, the police concluded they could not prosecute without Anna testifying.

I understood this dilemma, validated Anna's right to decline a traumatic trial, and discussed how Mark could best support and protect her. The most apparent and surprisingly controversial strategy was to protect Anna from her cousin by insisting that the cousin stay entirely away from Anna and not attend any family event where she and her family were present. I was impressed with Mark's steadfast commitment to protecting his daughter. His desire for the cousin to repent and experience divine forgiveness also impressed me. Unfortunately, the family did not feel the same way. They went ballistic over Mark's new boundaries. This was quite unexpected. The "black sheep" cousin was always an outlier in this deeply pious, biblically focused family. The cousin's father had been a deacon and Sunday School teacher for as long as anyone could remember. So, when the father asked to meet with Mark at a local restaurant, Mark expected to hear an apology for the destruction his son had wrought, perhaps followed by some clarifying questions regarding Mark's boundaries. Instead, within seconds of being seated, this father tore into Mark, venomously declaring, "You have no right teaching anyone the Bible! You know nothing of biblical forgiveness. God won't forgive you if you don't forgive others, including my son." Mark was initially speechless. He had been sucker punched from the book of Matthew.

Mark's devastating experience vividly illustrates the potential for biblical passages about the Christian life to be weaponized against survivors and their protectors. In this chapter we will focus on five key passages, starting with the forgiveness passage used against Mark and Anna.

1. MATTHEW 18:21-22, 35

"Then Peter came to Jesus and asked, 'Lord, how many times shall I forgive my brother or sister who sins against me? Up to seven times?' Jesus answered, 'I tell you, not seven times, but seventy-seven times . . . . This is how my heavenly Father will treat each of you unless you forgive your brother or sister from your heart.'"

Mark and Anna's very real and tragic story is a shockingly common one. It begs us to clarify what biblical forgiveness explicitly means. Will God refuse to forgive rape victims who refuse to reconcile with their unrepentant, dangerous abusers? Matthew 18 teaches the opposite, but if you only look at verses 23–35 (the story of the unforgiving servant), you might terribly misconstrue Jesus's words.

The Context Clarifies Forgiveness

The forgiveness teaching in Matthew 18 does not begin in verse 21 but in the preceding paragraph (vv. 15–20), where Jesus discusses what to do when "your brother [or sister] sins against you" (v. 15 ESV). You are to go to them and "point out their fault" (bring to light, expose, rebuke). If they listen, you have "won them over" from their destructive, hell-bent path (v. 15). The word "listen" (*akouō*) used here means "give careful attention to, heed."[1] Commentators agree that "hear" in this text describes not just hearing words but a decisive, life-altering response—that is, repentance. If the one in sin doesn't listen, you must take another with you and confront them again. You must take them to the church if they still don't repent. If they refuse to listen to the church, they are to be excommunicated from the community and treated as a gentile or a tax collector (i.e., as an outsider alienated from the community). In other words, those who sin against us should be confronted and allowed to turn from their destructive sin. (We saw earlier in chapter 5 that Matthew 18 does not mean that abuse victims need to confront their abusers.) If the sinner doesn't repent, they forfeit being in a relationship with others in the community. Failing to repent prohibits reconciliation. This is reiterated in Luke 17:3: "If your brother or sister sins against you, rebuke them; and *if* they repent, forgive them." The father of Anna's rapist wholly ignored and violated this portion of Matthew 18 and incorrectly deduced that biblical forgiveness simply means letting go of all consequences for another person's destructive sin. This is a grave misunderstanding of biblical teaching.

A Clarifying Parable

What does the next section of Matthew 18 teach us about forgiveness (vv. 21–35)? It begins with Peter, after hearing Jesus discuss what to do when a brother or sister sins against you, asking how often we must forgive. Peter suggests a limit of seven times. This is a very generous suggestion, since ancient rabbis said three was the maximum number of times you might (but didn't have to) forgive someone. Jesus corrects Peter and says to forgive seventy-seven times; in other words, in an unlimited manner. As often as they repent, you forgive them. To clarify this principle, Jesus tells a story of a servant whose master forgives a huge, unsurmountable debt but, in turn, refuses to forgive a fellow servant who owes him a lesser debt. He has no pity on this fellow servant but abuses him and throws him in prison. This is the context of Jesus's summary words in verse 35, affirming that God will not forgive us if we, after being forgiven by God, arrogantly refuse to forgive others. This point is simply that forgiven people forgive others. If we (like this cruel, merciless servant) are characterized by a hard heart that refuses to forgive others, it may indicate that we have not truly experienced God's forgiveness. We must not make more out of this text than is here. Just because in this parable forgiveness is described as letting go of a debt, we must not press this beyond the point of the parable, as if "letting go of a debt" is a formal definition of forgiveness. It isn't.

FORGIVENESS AND CONSEQUENCES

One of the biggest challenges with understanding biblical forgiveness is that Scripture describes but doesn't strictly define it. The most common Greek word in the New Testament for forgiveness (*aphiēmi*) means "to let go." But what is an abuse victim to let go of?[2] Boundaries? Consequences? Revenge? The story of the unmerciful servant in Matthew 18 gives us important insights into the positive and negative aspects of forgiveness. Negatively, we see that forgiveness involves letting go of hatred and attempts to get revenge on others for hurting us (cf. Rom 12:17–21; Eph 4:31). In the Matthew 18 parable, the unmerciful servant beat, choked, and threw into prison the man who owed him money. He sought revenge against one who had financially harmed him. Matthew 18 also highlights the positive aspect of forgiveness—namely, extending grace or mercy to others. Mercy is what the unforgiving servant didn't possess. He had no concern whatsoever for the other servant's plight or well-being. Matthew 18 also teaches that mercy does not preclude boundaries and does not require reconciliation with a dangerous person. Matthew 18:15–20 clarifies this with the guidelines for church discipline of an unrepentant member.

Even when a destructive sinner does repent, this does not preclude serious consequences. For instance, after King David's sexual abuse of Bathsheba, murder of her husband Uriah, and murder of other Jewish soldiers innocently caught in David's cover-up scheme, David truly repented, stating without qualification or blame shifting, "I have sinned against the LORD" (2 Sam 12:13). Immediately Nathan the prophet declared, "The LORD has taken away your sin" (v. 13). Yet Nathan goes on to say, "But because by doing this [power rape and murder] you have shown utter contempt for the LORD, the son born to you will die" (v. 14). Similarly, in Numbers 14, after the Israelites rebelled, refused to go into the promised land, and prepared to stone Moses to death (vv. 1–10), they apparently repented because God announced that he had pardoned them (v. 20). Yet he pronounced grave consequences for their rebellion and attempted abuse: "I have forgiven them. . . . Nevertheless, as surely as I live . . . not one of them will ever see the land I promised on oath to their ancestors. No one who has treated me with contempt will ever see it" (vv. 20–21, 23). Later in this same chapter, some of the Israelites mistakenly assumed that the consequences had been lifted since they had confessed their sin and been forgiven by God. They presumptuously tried to enter the land but were utterly routed in battle (vv. 40–45). Genuine repentance does not eliminate all consequences, particularly for highly destructive sins such as abuse.

In summary, forgiveness involves letting go of our attempts at revenge and extending appropriate grace to the ones who hurt us. However, it does not eliminate all consequences for the offender and does not necessitate reconciliation with abusers.

2. MATTHEW 5:22

"Anyone who is angry with a brother or sister will be subject to judgment."

Sinful Anger?

Countless times, I have seen abuse survivors condemned by church leaders for being angry at their abusers or those who failed to protect them from their abusers. Recently I listened to several online sermons in which the pastor mocked those who had experienced racial

injustice, sexual harassment, or sexual assault for their "victim pos-
turing" and indicted them for their "sinful anger and bitterness." Is it
acceptable for abuse victims to be angry? Many argue that virtually all
anger over what others have done to us is sinful. Counselor Ed Welch
states: "Ninety-nine percent of my anger is sinful; I don't want to give
tacit permission to my frustration by calling it righteous indignation. I
am on safer ground if I am angry because of what was done to another
person. If I am angry because of what someone did to me, I am *always*
wrong" (emphasis mine).[3] While Welch rightly cautions us against
the danger of anger, is it always sinful to be angry at injustices we
suffer? We've already seen that Jesus condemned anger in Matthew
5:22. Many other passages issue similar warnings—we are to refrain
from anger (Ps 37:8), put it away (Col 3:8), and not make friends
with someone given to anger (Prov 22:24). But biblical teaching on
anger is quite robust and must be nuanced. Anger is not universally
condemned, particularly in cases of grave injustice against oneself
or others. Scripture calls us to "be angry and do not sin" (Eph 4:26
ESV). Jesus condemned gratuitously insulting anger while modeling
righteous anger (Mark 3:5). In this same article, Welch argues that
Jesus was never angry at injustices done to him, only injustices done
to others. These binary categories are not as clear-cut as Welch would
have us believe; his assertion is untenable. In Mark 3:5, Jesus looked
around at the Pharisees "in anger" at their hard-heartedness. They
were hard-hearted toward the disabled man whom Jesus wanted to
heal, and toward Jesus himself. Their hard-heartedness was so great
that we read in the following verse they were scheming to kill Jesus.
This angered him! While Jesus's anger is aroused when God or people
are dishonored (Matt 21:12–14; Mark 10:13–14), he is also grieved
and angered when people dishonor him. This is seen most clearly at
the end of the age when Jesus pours out his wrath on his enemies
(Rev 19:11–21).

Similarly, in the lament psalms, the writers express great anger toward their abusive enemies. This is particularly evident in the imprecatory psalms, in which the writers ask God to slay and consume their abusive adversaries.[4] In the individual lament psalms, the writers, based on their own experience of mistreatment by evildoers, express their great anguish and anger over their oppressive and abusive mistreatment. These psalms refute Welch's claim that anger at grave injustices that we experience is sinful. While the proper use of imprecatory psalms for New Testament-era believers is debated, I am convinced that they give us a model for responding to abuse. After all, they are inspired Scripture, are quoted repeatedly in the New Testament, and other New Testament passages issue similar imprecations against one's enemies (Acts 13:9–11; Rev 6:6–11).[5]

God's Anger

It is essential to recognize that the anger or wrath of God is a dominant biblical theme found in hundreds of different passages. Two of the most frequent causes of God's anger are dishonoring God our Creator (particularly through idolatry) and dishonoring humans made in God's image (through abuse and oppression). Earlier in Proverbs 6:16–19, we saw that five of the seven shortlisted sins God most hates involve some form of abuse. God declares his abhorrence of unrepentant abusers (Pss 5:6; 11:5). His raging anger toward spiritual leaders who abuse and rob people of their rights cannot be assuaged (Isa 10:1–4). God was furious when the Israelites practiced fatal child abuse as a form of perverted pagan worship (2 Kgs 17:17; Ezek 16:20–36). God's "anger burns against" spiritual leaders who don't protect the vulnerable and instead allow them to be abused (Zech 10:3). Godly people reflect God's heart and values. They are angry at what makes God angry, particularly abuse and oppression (Exod 11:8; Neh 5:6). In their profoundly insightful book on emotions, Alasdair Groves and Winston Smith caution that while anger is the most dangerous human emotion, anger "at its best communicates protective love for what God loves."[6] *Failing to be angry at abuse is ultimately a failure to love.*

In summary, abuse victims have every right to be angry at what was done to them, just as God is furious that they were abused. Spiritual leaders who point an accusatory finger at angry survivors, while failing to be angry that these survivors were abused, stand condemned. They utterly fail to model the values and passions of God.

3. PHILIPPIANS 2:3-4

"Do nothing out of selfish ambition or vain conceit. Rather, in humility value others above yourselves, not looking to your own interests but each of you to the interests of the others."

Sheila didn't know where else to turn. Her sixteen-year marriage felt like a sham. Her husband was a highly intelligent attorney who demanded absolute obedience from everyone in the household, including Sheila. Over the years, he had become increasingly caustic and cruel. While Tim spent money quite liberally on himself, he demanded that Sheila account for every dollar she spent. He took away her meager monthly "allowance" at the slightest whim. Tim seemed to go out of his way to ridicule and mock her, often in public. He had recently entered her closet and taken the two new outfits her parents had given her for her birthday. Tim sneered and declared, "You don't deserve them. And you are too fat to wear them." For most of their marriage, Sheila was simply numb, going through the motions and trying to be a godly wife. But years of chronic mistreatment were finally melting her numbness into simmering anger. So she went to her pastor for help. He listened attentively, but the expression on his face told her he wasn't sympathetic to her plight. He picked up his Bible and read chapter two of Philippians. He postulated that her problem was focusing on her "rights" when, in reality, believers have no rights. His solution? Let go of her rights like Jesus did.

"No Rights" Teaching

This type of "you have no rights" teaching is promulgated by all too many conservative Christian leaders. Based mainly on Philippians 2:3–4, it goes like this. When mistreated, we should not get angry but must recognize that we don't have any rights. Claiming our rights only leads to conflict, anger, and bitterness. We must learn to give our rights over to God. John and Janie Street argue that "unrighteous anger . . . is always consumed with being denied personal rights."[7] Similarly, Nancy DeMoss Wolgemuth denies that a Christian wife has a right

- to be respected and loved,
- to an equitable wage, and
- to be valued by her husband.[8]

Other "no rights" advocates assert that Jesus wants us to give up the right to personal property, the right to our comforts, and the right to be well-treated. If this is accurate, then Sheila's pastor is correct. Sheila has nothing to be angry with or complain about, no matter how abusively or contemptuously her husband treated her. Is this true? Do Christians have no "rights" that should be respected by others? For abuse victims, this is a critically important issue.

The Context of Philippians 2:3–4

In the previous section, we discussed the issue of righteous anger. Here we discuss whether Philippians 2 teaches that believers have no rights. Let's start where we always should by noting the immediate context of Philippians 2:3–4. In the preceding two verses, Paul addresses the issue of Christian unity. There was conflict and disunity in this congregation (e.g., in 4:2 Paul appeals to two women by name who were apparently at odds with each other), and Paul was deeply concerned that the Philippian believers be more united, learning to love and serve one another (1:27; 2:20–21). In 2:3, Paul makes a particular appeal, saying they should "do nothing from selfish ambition or conceit"; instead, each is to "look not only to his own interests, but also to the interests of others" (v. 4 ESV). Notice that Paul doesn't say they shouldn't consider their own needs. Rather, they should not *only* look to their *own* needs or interests. Paul doesn't deny personal rights. Instead, his point is that we are not to be self-absorbed. We are to consider the needs of others and be willing to put others' needs above our own. Then he gives the example of Christ, who laid aside his divine glory and privileges to come to earth to save fallen humans (vv. 5–8). In other words, Jesus was willing to prioritize others' needs above his own needs and legitimate privileges. Furthermore, Jesus didn't cling to his divine "rights" in the incarnation (particularly the "right" to be honored as God, which is alluded to in v. 6). Jesus didn't lose this right. After his death and resurrection, God the Father exalted him to his proper position of honor. One day, Jesus will receive what is due from every created being—they will bow their knees before him and proclaim him Lord (vv. 9–11)!

In summary, Philippians 2:1–11 teaches that believers have fundamental rights and needs, but we must not focus solely on ourselves. Sometimes God will direct us to deny specific needs or rights for the sake of others. This is dramatically different from asserting that we have no real rights and therefore no basis for grievance when our rights are trampled on. Ironically, this letter was written to Christians living in the same city in which Paul was willing to not use his Roman legal rights to avoid a beating (Acts 16:37). However, later in his ministry, Paul did exercise his Roman legal rights to avoid languishing in prison in Caesarea (Acts 25:11). Even when God led Paul to not use his legal rights, he affirmed having them. He shamed the Philippian authorities for violating his legal rights (Acts 16:37–39)!

Paul declares his right to financial support from the churches he was serving and a right to have a Christian wife join him. Yet Paul, directed by God, chose not to exercise those rights (1 Cor 9:3–6). However, the other apostles did exercise these rights (1 Cor 9:5). Again, the idea that the believer has no rights and no basis to complain when their rights are trounced on is illogical and utterly unbiblical.

The Biblical Basis for Human Rights

Let's take this a step further. What exactly are our natural "rights"? What are they based on? The "no rights" advocates often (legitimately) assert that many Americans are so preoccupied with "their rights" that they claim a seemingly endless list of them. As a result, virtually anyone and everyone can claim victim status. But we must not let this distorted approach to rights hijack the discussion and distort God's truth. Biblically, our human rights are based on our creation as God's image bearers. This gives humans unique worth and dignity. God made us "a little lower than God"[9] and "crowned [us] with glory and honor" (Ps 8:5). Therefore, to mistreat or dishonor a person is, in a real sense, to dishonor God himself. As image bearers, humans are innately worthy of being treated with respect and dignity. This helps us understand why mistreating humans is such a serious offense to God. Scores of Scripture passages proclaim God's condemnation and rage at injustice, abuse, and oppression (e.g., Isa 59:1–20; Amos 1–8).

Furthermore, God expects his people, particularly spiritual leaders, to champion the rights of the vulnerable and oppressed. "A righteous man knows the rights of the poor; a wicked man does not understand such knowledge" (Prov 29:7 ESV). A godly leader will "speak up for those who cannot speak for themselves, for the rights of all who are destitute" (Prov 31:8). God promises to harshly judge leaders who fail to promote the well-being of the vulnerable and "defend the rights of the needy" (Jer 5:28 ESV; cf. Isa 10:1–4).

In conclusion, Sheila deserved to be treated with dignity and respect, like every other woman (and man). She had every right to feel hurt and angry at her abusive husband.

4. PHILIPPIANS 4:6

"Do not be anxious about anything."

Jill was grocery shopping at a discount store near her home. As she rounded the corner with her cart, she faintly caught sight of a man at the end of the aisle. She had never seen him before. Before she had time to process what had just happened, her heart began to race, her head began to spin, and a sense of panic overwhelmed her. She needed to track where she was in time and place. It felt like a nightmarish, out-of-body experience. Thankfully, she had been working with a skilled trauma counselor and quickly began to practice some of the grounding exercises her therapist had taught her (slow, deep breathing, tuning in to her five senses to reconnect with her body, reminding herself where she was—in the store, in a safe place, etc.). Before long, her body began to calm down, and after a few minutes she could quickly finish shopping. What was the essence of Jill's problem? What caused her extreme anxiety and foreboding sense of fear?

Fear, Anxiety, and Sin

According to some Christian leaders, Jill's fear and anxiety were evidence of sin. Thus, she needed to repent of her fear and learn to trust (fear) God. Counselor Heath Lambert asserts that even a PTSD diagnosis and its classic symptoms—as Jill experienced—are clear indicators of sin. Lambert states: "These sorts of physical symptoms don't mean that our sinful fear is anything other than sin."[10] Such counselors appeal to Scripture passages about not being anxious and not fearing to prove that anxiety and fear are inevitably sinful. Is this actually what Scripture is saying?

As we have seen with many other topics, biblical teachings on fear and anxiety are complex and multilayered. We must not draw premature conclusions but rather look at the breadth of Scripture to build a theology of fear and anxiety. We should also note that fear and anxiety are closely related but not identical. Anxiety is a generalized sense of emotional discomfort based on identifiable or unidentifiable concerns. Fear is a sense of dread based on future harm. Before we specifically look at anxiety and fear, which most abuse survivors experience intensely, let's make a few general observations about emotions.

Many of us grew up in evangelical contexts in which emotions were downplayed or even ridiculed. We were told, "You can't trust your emotions. They lead you astray. You must stand on truth. Right thinking is the key to the Christian life." Worse yet, masculinity was tied to being rational and not emotional (like women). Such teaching, explicitly or implicitly given, is exceedingly harmful. God himself is an emotional being. (We will elaborate on this in the next chapter.) He has made us, in his image, as emotional beings. Perhaps the most important truth to recognize about emotions is that while they are not infallible (neither are our minds), they are indispensable signals of our inner life. They particularly tell us about what we value and what we love.[11] Before determining whether an emotion is healthy or unhealthy, sinful or innocent, we need to ask what our emotion is telling us about our inner life. Once we begin to do this, we are much better prepared to bring Scripture to bear in assessing our feelings.

Anxiety and Scripture

Let's begin by looking at anxiety. Philippians 4:6 does admonish us not to be anxious about anything. The Greek word used here for anxiety (*merimnaō*) means "to be apprehensive, be (unduly) concerned."[12] Interestingly, the definitive Greek lexicon I've cited adds "unduly" to this definition. In other words, anxiety is not unequivocally condemned. Paul warns against *excessive* or *unjustified* anxiety. Philippians 4:6 helps to clarify unhealthy anxiety by giving us the antidote. Instead of being anxious, he tells us to "in every situation, by prayer and petition, with thanksgiving, present your requests to God." This suggests that unhealthy anxiety results from failing to look to God for help. Paul's admonition is similar to Peter's in 1 Peter 5:7: "Cast all your anxiety on him because he cares for you." We will become unduly anxious when we have not gone to Christ with our concerns and are trying to cope on our own. However, there are many examples of godly individuals in Scripture who were looking to God, crying out to him, who still experienced great anxiety. We must not falsely condemn them (or ourselves) for any and all anxiety. For starters, let's note that the same Greek word Paul uses here for "anxious" he uses in a positive sense earlier in this epistle. In 2:20, he speaks of Timothy's deep "concern" for the Philippians.

Furthermore, in this same letter, Paul says he desired to send Epaphroditus to minister to them so that "I may have less anxiety" (Phil 2:28). This is very similar to Paul's "anxiety for all the churches" (ESV) referenced in 2 Corinthians 11:28. Not all anxiety is sinful. Again, we should prayerfully ask God what our anxiety tells us about our hearts. Paul loved the Philippians, and that concern led to a measure of anxiety. Furthermore, Paul hadn't lost sight of God's power or promises. But he still felt anxiety over those he loved.

In the case of abuse survivors, anxiety may result from concerns about their well-being in light of past and potential future threats.

While we are to take all concerns to God, this doesn't instantly eradicate all emotional angst. There are many other examples in Scripture of godly individuals who experienced great anxiety over very real concerns. The Hebrew prophets and the lament psalmists repeatedly express great emotional pain, including worry over their own well-being, even though they were taking these concerns to God (e.g., Pss 22; 44). Taking our concerns to God is one of the most unmistakable pieces of evidence that we honor him with our anxiety.

Anxiety, Faith, and PTSD

Finally, let's come back to Jill's story. Was her anxiety and fear simply a lack of faith in God? Such an assertion reveals a glaring misunderstanding of neurobiology. Scientifically speaking, her symptoms were a direct result of fear. But this was not fear she was fully conscious of or in immediate control over. We now have an overwhelming amount of scientific data on what trauma does to the brain.[13] We know, based on brain scans and other rigorous scientific research, that trauma changes the way the brain functions. As the psalmist declares, we are "fearfully and wonderfully made" (Ps 139:14). Nowhere is this more evident than in our intricately fashioned brain and nervous system, which are exquisitely designed to sustain and protect us. Much of this process occurs through autonomic systems, which we are not in conscious control over. For instance, our brain subconsciously controls our breathing, digestion, heart rate, and hormone production. Concerning trauma, a part of our "not conscious" brain, the amygdala, is primarily responsible for regulating emotion and memory. The amygdala receives input from our five senses. When it senses danger (based on previous experiences), it immediately launches a "fight, flight, or freeze" sequence based on the release of fast-acting stress hormones such as adrenaline. This biological system is what creates classic trauma symptoms, such as Jill experienced. In her case, sensory data, which Jill was not fully aware of (e.g., a man's profile, a color, a scent), which the subconscious part of her brain interpreted as danger, sounded an alarm in her body. The surge of hormones told her muscles to contract, her heart rate to spike, her breathing to alter, etc. These processes also disconnected her from her immediate physical surroundings and created mental confusion. These automatic biological responses had little or nothing to do with Jill's conscious thoughts, let alone her lack of faith. It is worth noting that we have several somatic descriptions in Scripture of classic trauma symptoms, with no implication whatsoever that the godly individuals experiencing them lacked faith—heart palpitations, muscle trembling, quivering lips (Hab 3:16; Nah 2:10), altered blood flow resulting in pale skin (Dan 7:28), muscle weakness and dry mouth (Ps 22:15).

How Jill responded to this troubling, triggering event is where faith comes in. In addition to the grounding techniques, Jill's counselor taught her to practice breath prayers, to journal, and to claim God's promises in Scripture. These practices helped her grow in faith and God's peace. Jill, like all abuse survivors, did need to keep growing in faith, though lack of faith did *not create her PTSD or its disturbing symptoms.*

Fear

This is an excellent place to segue into the biblical subject of fear. While some assert that other than fear of God and fear of sin, all fear is sinful, this is not what Scripture teaches. Yes, Scripture many times in a variety of ways admonishes us to "fear not." For instance, "do not fear" and "do not be afraid" occur a combined eighty-seven times in Scripture (NIV). Fear can be very destructive and sinful. Fear of the people caused Saul to disobey God and led to his downfall (1 Sam 15:24). Fear of the inhabitants of Gerar caused Isaac to lie and expose his wife Rebekah to sexual assault (Gen 26:6–11), just like his father Abraham had done. Fear caused a generation of Israelites to sinfully distrust God and forfeit the promised land (Num 13–14). Fear of the Judaizers caused Peter to sinfully dishonor gentile Christians (Gal 2:11–14). We could go on and on, noting the dangers of fear. But abuse survivors need to recognize that while some fear is harmfully sinful, some fear is normal and healthy.

First of all, let's note that fear is a signal that we might be in danger. While this signal is not infallible, it is normal and invaluable in many contexts. For instance, in Amos 3:8 the prophet rhetorically asks: "The lion has roared—who will not fear?" In other words, the standard and healthy response to a dangerous animal's roar is fear. Gavin De Becker, one of the world's leading authorities on the physical protection of public figures, argues that one of the most important ways to avoid interpersonal violence is to listen to our intuitive sense of fear. Thus, he titled one of his most influential books *The Gift of Fear*.[14] Proverbs 22:3 affirms the benefits of healthy fear: "The prudent see danger and take refuge, but the simple keep going and pay the penalty." While "fear" is not explicitly mentioned in this verse, it is implied. Most often, fear warns us of danger. And we must learn to heed its signal. Abuse survivors are often numb to the very emotions that can protect them. So learning to hear and appreciate an internal sense of fear, particularly regarding other people who may be unsafe, is very important. It is quite normal to experience fear of individuals who have harmed us in the past, even if they are not a danger in the present.

Second, let's note that while Scripture most often condemns fear, there are numerous instances in which it isn't condemned, particularly in cases of extreme danger. Godly individuals in Scripture respond to threats with fear. Isaiah the prophet acknowledged that in light of the coming judgment by the Babylonians, "fear makes me tremble" (Isa 21:4). Similarly, the lying prophets' words caused Jeremiah to admit that "all my bones tremble" (Jer 23:9). In response to the violent threats of the wicked, the psalmist declares, "Fear and trembling have beset me; horror has overwhelmed me" (Ps 55:5). The apostle Paul confided to the Corinthians, "I came to you in weakness with great fear and trembling" (1 Cor 2:3; cf. 2 Cor 7:5). We see in the context of this verse that Paul is not recounting a sinful condition, because he immediately notes that despite his fears he came "with a demonstration of the Spirit's power so that your faith might not rest on human wisdom, but on God's power" (1 Cor 2:4–5). In each of these instances, godly characters in Scripture experienced fear over impending and potential threats, and they learned to trust God in the face of those fears. What we do with our fears is most essential. Do we let them shackle us, or do we turn to God and act in obedience and faith? Tristen and Jonathan Collins help us unpack this principle. They note:

> Until creation is renewed, there will always be danger in our world, from lions and tigers to dishonest schemers; it is OK to feel fear in the face of dangers, to let that fear help us fight back or get away safely. What's not OK is to be dominated by fear—to let it haunt you and rule you, to let fear get in the way of doing what God has asked you to do.[15]

In summary, fear can debilitate any believer, particularly an abuse survivor. But fear is a normal response to danger and can protect us. The key to growth and health is to learn to recognize our fears and, with God's help, not let them dominate us. Like the apostle Paul, we can learn to act in faith and obedience despite our fears.

5. JAMES 2:10

"For whoever keeps the whole law and yet stumbles at just one point is guilty of breaking all of it."

Jonnie was a very popular pastor. His sermons were masterfully delivered with a perfect blend of humor and application. He was a strong and effective leader. Under his pastorate, Bethel Church had tripled in size. So the congregation went into an uproar when rumors began to spread that ten years earlier, when he was a twenty-six-year-old youth pastor, he had an "affair" with a sixteen-year-old girl in the youth group. While there was extensive corroborating evidence that he had had a sexual relationship with this minor-age girl, the statute-of-limitations laws in this state prevented authorities from filing charges. Jonnie eventually gave a weak apology for a "mutually consensual inappropriate relationship long ago" and asked the congregation to "forgive me just as Jesus has." A large portion of the church immediately went to his defense.

The primary biblical argument his supporters effectively used to shut down Jonnie's critics was drawn from James 2:10. It went like this: "All sin is the same in God's eyes. If you've broken one biblical commandment, it is as if you've broken all the commandments." The clear implication is that anyone criticizing Pastor Jonnie and arguing for his removal is a self-righteous hypocrite who doesn't understand the biblical doctrine of sin. The assertion "all sin is the same in God's eyes," drawn from James 2:10, is very often leveraged against those who seek to hold abusers accountable for their actions. Sometimes abusers themselves leverage it. Several years ago I was watching a documentary on prisoners serving life sentences for capital murder. This episode featured a man on death row who had brutally murdered a pregnant woman and her child (with a shovel), and shortly afterward raped and killed another woman. He "found God" in prison and, on death row, led regular Bible studies for the other inmates. The interviewer asked him what he would say to the family members of his victims who might be troubled by his unofficial role as prison chaplain. His response was unflinching and chilling: "Those people need to understand that all sin is the same to God. In his eyes, there is no difference between murder and stealing a cracker."

All Sin Is the Same

Is all sin the same in God's eyes? This critically important question deserves a nuanced answer of yes and no. One characteristic of sin, sometimes called the "absolute" nature of sin, highlights the commonality of all sin. All sin violates the character and commands of a holy God. All sin separates us from God (Rom 6:23; Gal 3:10). All sin renders us in need of forgiveness and a savior. Let's relate this to James 2:10. The context of this verse is an extended condemnation of partiality toward the rich at the expense of the poor (Jas 2:1–13). It appears that these believers prided themselves on their fidelity to God's law (vv. 8–11) yet minimized the importance of loving their neighbor, particularly their poor neighbor (v. 8). This is the immediate context in which James declares "whoever keeps the whole law and yet stumbles at just one point is guilty of breaking all of it." In other words, James is cutting through their self-righteousness and showing that failing to love the poor leaves one guilty before God regardless of how many different commands one may have kept. As one of the ancient rabbis put it, "to break one command is to defy God who commanded the whole [law]."[16] So, in the absolute sense, Jonnie's sexual abuse made Jonnie a divine-law-breaking sinner in need of a savior, just like every other human being in his congregation. But we must not stop here.

All Sin Is Not the Same

There is another essential aspect of sin taught throughout Scripture. We might call this the "graded" nature of sin. Scripture and common sense clearly show that Jonnie's sin of statutory rape is not the same as most other types of sin. Sin has a graded quality. Some sins are far worse than other sins. Jesus himself declared that the Pharisees who handed Jesus over to Pilate were guilty of "a greater sin" (John 19:11). As Cornelius Plantinga eloquently puts it,

> All sin is equally wrong but not all sin is equally bad. Acts are either right or wrong, either consonant with God's will or not. But among good acts some are better than others, and among wrong acts some are worse than others. . . . The badness or seriousness of sin depends to some degree on the amount and kind of damage it inflicts, including damage to the sinner, and to some degree on the personal investment and motive of the sinner.[17]

Common sense should inform us that while lust in one's heart makes one just as guilty as the actual physical act of adultery, and anger in one's heart makes one just as guilty as the act of murder (Matt 5:21–28), the latter are much worse because they create more destructive consequences. If one lusts about raping a woman, that lust is just as sinful as actually raping her. But no one in their right mind would say that lust and rape are the same in God's sight. We have already seen that Scripture singles out a short list of sins that are worse than others. Abuse, be it verbal, physical, or sexual, is repeatedly singled out as sin that God particularly hates; it is an "abomination" to him (Deut 12:31; Ps 11:5; Prov 6:16–19). Abuse merits far harsher punishment than most other sin (Gen 9:6; Deut 22:25–26).

Let's give a final, brief explanation of the graded nature of sin. While all sin separates us from God and causes spiritual death, there are gradations of punishment for sin based on:

- *one's knowledge* (Matt 11:24; Luke 12:47–48; 1 Tim 1:13: "I was shown mercy because I acted in ignorance and unbelief");
- *one's willfulness* (Lev 4:22–23; Num 15:27–31);

- *degree of deviation from the plan of God* (Lev 20:16, bestiality);
- *consequences upon society in general or individuals in particular* (Lev 20:9–27; Deut 12:31).

Based on these criteria, we can quickly see that Jonnie's sexual abuse was a most serious sin, warranting more severe consequences. Pastors should have a much greater knowledge of Scripture and should be held to a much higher standard of behavior. Teachers of Scripture "will be judged more strictly" (Jas 3:1). Feeding your lusts on the vulnerable sheep you are charged with protecting is a destructive distortion of God's plan for spiritual leaders. Sexual abuse creates some of the greatest destructive consequences imaginable. In summary, Jonnie and the incarcerated rapist and murderer are sinners in need of forgiveness, just like the rest of us. None of us have any room to boast. We all need God's grace. But we are not all murderers and rapists, and abuse is a much worse and more destructive sin than most other types of sin. In short, God does not view rape and murder as the same as stealing a cracker. Nor should we.

Now that we have surveyed "poisonous" understandings of biblical passages on the family, church, abuse victims, and spiritual life, we will focus on the Bible as life-giving medicine. Since most abuse survivors have been retraumatized by the responses of others who learned about their abuse, we will begin the medicine section by unpacking *God's* response to abuse.

Part 3

THE HEALING ROLE
OF SCRIPTURE

Chapter 9

GOD'S RESPONSE TO ABUSE

God is love. That is why he suffers. To love our suffering world
is to suffer. . . . The tears of God are the meaning of history.
—NICHOLAS WOLTERSTORFF, *LAMENT FOR A SON*

The Lord said, "I have indeed seen the misery of my
people in Egypt. I have heard them crying out because
of their slave drivers, and I am concerned about their
suffering. So I have come down to rescue them."
—EXODUS 3:7-8

At the height of World War II, Primo Levi, a brilliant Italian
chemist, lost his job. He lost his home. He lost his freedom.
Though he was not particularly religious, Levi's Jewish ancestry
ultimately led to his imprisonment in Auschwitz, the gigantic exter-
mination camp in Poland. Levi recounts a recurring dream during
his incarceration. Levi felt warm joy as he dreamed that he had
been liberated from the death camp and returned to his family and
friends. There was much he needed to tell them about his hellish
experiences. But in his dream, as he turned to his listeners and began

recounting his ordeal, he became aware that no one was listening. His closest community was "completely indifferent" and stared right through him. Worst of all, in his dream his sister got up while he was speaking and quietly left the room. Levi then knew. His own flesh and blood could not see him. This recurring nightmare resulted in a "desolating grief," a "pain in its pure state."[1]

While Levi experienced the most extreme forms of evil and suffering, his dream is the nightmare experience of most abuse survivors. For most, their deepest "pure state" pain flows out of *not* being seen, believed, or listened to—particularly by those who should: family, intimate friends, and spiritual leaders. When Mending the Soul surveyed over fifty adult survivors of childhood sexual abuse and parents of sexually abused children, we found that 61 percent of the respondents had disclosed the abuse to their families. But they were more than twice as likely to be disbelieved as believed. Furthermore, the vast majority of those who disclosed the abuse to their churches were not believed and not supported. Sadly, when the people you rely on the most for validation and support don't even believe that the abuse happened, it is quite natural to project this experience onto God, the ultimate authority. We can conclude (consciously or subconsciously) that the almighty God of the universe isn't truly seeing our pain, hearing our cries, or working on our behalf. We conclude that he doesn't care. In our pain we must let Scripture reveal God's heart—his response to our suffering. We must let him, not Satan, tell us the truth about how our Creator responds to our pain. Thankfully, there is *abundant* biblical information.

Let's start with the most significant single event in Old Testament Jewish history—the exodus. Scripture tells us that the Israelites had been in Egypt for four hundred years. Initially, due to God's providential elevation of Joseph to a position just under Pharoah, the Israelites experienced great prosperity. This began to change when new Egyptian leaders emerged who were threatened by the Israelites' population growth. This led to fierce oppression. The Jews became slaves under cruel despotic masters who "worked them ruthlessly" and "made their lives bitter with harsh labor" (Exod 1:13–14). The Hebrew word translated "ruthlessly" denotes being ground, crushed, savaged by violence. Abuse was crushing them. Not only had the Israelites lost their freedom and well-being, but the Egyptians sought to destroy their future. They schemed to slaughter every Jewish baby boy (vv. 15–16). The Israelites were being suffocated! How did God respond to their suffering? Scripture gives a powerful description:

> The LORD said, "I have indeed *seen* the misery of my people in Egypt. I have *heard* them crying out because of their slave drivers, and I am *concerned* about their suffering. So I have *come down* to *rescue* them from the hand of the Egyptians and *to bring them up out* of that land into a good and spacious land. (Exod 3:7–8, emphases added)

Notice how God responds—he sees, hears, feels, and comes down to rescue. We'll explore each of these four responses.

GOD SEES

Scripture declares that God sees (knows) absolutely everything that happens throughout human history. He never blinks. "Nothing in all creation is hidden from God's sight" (Heb 4:13). He knows everything about us. He sees every single injustice we suffer, all the pain we endure, and every trial we face (Hos 13:5; Rev 2:13). He acknowledges and affirms faithful service (Rev 2:19). He even keeps track of the number of hairs on our head (Matt 10:30). God's knowledge is incomprehensible. He sees and knows:

- *Every possible fact about my life—everything I experience, feel, and think.* "You have searched me, LORD, and you know me. You know when I sit and when I rise; you perceive my thoughts from afar. You discern my going out and my lying down; you are familiar with all my ways" (Ps 139:1–3).
- *The hidden thoughts and longings of my human heart.* "The LORD searches every heart and understands every desire and every thought" (1 Chr 28:9).
- *Every word I will utter before I have spoken it.* "Before a word is on my tongue you, LORD, know it completely" (Ps 139:4).
- *Each baby before it is born.* "Before I formed you in the womb I knew you, before you were born, I set you apart" (Jer 1:5).
- *Everything about my life, including the details of my physical body and the number of days I will live.* "Your eyes saw my unformed body; all the days ordained for me were written in your book before one of them came to be" (Ps 139:16; cf. Ps 37:18).
- *Every event of my life before they occur.* "New things I declare; before they spring into being I announce them to you" (Isa 42:9).
- *The smallest details of the natural world.* "I know every bird in the mountains, and the insects in the fields are mine" (Ps 50:11).

What comfort this all-encompassing scope of God's knowledge is to each of us who know him! There is nothing he does not know about you and me. We are his children, and he comforts us by assuring us that he sees and is near: "I am the good shepherd; I know my sheep, and my sheep know me" (John 10:14). When no one else sees or cares, take great solace in the truth that God sees it all—including the cruel choices of our abusers! He sees every single malevolent act. He knows the twisted thoughts inside evildoers' hearts (Ezek 11:5–6). He knows these things, no matter how cleverly they have hidden their corrupt deeds and desires and deceived those closest to us. *Nothing* is hidden from God's sight! The artwork below is titled, "The Lord Is My Shepherd." It gives a great visual of how God sees his children, all the evil they face, and responds by carrying them though the dark valley.

The Lord Is My Shepherd
Credit: James VanFossan

In an act of supreme perversion against the good character of God, abusers pretend God doesn't see their evil acts. Psalm 10 condemns violent men whose mouths are filled with lies and who scheme to ambush and crush the innocent. These contemptible abusers delude themselves into thinking that God overlooks their abuse. They tell themselves, "God will never notice; he covers his face and never sees" (v. 11; cf. Ezek 9:9). God does see! He keeps track of the exact number and greatness or severity of abusers' sins against their victims (Amos 5:12). Such intimate knowledge of perpetrators should be a source of great comfort to survivors, particularly when the very people who should be listening to victims' cries refuse to listen.

After recounting the abusers' foolish arrogance, the psalmist takes comfort in the fact that God does see and does care. The psalmist prays this truth back to God (a most helpful prayer practice for survivors): "You, God, see the trouble of the afflicted; you consider their grief" (Ps 10:14). God himself reminded the discouraged, weary Israelites who had been exiled to Babylon that he saw their plight. Their way was not hidden from him; he had not disregarded their needs (Isa 40:27). God saw the Israelites' suffering in Egypt, and he sees the suffering of every human being who has ever lived. God has been carrying your pain.

GOD HEARS

God sees our anguish and hears our cries. Every word we think, whisper, or shout, God hears and cares.

> Sarah survived. That's what she did best. She trusted no one. Every relationship she had known had been one of exploitation and betrayal. Her fiercest anger, though, was reserved for God.

She loathed and blamed him for every bit of misery she had endured. This created a bit of tension at the beginning of our relationship. I was a pastor's wife and therapist. She was a runaway whose teen years were spent transactionally, being bought and sold on our city's streets. Her sex crimes detective introduced us, and we began an unlikely friendship.

We would meet anywhere she felt comfortable: hotel rooms, McDonalds, restaurants, and city parks. Our first meeting was in a juvenile detention facility. I spent four hours that first afternoon listening to the stories that fueled her intense hatred of God. I wanted to know her and to understand. The first day we met, she was so amped up she would not sit down. She stomped and raged and yelled. When she caught her breath, she asked me how much I was being paid to spend time with her. Even though she was not immediately convinced, I explained that I lost money spending time with her because I wasn't logging work hours in my "day job." I wanted to know her, I explained. I shared openly about my background, that I did have a relationship with Jesus that was hard won—that he and I had battled it out until I knew I could trust him. I explained that an intimate relationship with Jesus had replaced religion in my life. I explained that his love for me broke through to my cold, betrayed heart, that nobody loved us as he did, and that I worked for a Christian nonprofit that created accessible trauma-care resources for people from hard places. I understood her anger. I had lots of it too.

She began to talk, pouring out story after story of abuse, most of it sexual and spiritual. She shared accounts of pastors and Christian men who had abused and used her. *How could she trust a God like that?* My heart had been repeatedly shattered. I asked her to tell me all the religious words that triggered her so that I could remember not to use them. I wrote as she talked, and the list filled two sides of my paper. In the four hours we were together, I bore witness to atrocity after atrocity, much of it perpetrated in Jesus's name. It wasn't perfect. My tears flowed. Thus began our friendship.

A year went by, and one day, she asked if I had an office. I told her I used to own a clinic with many offices but that I had transitioned to community-based care through Mending the Soul so I could help more people. Now I have another office, I explained; it was a suite of rooms in a church that had given me space to use as needed. It was freely given by a pastor who wanted to help people who didn't have adequate support. That got her attention. She asked to meet this man. I was nervous about connecting them but knew she was ready. By this time, we had talked through her abuse history without any mention of God, Jesus, or prayer. She needed safety, and I was committed to giving it to her. After hearing about this man, she asked to meet him in the office that he had provided for "girls like her" so she could say "thank you." My heart soared!

It was arranged for the following week. Pastor Brad is a big, husky guy with a smile a mile wide. He was more eager to meet her than she was nervous to meet him. I'll never forget that day. She walked in, slowly running her fingers on everything in the room. It was a beautiful space. I could tell she felt safe and loved there. Brad sat across from the two of us. She began to talk and poured out her fury at God and the faith leaders who had abused her. He listened with silent tears falling down his face. *I'm sorry*, he repeated over and over. *I'm sorry.* She eventually softened and began to cry too. He apologized for the sexual and spiritual abuse she had experienced by religious leaders. He stood in the shoes of all those men and took it: her rage, her language, her accusations, her shattered stories. When she grew quiet, he thanked her for trusting him enough to be honest. He told her, in the future, to come to the church whenever she needed anything and that these doors would always be open. He needed her help to learn how to support her better and others like her—he was proud of her strength and courage. He left, and she was quiet for a long time. Eventually, she leaned over and whispered, "You can pray with me now."

—STORY RECOUNTED BY CELESTIA TRACY

Brad listened because he knew God was listening, and Sarah desperately needed to be heard. Brad listened to be changed by what he heard. As we feed on Scripture and know God's promises to attend to our cries, we can slowly believe we're worth listening to. In time, we can offer the same gift of presence to others. Listening is a powerful transformative tool. In Scripture, seeing and hearing are inextricably linked. *God hears the cries of the oppressed.* God saw the suffering of the Israelites' and heard their cries, just as he sees and hears you.

Following is a short description of some key passages and principles regarding God's response to victims' cries.

- *God sees our anguish and listens to our cries.* When we are overwhelmed with the effects of abuse, we are invited to call out to God continually, "evening, morning and noon," in our distress. God promises to "hear" the voice of survivors tormented by their anxious thoughts, who are "distraught" by their abusers' threats, whose hearts are "in anguish," and who are "beset" by "fear and trembling" (Ps 55:2–5, 17; cf. Ps 34:4–6).
- *God sees every evil deed and hears victims' cries—we are not forgotten!* God sees it all. God knows. When you are hurt by a person who, with arrogance and duplicity, covers his abuse with a false, pleasing persona to hide his sin from others so that you won't be believed, you can gain confidence from the psalmist who declared, "Does he who fashioned the ear not hear? Does he who formed the eye not see?" (Ps 94:9).

- *When we feel alone amid dangerous people, including family members and community leaders who collude with abusers "skilled in doing evil" (Mic 7:2–6), we must cry out to God, knowing that he will hear us.* He never gets tired of us coming to him for help. We can proclaim with the prophet Micah: "But as for me, I watch in hope for the LORD, I wait for God my Savior; my God will hear me" (Mic 7:7).
- *When evildoers prosper, particularly when they wear a false cloak of righteousness, we can take confidence that God will listen to our humble cries.* "The LORD is far from the wicked, but he hears the prayer of the righteous" (Prov 15:29; cf. John 9:31).

We will close this section by noting a closely related passage in Psalm 56:8 where the psalmist declares: "Record my misery; list my tears on your scroll—are they not in your record?" This significantly qualifies how God listens to his children's cries. He keeps a "record" of our pain and stores our tears in a (metaphorical) bottle. In other words, our loving heavenly Father listens and remembers our anguished cries.

GOD FEELS

Dr. Morrey, one of the world's leading orthopedic elbow surgeons, turned to face Celestia after reviewing her X-rays and an MRI of her left arm. She had just returned from the Democratic Republic of the Congo after training extensively for over a month. Upon arriving home with extreme exhaustion, she was very sick and unable to get out of bed. Her weight had plummeted fifty pounds. We rushed her the next day to her specialists at Mayo Clinic in Rochester, Minnesota.

Fifteen years earlier, Dr. Morrey implanted a Hoffman-Morrey titanium device in her elbow to replace her severely damaged joint and bone. He knows more about elbows than virtually anyone alive and has written the definitive textbook on this most complex joint. Celestia was his youngest patient to receive this device. From the beginning he had fought hard to keep her from losing her arm. He knew Celestia's elbow better than any other human being. Early that morning, he was sitting on his black stool in front of the scans, and after quietly examining each one he turned to face her with tears on his face: *Why did you wait so long to come and see me? You have a systemic infection that is at least a year old. It has eaten most of the little bone left in your arm. We will be admitting you immediately to the hospital so I can operate in the morning. I don't know if I can save your arm. I will do everything I can. I am very sorry. We are in God's hands now.* Celestia's pain had become his pain.

Celestia recounts regarding that day:

> I've never felt such compassion from a doctor. By that time, Dr. Morrey had been my surgeon for over sixteen years. He had operated on my left arm seven times, each time attempting to save the elbow God had given me. Skin, fascia, and bone had been harvested multiple times in valiant attempts to save my elbow. That morning, as I sat in his office, he shamelessly cried. It was devastating news. I could tell—he didn't think my arm could be saved. His palpable love and compassion helped me transcend the intense pain and shock of what I was being told. He was present with me. He didn't rush but helped me process the terrible state of my arm and an unidentifiable infection. The power of presence. It heals. That's what Dr. Morrey gave me over and over again.[2]

Let's project this illustration onto God. He sees and understands everything about us. But superior knowledge in itself provides limited comfort. Does the God who knows also care? More pointedly, does our pain cause him pain? This is a critically important question for those who suffer. And the theological answer to this question is surprisingly complex. For most of the church's two-thousand-year history, most theologians have asserted that God is "impassible," that is incapable of emotion in response to humans. It means that "God cannot be acted on or even affected emotionally by anything in creation."[3] One advocate of "strong impassibility" states this quite starkly, asserting that our sins "do not affect God," for he, "like the clouds above," is not impacted by human actions or experiences.[4]

Unless you have formally studied theology, the possibility of God not feeling the actions of humans may well be surprising and unsettling. I also find the idea that God has no emotions to be troubling and biblically unsupportable. So we must pursue this a bit further. We won't get into the technicalities of this debate, but a basic understanding of divine passibility or impassibility is critical to understanding God's response to human suffering. After all, Exodus 3:7 says that when God saw the Israelites' misery and heard their cries, he was "concerned about their suffering." This suggests a strong emotional response by God. But before we give biblical support for divine passibility, let's further clarify the chief concerns of its opponents.

Let's introduce the arguments of divine impassibility by returning to the story of Celestia's surgeon, Dr. Bernard Morrey. Is empathy in and of itself sufficient for healing? Actually, it is not. What if Dr. Morrey was so compassionate that he was completely overwhelmed with sorrow at Celestia's condition, and it threw him into a paralyzing depression, and he couldn't continue treating her? Or what if he was so enraged at Celestia's physicians for failing to correctly diagnose her bone infection that he couldn't steady his hands enough to perform her life-saving surgery?

While these examples may sound silly, they illustrate the primary concerns of the early church fathers, which prompted them to assert repeatedly that God was "impassive." They wanted to distinguish the Almighty, unchanging God of Scripture from the fickle, emotionally volatile Greco-Roman gods. Modern evangelical proponents of divine impassibility are also concerned with guarding against recent theological models, particularly open theism, which asserts that God is not all-powerful or all-knowing. He learns and grows as human history unfolds. He experiences profound emotional change and grief when surprised at the bad things that happen to humans.[5] Modern proponents of divine impassibility are mainly concerned with denying the possibility of God being emotionally overwhelmed or manipulated by his creation.[6] Furthermore, they are concerned with doing justice to biblical assertions that God is self-existent (John 5:26), unchanging (Heb 13:8), and independent (Isa 40:13–15).

The latter affirmation is essential to those who affirm divine impassibility, since Scripture teaches that God is complete in himself. He doesn't need humans to add anything to his perfect nature or to sustain his glorious existence. As Paul stated to the pagan Athenians, "The God who made the world and everything in it, being Lord of heaven and earth, does not live in temples made by man, nor is he served by human hands, as though he needed anything, since he himself gives to all mankind life and breath and everything" (Acts 17:24–25 ESV). Similarly, Isaiah declares, "Who has measured the Spirit of the LORD, or what man shows him his counsel? Whom did he consult, and who made him understand? Who taught him the path of justice, and taught him knowledge, and showed him the way of understanding? Behold, the nations are like a drop from a bucket" (Isa 40:13–15). In other words, God is complete in his perfect being. He needs nothing from creation to enhance or add to his perfection. God the Father, Son, and Spirit from eternity past have enjoyed a perfect love relationship (John 17:5). God did not need to create humans to experience intimate relationships.

The triune God knew that humans would sin and that the cost for redeeming humans would be for the Son to leave the perfections of heaven to come to a sinful earth, suffer, and die (Phil 2:5–8). In creating humans, God voluntarily chose to suffer. As we will soon see, God's suffering was not limited to Jesus's suffering in his humanity on earth. Instead, *the whole Trinity freely chose to enter into an affective relationship with humans in which God "makes himself vulnerable to pain and suffering."*[7] This point is critically important for abuse survivors. In his classic work on the cross of Christ, the late John Stott notes, "In the real world of pain, how could one worship a God who is immune to suffering?"[8]

What biblical data suggests that God emotionally responds to humans? More pointedly, does Scripture expressly affirm that God suffers?

Scripture Ascribes a Broad Range of Emotions to God

There are hundreds of passages in Scripture that attribute emotion to God. David Lamb identifies seven emotions that are most frequently attributed to God in Scripture. For instance, in the Psalms, God is said to:

> hate (5:5; 11:5; 45:7)
> get angry (6:1; 30:5; 78:21)
> be jealous (78:58; 79:5)
> be grieved (78:40)
> be delighted (18:19; 22:8; 35:27)
> be merciful (25:6; 28:6; 103:4)
> love (5:7; 25:6; 136:1–26)[9]

Strong impassibilitists argue that such biblical references to God's emotions are simply anthropopathisms (attributing human emotions to a nonhuman being) and are not meant to be taken literally, just as references to God having hands, eyes, or wings are not meant to be taken literally.[10] But Scripture tells us that God is spirit; he doesn't have body parts (John 4:24; Col 1:15). Thus, statements of God's right hand, eyes, etc. are metaphorical statements intended to convey a truth about God (his knowledge, his strength, etc.). On the other hand, Scripture never states or implies that God doesn't have emotions. Over and over, it expressly says he does. We must let Scripture shape our theology. I am convinced that Scripture reveals that God is very emotional. As Celestia loves to say, particularly when people apologize for crying, "Don't apologize; no one is more emotional than God."

God's Emotions Are Robust Responses to Humans

Most of the descriptions of God's emotions in Scripture are in response to humans—his posture toward them or his response to their actions or condition. Scripture from Genesis to Revelation reveals that God is deeply affected by and responsive to humans. He delights in those who are righteous (Prov 11:20), is fiercely angry at evildoers (Ps 7:11), is jealous over his wayward people (Deut 32:16), is tenderly compassionate toward his feeble children (Ps 103:13–14), laments when he must judge (Jer 9:10–11), rejoices over his children (Zeph 3:17), and grieves at human misery (Isa 63:9). Based on Scripture, it is inconceivable to say that God isn't affected by our sin, prayers, or suffering. His broad emotional responses show how responsive God is toward his creation. He cares deeply for us.

God's Children Cause Him Pain

God experiences a wide range of emotions, including deep heartache and sorrow over the suffering of his people due to the consequences of sin. Sin and pain are inseparably linked. We were created to experience blessing. Sin distorts and steals God's desired state of shalom (wholeness, flourishing), leading to pain and disorder. God grieves over this broken state, even when we bring such pain on ourselves. Jesus lamented over the coming judgment on the inhabitants of rebellious Jerusalem. Their impending, self-inflicted pain caused Jesus's pain. Jesus plaintively cried out: "Jerusalem, Jerusalem, you who kill the prophets and stone those sent to you, how often I have longed to gather your children together, as a hen gathers her chicks under her wings, and you were not willing. Look, your house is left to you desolate" (Matt 23:37–38). Grief over human suffering extends to the whole Godhead—Father, Son, and Spirit. Many of the strongest texts that affirm God's painful emotions over human misery are found in the Old Testament. The following are a few of the most significant texts.

Genesis 6:6

"The LORD regretted that he had made human beings on the earth, and his heart was deeply troubled."

This is a substantial text describing God's emotional sorrow and pain. God made humans in his very image to mirror his character. He gave them potency over creation to care for it as his royal representatives. Instead, they were using their power to assault and murder fellow image bearers. God's beautiful creation "was corrupt in God's sight and was full of violence" (Gen 6:11). Notice God's response to this dreadful twisting of shalom, evidenced by widespread physical abuse. God's "heart was deeply troubled" at the broken human condition. The Hebrew word translated "regret" (*naham*) does not mean that God was having second thoughts regarding having made humans. As Millard Erickson notes, the passive form of the verb *naham* used in this verse is best translated "to suffer emotional pain."[11] The statement at the end of the verse confirms this reading—God was "deeply troubled." God experienced deep pain over human brokenness, precipitated by physical abuse and murder. Abuse destroys life. It causes physical and relational pain. And it pains God.

Hosea 11:8

"How can I give you up, Ephraim? How can I hand you over, Israel? How can I treat you like Admah? How can I make you like Zeboyim? My heart is changed within me; all my compassion is aroused."

In the context of Israel experiencing judgment for her idolatry, God expresses his compassionate sorrow over her pitiful state. He laments over her wretched condition and says he can't abandon her. His compassion was so great that it caused him emotional pain.

Isaiah 63:9

"In all their affliction he was afflicted, and the angel of his presence saved them; in his love and in his pity he redeemed them; he lifted them up and carried them all the days of old." (ESV)

This verse appears in a passage recounting the loving faithfulness of God to his people over many generations. Repeatedly the Israelites suffered greatly due to their unfaithfulness, and yet God continued to be compassionate toward them. Over and over, he delivered and preserved them. But more than that, in all of their afflictions God himself was afflicted. This biblical phrase tells us that God's rescue "involves far more than merely delivering people from their afflictions; it requires participation in the afflictions with the afflicted."[12] God suffers with his suffering children.

Jeremiah 31:20

"Is not Ephraim my dear son, the child in whom I delight?
Though I often speak against him, I still remember him.
Therefore my heart yearns for him; I have great compassion
for him," declares the LORD.

This verse is also in the context of unfaithful Israel (Ephraim, the northern kingdom), who had suffered greatly due to her sin. While she forgot the covenant with her God, he had not forgotten her. While her heart strayed after other lovers (idols), God's heart was painfully moved with compassion toward her. The Hebrew language used here for a yearning heart is metaphorical and refers to churning intestines. This phrase indicates intense, painful grief over a beloved, wayward child. God's compassion causes him to suffer over his children. Similarly, Hosea 11:8 describes God's emotional pain over Ephraim: "My heart recoils within me; my compassion grows warm and tender" (ESV).

Many other Scripture passages describe God's sorrow, particularly over human sin and its tragic, destructive results. In addition to Jesus's lamenting over Jerusalem in Matthew 23, many other passages describe God's sadness over his children's sinful choices as they strayed from the path of covenant blessing (e.g., Jer 2:1–8; 3:19–20; Hos 6:4). David Lamb notes that numerous passages, such as Ezekiel 6:9 ("I have been broken," ESV), describe God as broken, crushed, and grieving. Additionally, Lamb notes many other texts that describe God's (metaphorical) tears over broken, sinful humans (Isa 16:9; Jer 9:10–11).[13] Finally, let's note that God the Holy Spirit grieves over the broken creation. In Romans 8:18–25 Paul describes the effects of the curse on all creation, resulting in great pain— "the sufferings of this present time" (v. 18 ESV). He says that we believers and all of creation "groan" as we wait to be delivered from the brokenness of our fallen world (vv. 22–23). Paul goes on to say that we often don't even know how to pray correctly in our human weakness. Hence, the Spirit "groans" intercessory prayers on our behalf ("the Spirit himself intercedes for us with groanings too deep for words," v. 26 ESV). The word used here for "groan" in verse 26 (*alalētos*) refers to wordless sighs. The verbal form of this word group indicates loud wailing (Mark 5:38). Contextually, the Spirit's groanings are best understood as cries of lament on behalf of believers who are suffering. God the Spirit grieves for and with us.

In summary, we worship a God who intimately relates to his creation. Far from being the "unmoved mover" of the Greco-Roman pantheon of gods, or the emotionally unmovable god of strong impassibility, the God of Scripture is more emotional than any human. He is passionate. He loves, hates, mourns, and anguishes. He has chosen to hurt when we hurt. As Christian philosopher Nicholas Wolterstorff notes from his wrestling with grief after the death of his son, "God is not only the God of the sufferers but the God who suffers. The pain and fallenness of humanity have entered into his own heart. . . . Instead of explaining our suffering, God shares it."[14]

GOD COMES TO RESCUE

Sheila stood in front of me erect, every muscle tensed. She was flooded with emotion—rage, fear, and confusion. Then she blurted out, "Where was God when I was being raped. Where was he?" My heart broke for this adolescent. In over forty years as a seminary teacher and pastor, I've been asked thousands of questions, but this one is, without doubt, the most difficult. Numerous "Sheilas" on multiple continents have asked this same question. As I write these words, I'm slated in six weeks to lead a small team to "the triangle of death" in Eastern Congo to meet with our Mending the

Soul master trainers. They continually witness the worst atrocities imaginable.

"Where was God when . . ." will undoubtedly be on their lips, for themselves and those they serve. This is hands down the most painful, vexing question any human being, let alone a theologian or pastor, can ever hear. The first "Sheila" asked me this question almost thirty years ago. I didn't have a perfect answer then. I don't have a complete answer now. But in my wrestling with God over the decades, he has given me a partial answer that gives me more than enough confidence to believe his promises, to keep pursuing him, and to entrust abuse survivors to his care. The heart of the answer to, "Where was God when?" is found in "God came down."[15] For the enslaved Israelites, God coming down meant God acting to deliver them from Egypt. But the supreme act of God coming down to rescue is seen in Jesus. Jesus coming down is the fullest answer to "Where was God when . . ."

Jesus Came Down

In the previous chapter, we noted Jesus's astounding conde-scension, as referenced in Philippians 2:5–11. This was indeed the most significant "coming down" in human history. Jesus, the divine Son of God, dwelt in heaven from eternity past in perfect intimacy within the Godhead. He experienced perfection and joy, worshiped ceaselessly by holy angels (Isa 6:1–3; Rev 4:8). Yet he voluntarily chose to come down to the lowest possible depths. As Paul says in Philippians 2:7, Jesus "made himself nothing by tak-ing the very nature of a servant, being made in human likeness." "Likeness" does not suggest he only appeared human. The Greek word (*homoiōma*) used here emphasizes likeness and similarity, not identity. Christ was like other human beings in all respects, but he also remained fully divine. His true "identity" differed from any other human. He was the divine Son of God who took on humanity. In taking on human flesh, Jesus entered the vortex of human suffering, abuse, and evil. Consider the fact that in Jesus's first months of earthly life, King Herod slaughtered all of his young male peers in Bethlehem. This evil atrocity led to Jesus and his parents becoming poor refugees in a foreign country (Egypt; see Matt 2:1–23). When he became a man, numerous times the religious leaders, and even his fellow villagers in Nazareth, tried to kill him (Mark 11:18; Luke 4:28–29). Jesus's heart was broken when his cousin John was beheaded at the hands of a wicked public official (Matt 14:6–13). Throughout his earthly life, Jesus repeatedly witnessed terrible suffering and responded with compassion (Matt 9:36; 20:34; Luke 7:13). Jesus wept when his dear friend Lazarus died (John 11:35). From the earliest moments of his earthly life until the last second of his gruesome death, Jesus experienced evil and suffering. He tasted blood and tears. Jesus understands human suffering and evil because he came down and experienced it. Not only did he experience evil and death, but through the cross he defeated them.

Jesus Died

Paul goes on in Philippians 2:8 to say that Jesus "humbled himself by becoming obedient to death—even death on a cross!" This is the crux of the answer to Sheila's haunting "where is God" question. (Ironically, the word *crux* comes from the Latin word for "cross." Even the English language reflects the monumental significance of Jesus's death!) Crucifixion was indeed one of the most sinister forms of torture ever devised. It created the most extreme physical and emotional pain. The humiliation or shame it engendered was a big part of the emotional pain. Evildoers, ancient and modern, understand the devastating power of shame and often strategize to humiliate their victims in every way possible. For the Romans, shame was the primary intention of crucifixion. Jerome Neyrey argues that Roman crucifixion "at every step entailed a progressive humiliation of the victim."[16] He lists numerous ways crucifixion shames the victim: it was the punishment of those considered the most shameful; it followed "status degrading" public trials; it included torture while nude, which often maimed the body and caused the victims to soil themselves with urine and or excrement; it included carrying the cursed cross; it involved the confiscation of one's clothes and public execution while nude; it stripped the victim of all power through pinning one's hands and feet to the cross; it was a form of crude public entertainment and ridicule; it often denied victims an honorable burial—their bodies were left to rot on the cross or be devoured by scavenger animals and birds. Truly, crucifixion was the ultimate experience of shame, disgrace, and evil.[17] Other than having his body left on the cross to rot, Jesus experienced every aspect of the shameful evil that Neyrey describes. In light of the obscene nature of crucifixion, we can understand why the Romans, most of whom had probably witnessed numerous crucifixions, were highly reluctant to discuss it or even think about it. The influential Roman philosopher Cicero admonished his readers, "The very word 'cross' should be far removed not only from the person of a Roman citizen but from his thoughts, his eyes, and his ears."[18] For the Romans, the Christian gospel of Jesus coming down and dying on the cross was sheer foolishness. Likewise, to the ancient Jews for whom dying on a tree was a curse, the gospel was an offensive stumbling block (1 Cor 1:23). Yet Paul says that the cross of Christ is the very foundation for all of life (1 Cor 2:1; Gal 2:20).

Jesus Rose

Resurrection means that the worst thing is never the last thing. . . . The worst isn't the last thing about the world. It's the next to the last thing. The last thing is the best. It's the power from on high that comes down into the world and wells up from the rock-bottom worst of the world like a hidden spring. Can you believe it? The last, best thing is the

laughing deep in the hearts of the saints, sometimes our hearts even. Yes.
You are terribly loved and forgiven. Yes. You are healed. All is well.
—Frederick Buechner, *The Final Beast*

Let's now come back to Philippians 2. After noting the depth of Christ's humiliating condescension, Paul dramatically pivots. He declares that after Christ's crucifixion "God exalted him to the highest place and gave him the name that is above every name, that at the name of Jesus every knee should bow, in heaven and on earth and under the earth, and every tongue acknowledge that Jesus Christ is Lord" (Phil 2:9–11). Jesus did not remain in the grave. If he had, we would truly have no hope. Evil, abuse, and death would have been victorious. But in the darkest hour of human history, God performed the greatest miracle: he raised Jesus from the dead. Jesus's death broke the power of Satan, sin, and evil (cf. Col 2:14–15; Heb 2:14–15). Paul references this cosmic victory in Philippians 2:10–11 by saying that one day every knee on earth, in heaven, and under the earth will bow and every tongue confess that Jesus is Lord. In essence Paul is asserting that every created being, human or angelic, child of God or enemy of God, will one day yield in complete surrender to Jesus. This is very similar to what Paul describes in Colossians 1:20, where Paul says that through Christ's blood shed on the cross God has and will "reconcile to himself all things, whether things on earth or things in heaven, by making peace through his blood, shed on the cross." This is a cosmic reconciliation in which heaven and earth (including all created beings) are put back into their originally created order under the authority of Christ. Christ's death and resurrection will soon bring about complete shalom.

Jesus Will Return

Scripture declares that Jesus's death defeated sin, death, and evil, but this malevolent trifecta still appears alive and well. Sheila's haunting "where is God" question is not fully answered. In chapter 3, we discussed the nature of the New Testament epistles and noted that they reflect an "already" but "not yet" framework. Jesus's death and resurrection brought new life and defeated death, but this is just the first stage of the final defeat. We see this when the writer of Hebrews applies Psalm 8:4–6 to Jesus (Heb 2:6–8a), noting that Jesus has been crowned with glory and honor (in his resurrection and exaltation), and everything in creation has been put under his feet. Yet in the next line, the author acknowledges that "at present, we do not yet see everything in subjection to him" (Heb 2:8b ESV). In other words, the world is still in disorder and rebellion. Evil and suffering continue, seemingly unabated. Jesus's death and resurrection struck a fatal blow, but the final defeat is yet to come. Satan, the god of this world who promotes evil, abuse, and suffering, will only be fully banished forever when Jesus returns.

The book of Revelation gives one of the most explicit biblical pictures of this age's "already" but "not yet" nature. In Revelation 1, John says that Jesus is "the firstborn of the dead, and the ruler of kings on earth," who "has freed us from our sins by his blood" and has "made us a kingdom, priests to his God and Father, to him be glory and dominion forever and ever" (Rev 1:5–6 ESV). John is highlighting the victory gained through the cross. Jesus rose from the dead, broke the power of sin, and made us citizens of a new kingdom. And this Jesus reigns supreme, and to him belongs "glory and dominion forever" (v. 6; cf. 5:13). This is the "already" of what Jesus has accomplished. But the very next verse notes that there is more to come, for "behold, he is coming with the clouds, and every eye will see him" (v. 7 ESV). The following verse (v. 8) adds that Jesus is "the Lord God, 'who is and who was and who is to come, the Almighty.'" Jesus came the first time as a lamb, and in his death and resurrection he inaugurated his kingdom's victory over evil. However, in the church age, Jesus is not yet fully reigning; thus, sin and evil continue.

Interestingly, the predominate title for Christ in Revelation 4–22 is "Lamb." It is used twenty-seven times to refer to Jesus. A lamb is a sacrifice for sin, not a mighty, roaring lion who conquers. But Jesus is both (Rev 5:5–6). Revelation 4–17 describes the "already" (this present age) in which Satan and evil are still ravaging the world. This highlights Jesus as the powerless, meek Lamb. Revelation 18–22, however, highlights the "not yet" inaugurated at Jesus's return. These chapters showcase Jesus as the lion who will utterly and eternally defeat Satan and evil. John described this clearly: "'"He will wipe every tear from their eyes. There will be no more death" or mourning or crying or pain, for the old order of things has passed away.' He who was seated on the throne said, 'I am making everything new!' Then he said, 'Write this down, for these words are trustworthy and true'" (Rev 21:4–5). This is God's magnificent promise. He will establish shalom throughout all creation. The day is coming when there will be no more evil, abuse, or suffering. Satan's days of destruction are drawing to a close.

So, we live in the tension of the "already" but "not yet." Jesus came down to rescue us. The cross shows us where God is when evil occurs. But we must patiently wait for Jesus's return, trusting that he will fulfill his promises. His promises are "trustworthy and true."

CONCLUSION

I want to tie this chapter together by sharing some journal entries. I wrote what follows in 2017 while on a five-day silent prayer retreat. Celestia and I scheduled this retreat because we sensed from God that our upcoming Congo intensives would be particularly difficult. This was the conference I mentioned earlier on the site of a horrific massacre in the late 1990s. We had spoken to several people who had witnessed this mass killing. Such horrific evil has haunted me over the years. So I went on this five-day retreat, reflecting on the question, "Where is God when people suffer terrible evil?" While wrestling with God in the prayer garden on the second day of the retreat, he powerfully spoke to me. As I sat under a cracked and weathered statue of Jesus, with his arms outstretched to the world, I heard God whisper:

- I am Immanuel, "God with you." I am in the Congo. I see and feel all the suffering.
- Keep coming to me with your pain and the suffering around you.
- Trust me to take care of my people. They are mine. You aren't responsible for them. You can't heal them; I can and will. Just be there in my name, and I will be present through you.
- Your tears and heartache for their suffering are my tears and heartache.

I then wrote the following response to God:

God, please keep speaking. Sometimes, the suffering you allow, which you could stop, makes me want to run from you. I want to lean away and not trust. But Jesus, even in your resurrected body, you bear scars in your hands and side. You were and are broken for the sins of the world. Let my pain over the brokenness around me drive me to you. Let it be the fodder to deepen my experience of your love for me and your agony over human suffering. Lord, I believe. Help my unbelief (Mark 9:24).

As expected, it was one of our most arduous trips to Africa. We've done many more trips since then. We've continued to wrestle with, "Where is God when . . . ?" But God's voice in this retreat has significantly changed my perspective. I am more convinced than ever that the image of Jesus suffering on the cross and his outstretched arms with scars on his resurrected body are the best answer to, "Where is God when . . . ?"[19] He is here with us. He sees our misery, hears our cries, is moved by our pain, and comes to rescue us. And soon he will make all things new (Rev 21:5).

How God would respond to his children's suffering isn't explicitly stated in Exodus 3:7–8 but is revealed a few verses later: "I am sending you to Pharaoh to bring my people the Israelites out of Egypt" (v. 10). God acted *through* his servant Moses. God called him to be the human agent of deliverance, just as God expects his people, from ancient times to the present, to respond sacrificially to human suffering. This is a huge theme in Scripture. We will make it the focus of the next chapter.

Chapter 10

GOD'S MANDATE TO PROTECT THE VULNERABLE AND CARE FOR THE ABUSED

That justice is a good thing, a fine goal, even a
supreme ideal, is commonly accepted. What is lacking
is a sense of the monst rosity of injustice.
—ABRAHAM HESCHEL, *THE PROPHETS*

This is what the LORD says: Do what is just and right. Rescue
from the hand of the oppressor the one who has been robbed.
Do no wrong or violence to the foreigner, the fatherless or the
widow, and do not shed innocent blood in this place. . . .

"He defended the cause of the poor and needy,
and so all went well.
Is that not what it means to know me?"
declares the LORD.
—JEREMIAH 22:3, 16

I will never forget my first day in preschool. I was so excited I couldn't sleep the night before. Even as a four-year-old, I yearned to share the school experiences that the older kids described. Over a half century later, I can vividly recall that day. We played games, enjoyed snacks, and returned to a cool classroom after recess for story time. But my most poignant memory from that day was arguing with another boy. We started talking about our families, particularly our fathers. He bragged that his dad worked for the Salt River Project and made water flow into the canals. I bragged that my dad worked for Reppel Steel Company and built huge buildings. After he suggested that his dad might throw me and my dad into one of the canals, things quickly escalated into "my dad can beat up your dad." The fact of the matter was that I had never seen my father beat up anyone, let alone one of my peer's dads.

Nevertheless, I had absolute confidence that he *could* and *would* protect me if I was threatened. I was so confident of this hypothesis that I almost got into a fight to prove it! While one might question my four-year-old communication strategy, I am incredibly grateful to have grown up with a father committed to my protection and well-being. I repeatedly witnessed his commitment to care for the vulnerable, particularly children, the elderly, and widows. Life would later temper my unbridled confidence, since my loving father was still a fallible, finite human and didn't and couldn't protect us from all harm. But the protection and care he did offer gave me a healthy paradigm. I learned that protecting and caring for the vulnerable is of utmost importance. It is not just a good thing to do. It is a vital thing to do regardless of the cost.

Decades later, after much life experience and theological training, I'm more convinced than ever that *protecting and caring for the abused and oppressed is one of the most essential tasks for the believer and the church.* You might think that this assertion would be uncontested. Unfortunately, that is not the case. Throughout

THE HEALING ROLE OF SCRIPTURE

this book we have noted numerous recent instances in which families, churches, and entire denominations have egregiously failed to care for abuse survivors and instead protected and cared for the perpetrators. Protecting sexual abusers has been such a problem throughout the evangelical world that some have referred to it as an "epidemic of denial."[1] Compounding this problem, many evangelical leaders are pushing back against "social-justice ministry," arguing that it is not part of the gospel and thus not the church's mission.[2] Kevin DeYoung and Greg Gilbert argue that the church's mission is solely to preach the gospel. It is not the church's task to restore shalom.[3] Furthermore, they argue that "we must not oversell" what the Bible says about justice.[4] Other Christian leaders go even further, arguing that social justice is a "serious hindrance" to the gospel.[5]

On the contrary, it would be impossible to overstate how much Scripture has to say about justice. The biblical mandate to protect the vulnerable and care for the abused is an overriding theme from Genesis to Revelation.

KEY TERMS

Justice, mercy, and the related phrase "social justice" are major themes in Scripture, each worthy of a book-length treatise. For our purposes, we will give a concise summary. Let's start with the biblical terms and then provide definitions. The most critical and frequent Hebrew words/word groups for "justice" are *tsedeq* and *mishpat*. Both of these are legal terms with overlapping but not identical meanings. *Tsedeq* is often translated as "right" or "righteous" and refers to that which is literally or morally straight (Ps 23:3), that which conforms to a correct standard. It is used of God and of his exemplary standards. It refers to laws or relationships that are as they ought to be. In other words, *tsedeq* describes the world as God intended. This helps us understand why God loathes injustice (Isa 5:7–9). It corrupts his good intentions of shalom for his creation (Gen 1:31).

This leads us to *mishpat*, which is also a legal term. It is used 424 times in the Old Testament, very often in contexts of abuse or oppression. Christopher J. Wright notes that in the broadest sense, "*mishpat* is what needs to be done in a given situation if people and circumstances are to be restored to conformity with *sedeq/sedaqa*."[6] In other words, *mishpat* refers to *corrective* or *restorative justice*. This has enormous implications for abuse victims. Often in the Old Testament these two terms/word groups (*tsedeq* and *mishpat*) are used together (Gen 18:19; Ps 33:5). Many evangelical scholars believe this is a case of *hendiadys*—two words used to express a single idea, which is best translated "social justice."[7]

Currently, "social justice" refers to a wide variety of concepts, some of which are biblically indefensible. However, we must not reject a biblical concept because some misuse it. The single word "justice" is somewhat incomplete to express a biblical theology of justice, because justice or injustice is always in a social (relational) context. Injustice reflects disordered and perverted relationships in which people are not being treated as they ought to be. Therefore, biblical justice must be social. As the Jewish scholar Abraham Heschel notes, justice "exists in relation to a person. An act of injustice is condemned, not because the law is broken, but because a person has been hurt."[8] Social justice is the wide-ranging corrective action required for fellow image bearers to be treated properly, with the fairness and dignity that their Creator gave them.

Biblical social justice involves two distinct but related activities. First, it involves *protecting the vulnerable*. This means advocating on their behalf and defending them against abusive systems and abusive people. "Speak up for those who cannot speak for themselves, for the rights of all who are destitute. . . . Defend the rights of the poor and needy" (Prov 31:8–9; cf. Isa 1:17). Second, social justice involves *caring for those who are suffering due to abuse and oppression*. In his final defense to his "friends," Job asserted that he was not suffering due to hidden sin. He cites social justice as prime evidence of his godly character. His life was so characterized by justice and mercy that it was like a proudly worn garment. "I put on righteousness [*tsedeq*] as my clothing; justice [*mishpat*] was my robe and my turban" (Job 29:14). His defense brings together both aspects of social justice. He states:

> I rescued the poor who cried for help,
>> and the fatherless who had none to assist them.
> The one who was dying blessed me;
>> I made the widow's heart sing.
> I put on righteousness as my clothing;
>> justice was my robe and my turban.
> I was eyes to the blind
>> and feet to the lame.
> I was a father to the needy;
>> I took up the case of the stranger.
> I broke the fangs of the wicked
>> and snatched the victims from their teeth.
>> (Job 29:12–17)

Oh, that every modern abuse survivor had a powerful Job in their life. Notice the breadth of Job's justice-and-mercy activity: he rescued, assisted, advocated, and aggressively defended. And notice the variety of vulnerable populations he aided: the poor, the fatherless, widows, people with disabilities, and the abused. Unfortunately, many anti-social-justice evangelicals understand biblical justice merely as equity or fair treatment for all parties.[9] In doing so, they inevitably minimize the prevalence of injustice against those with less power (e.g., women, the poor, ethnic minorities).[10] They also minimize the need to fight against injustice and protect victims.[11] Equity is certainly an aspect of biblical justice. We aren't to show partiality to the poor or the great (Lev 19:15). But the rich rarely need protection. There are almost no passages in Scripture arguing for the protection of the rich and otherwise powerful. It is the weak and the vulnerable who most need justice. This principle is clearly reflected in the repeated call to protect and not exploit orphans, widows, the poor, and aliens (e.g., Exod 22:22; Deut 10:18; 24:19).

Since the English word "justice" does not appear nearly as frequently in the New Testament, some have minimized its ethical significance. Part of the problem is that the most commonly used Greek word for "justice" in the New Testament (*dikaiosynē*) is most often translated as "righteousness." However, as is the case in the Old Testament, justice and righteousness are closely related. When *dikaiosynē* is used, it often can and perhaps should be translated as "justice"—that is, fairness, proper treatment that accords with God's righteous standards. Consider the following uses of *dikaiosynē* and *dikaios* in the New Testament. All of God's ways and judgments are just (Rev 15:3; 19:2; cf. John 5:30). God demands that elders in the local church are just (Titus 1:8). Godly people are to enforce justice (Heb 11:33). Jesus pronounced a special blessing on those who hunger and thirst after justice (Matt 5:6) and on those who are persecuted for the sake of justice (Matt 5:10).

Closely related to biblical justice is mercy. Often these two terms appear in the same passage. Zechariah the prophet declared: "Administer true justice; show mercy and compassion to one another. Do not oppress the widow or the fatherless, the foreigner or the poor. Do not plot evil against each other" (Zech 7:9–10). Notice that the call for justice and mercy is given in the context of abuse and oppression of the vulnerable. Oppressive and evil schemes lead to suffering, so justice *and* mercy are needed. This explains why the linking of justice and mercy (lovingkindness) is repeatedly found in Scripture (e.g., Jer 9:23–24; Mic 6:8; Matt 23:23).

This leads us to another rich, critically important biblical term, *hesed.*[12] It is used over 250 times in the Old Testament and is one of the most important words in the Hebrew Bible. I vividly remember my Hebrew professor in seminary explaining that *hesed* is such a rich word that it is impossible to convey its meaning with a single English word. It is used to signify loyal faithfulness (Ps 89:24 [89:25 MT]), graciousness (2 Sam 9:3), steadfast love (Ps 103:17), and mercy (Gen 32:11). The King James rendering of "lovingkindness" is perhaps the best single-word translation when *hesed* is used of God. The significance for abuse survivors is that *hesed* emphasizes God's faithfulness and mercy to his children, particularly when they are suffering. God tenderly cares for suffering people. He has compassion for those oppressed and wounded ("In you the orphan finds mercy," Hos 14:3 ESV). Furthermore, God demands that his people offer the same compassion to the hurting (Deut 10:18–19). We should finally note that the moral imperative of love is a dominant New Testament theme. Love conceptually encompasses both justice and mercy because it means treating another as having dignity and value and acting sacrificially to advance their best interests. Love summarizes Christian morality. Love fulfills the whole divine law and is the supreme Christian virtue:

- "For the entire law is fulfilled in keeping this one command: 'Love your neighbor as yourself'" (Gal 5:14).
- "Let no debt remain outstanding, except the continuing debt to love one another, for whoever loves others has fulfilled the law. The commandments, 'You shall not commit adultery,' 'You shall not murder,' 'You shall not steal,' 'You shall not covet,' and whatever other command there may be, are summed up in this one command: 'Love your neighbor as yourself'" (Rom 13:8–9).

- "And over all these virtues put on love, which binds them all together in perfect unity" (Col 3:14).

The most remarkable manifestations of religion (emotional experience, intellectual and theological understanding, faith, philanthropy, even martyrdom) are empty and worthless without love (1 Cor 13:1–3). Furthermore, love will endure forever and is greater than hope or faith (1 Cor 13:8–13).

We can already see from these short word studies that justice and mercy are extremely significant biblical themes. Furthermore, Scripture repeatedly calls for justice and mercy for those who have experienced abuse or oppression.

THE MORAL IMPERATIVE OF JUSTICE AND MERCY FOR THE ABUSED

To continue to build the case that justice-and-mercy ministry is a cardinal obligation for every believer and is integral to the mission of the church, I've organized extensive biblical data around several key themes or principles.

Justice and Mercy for the Abused and Oppressed Summarizes What God Requires of His People

Next week, I will visit a physician at Oregon Health and Science University for my annual physical exam. I work diligently to maintain my health, but I am not a medical doctor and need expert guidance. Let's imagine that after the doctor examines me and reviews my lab results, she briefly pauses and, in a sober tone, says, "Steve, you are already doing numerous good things to maintain your health. I'm glad you exercise regularly, don't smoke, and avoid processed foods. Those are all good and important.

But please listen carefully because I will summarize in ten words the most important thing you must do to maintain your health. Even if you increase your workouts to ten hours a day, run thirty marathons a year, and pay a professional chef $100,000 to prepare your every meal with the highest quality, nutritious ingredients, none of those things will matter if you miss what I'm about to tell you. Actually, every one of my patients with your same profile who didn't do what I'm about to tell you died within twelve months." You can imagine how attentive I would be to hear and heed my doctor's instructions. God has given us a similar urgent, critical directive. It is not optional. He summarizes concisely what he mandates of his people: *to doggedly pursue justice and mercy on behalf of the abused and oppressed.*

Let's start with Micah 6:8, one of the most well-known social-justice passages in all of Scripture. Micah wrote this short prophetic book in the eighth century BC to call Judah and Israel to repent lest they face God's sure judgment. The people (Mic 2:1–13) and the leaders (3:1, 9) are rebuked for their sins, particularly their oppression of the poor and vulnerable. Because it was "in their power to do it," evildoers schemed day and night to defraud and oppress the weak (2:1–2). Israel's leaders did not "embrace justice [*mishpat*]" but instead viciously abused the people (3:1–2). They were those who "tear the skin from my people and the flesh from their bones; who eat my people's flesh . . . who chop them up like meat for the pan" (3:2–3). Israel's rulers hated justice (*mishpat*), built Zion through bloodshed, and perverted judicial justice for the price of a bribe (3:10–11). The rich were "full of violence" (6:12 ESV), and the whole population lay "in wait to shed blood" (7:2).

It is into this maelstrom of systemic injustice and abuse that God's indictment thunders (Mic 6:1–2). In a case of extreme and tragic irony, God had faithfully delivered Israel from her oppression and slavery (6:3–5), yet Israel was now the oppressor and abuser of her own weak and vulnerable. So God rhetorically asks Israel what she thinks he wants from her. In a series of ascending requirements, the prophet asks:

> With what shall I come before the LORD,
>   and bow myself before God on high?
> Shall I come before him with burnt offerings,
>   with calves a year old?
> Will the LORD be pleased with thousands of rams,
>   with ten thousands of rivers of oil?
> Shall I give my firstborn for my transgression,
>   the fruit of my body for the sin of my soul? (Mic
>   6:6–7 ESV)

These hyperbolic suggestions set us up for the concise single sentence of what God desires from his people. This is the grand summary, the "what we absolutely must not miss or the consequences will be most dire" command. God requires us to "do justice," "love kindness," and "walk humbly" with our God (Mic 6:8 ESV). Let's make a few key observations on this poignant requirement.

- It is a full-throttled call to practice social justice in a context of abuse and oppression. God requires action, not lip service or policy statements. He is not interested in or impressed with mere articulations of justice or with good intentions. *We are to "do" justice.*
- It mandates us to pursue mercy for those who suffer. Abraham Heschel notes that the command "to love kindness" implies "an insatiable thirst, a passionate craving."[13] Again, God requires a full-hearted commitment to actively love those who are hurting. The people who please God passionately advocate and care for abuse victims. True compassion is costly.

- It requires us to focus on God first and then on those around us. "Walk humbly with your God" might seem somewhat discordant with "do justice" and "love mercy," but it is the necessary basis for both. Once we begin to see God for who he is, the merciful, just creator of the universe, we will vigorously pursue him and prioritize his concerns. The arrogant don't care about God, abuse, or human suffering. Their only concern is for themselves. As Bruce Waltke insightfully notes, "'Wickedness' is to serve self at the expense of the community," whereas "righteousness" means to "disadvantage self to 'advantage' the community."[14] For the humble who truly know and please God, practicing justice and insatiably loving the hurting is the only way to live. And this lifestyle is the only way to please the God revealed in Scripture.

We'll now apply the message of Micah 6:8 to the modern church. Is there any conceivable way a church or an individual believer who fails to protect and care for abuse victims is pleasing God? Micah gives us a crystal-clear answer—no! This is because justice and mercy for the abused and oppressed are essential for pleasing God. It is the "don't miss this no matter what" command of God. If we fail to practice justice and mercy, we cannot please God, regardless of all the other "good" things we do.

Micah is not the only biblical writer to make justice and mercy a summary of what God desires of his people. We find this same truth in Jeremiah 22. God warned ungodly King Jehoiakim against building wealth through injustice (Jer 22:13–14). Instead, he points Jehoiakim to his father King Josiah, who experienced great blessing from God. Josiah practiced "justice [*mishpat*] and righteousness [*tsedaqah*]. . . . He judged the cause of the poor and needy" (vv. 15–16 ESV). Then Jeremiah declares, regarding the social justice that King Josiah pursued for the vulnerable, "Is that not what it means to know me?" (v. 16). Much like Micah 6:8, Jeremiah gives us a stark, concise summary of what it means to know and please God. It is practicing social justice for the abused and oppressed. Similarly, in the New Testament, James 1:27 summarizes "pure religion" in two concise ways, one directed horizontally (to other people) and one vertically (toward a holy God). The first evidence of pure religion is "to look after orphans and widows in their distress" and the second is "to keep oneself from being polluted by the world." Again, a concise summary of pure religion is found in practicing social justice toward those who are suffering. As we have seen in other biblical passages, in singling out widows and orphans in distress, James highlights the need to extend justice and mercy to the abused and oppressed.[15] In the ancient world, widows and orphans were the most likely to be taken advantage of. Finally, in a more abbreviated form, Deuteronomy 16:20 declares, "Follow justice [*tsedeq*] and justice [*tsedeq*] alone so that you may live and possess the land the LORD your God is giving you." If the children of Israel were to experience God's richest blessings in the land God was giving them, their community had to be characterized by justice. It was indispensable.

Justice and Mercy for the Abused and Oppressed Are Based on the Character and Actions of God Himself

We would have no sure basis for defining, let alone practicing, justice and mercy apart from God (cf. Zeph 3:3–5). The very foundation for God's rule is justice and mercy: "Righteousness [*tsedeq*] and justice [*mishpat*] are the foundation of your throne; love [*hesed*] and faithfulness go before you" (Ps 89:14). Jeremiah, speaking to a people supremely characterized by injustice and oppression, points to God's just and merciful character as their only grounds for spiritual confidence: "Let the one who boasts boast about this: that they have the understanding to know me, that I am the LORD, who exercises kindness, justice and righteousness on earth, for in these I delight" (Jer 9:24). The implication is clear. Since God delights in justice and mercy, so should his people. Repeatedly God, in keeping with his character, affirms his commitment to provide justice and mercy for the vulnerable and afflicted:

- "A father to the fatherless, a defender of widows, is God in his holy dwelling" (Ps 68:5).
- "He upholds the cause of the oppressed and gives food to the hungry. The LORD sets prisoners free, the LORD gives sight to the blind, the LORD lifts up those who are bowed down, the LORD loves the righteous. The LORD watches over the foreigner and sustains the fatherless and the widow, but he frustrates the ways of the wicked" (Ps 146:7–9).
- "I know that the LORD secures justice for the poor and upholds the cause of the needy" (Ps 140:12; cf. 113:7–9).

The ethical implications of God being a God of justice and mercy should be patently clear. Because God is just and merciful and cares for the vulnerable and oppressed, he expects his people to do the same:

- "For the LORD your God is God of gods and Lord of lords, the great, the mighty, and the awesome God, who is not partial and takes no bribe. He executes justice for the fatherless and the widow, and loves the sojourner, giving him food and clothing. Love the sojourner, therefore, for you were sojourners in the land of Egypt" (Deut 10:17–19 ESV).
- "Endow the king with your justice, O God, the royal son with your righteousness. May he judge your people in righteousness, your afflicted ones with justice. . . . May he defend the afflicted among the people and save the children of the needy; may he crush the oppressor" (Ps 72:1–2, 4).

Justice and Mercy for the Abused and Oppressed Embodies the Kingdom of God and Enhances Our Gospel Witness

The revelation was truly heart breaking, but it wasn't unique. It felt like Groundhog Day. Another one of our friends had confided over dinner that her son no longer considered himself a Christian. He reasoned that he could no longer associate himself with a religion that blatantly and consistently perpetuated abuse, protected abusers, and blamed victims. He was done with it all! While one could rightfully argue that this is an extreme overreaction, the fact is that thousands of adolescents and young adults are leaving the Christian faith for the same reason. Celestia and I personally know dozens of parents who share this same tragic experience.

We can't begin to count the number of conversations we've had with unbelievers who refuse to consider the Christian faith because of the evangelical church's failure to address abuse and prioritize justice and mercy. This is what makes the argument that "social justice isn't the task of the church because sharing the gospel is our only mission" nonsensical, hollow, and painful. Prioritizing justice and mercy for the oppressed and abused dramatically enhances our gospel witness. It is quite notable that Jesus, after giving the Beatitudes that summarize kingdom values—and highlight justice and mercy—states: "Let your light shine before others, that they may see your good deeds and glorify your Father in heaven" (Matt 5:16). As we practice justice and mercy, we give the world a compelling picture of the character of God. In this sense it is a "gospel introduction."

Let's now connect this to the kingdom of God, which is the *rule of God*. We saw earlier that when Jesus came to earth, he inaugurated the kingdom, declaring that it had arrived (Matt 12:28). In this present church age, the kingdom reflects God's rule over his people. When Jesus returns in the future, the kingdom will be consummated and will reflect God's rule over all of creation (1 Cor 15:24–28). The church is the present community of believers who belong to the kingdom (Acts 8:12). Thus, the church should evidence the reign of God through compassion and social justice. John Stott states this well:

> The Kingdom of God is God's dynamic rule, breaking into human history through Jesus, confronting, combating, and overcoming evil, spreading the wholeness of personal and communal well-being, taking possession of his people in total blessing and total demand. The church is meant to be the Kingdom community, a model of what human community looks like when it comes under the rule of God, and a challenging alternative to secular society.[16]

In other words, as Christians live out key kingdom values, particularly justice and mercy, unbelievers get a stunning picture and taste of a God who is just, compassionate, and sacrificial in his love. For many, this is often the first step in being drawn to Jesus. Living out the gospel of the kingdom must never be separated from proclaiming the gospel. We are to proclaim the gospel in word *and* deed (1 John 2:6).

Now we can link the last two principles—*justice and mercy embody the character of God* and *justice and mercy embody kingdom values*. Both of these principles highlight the importance of demonstrating the character of God through our *acts* of justice and mercy.

Our daughter Abby lives with her family in western Uganda. Since 2007 she has joyfully served the poorest of the poor—street children, sex-trafficked women, impoverished families, and severely abused people. God has given Abby and her husband David a holistic work of justice and mercy. For the first ten years, Abby exclusively served street children and sex-trafficked women, two of the most traumatized and challenging populations imaginable. How does one break through to people who have known nothing but abuse and maltreatment, often by those who profess to be religious (Christians and Muslims)? How does one communicate truths about a loving heavenly Father to those abused and abandoned by their earthly fathers? In one of her early blog entries, Abby articulated her strategy of becoming "God in skin" to the most marginalized and abused. In other words, they and their staff lived out justice and mercy. She states:

> It is the most amazing blessing to work with street kids. I often feel sorry for anyone who has never gotten a chance. Yet working with street kids carries a heavy responsibility. You become the one person who doesn't beat them, who tells them you love them, that Jesus loves them, that they are special. . . . You become for them a picture of what God looks like and that is a heavy responsibility but one that I wouldn't trade for anything.
>
> As Christians we were made to utterly and completely change the way others see God, especially those stomped on by everyone else. . . . Every evening I put lotion on the boys at our house who want it (which is all of them) and rub their backs. Every time I do this I pray as I massage their scarred backs, legs, and arms that I am erasing just one of the scars on their hearts created by their physical wounds. . . . The boys have started initiating saying "I love you" to me and calling me mother Babirye [a familial name] instead of auntie. I know that God is answering my prayers.[17]

Abby and David have seen thousands of people come to saving faith in Christ through justice-and-mercy ministry. Celestia and I have also found justice-and-mercy ministry to be one of the most effective means of introducing people to Jesus. It powerfully enhances the gospel and draws people toward a loving God.

Justice and Mercy for the Abused and Oppressed Is Essential to Following the Life and Teachings of Jesus

To be a Christian is to be a follower of Jesus. His life and teachings must shape who we are and what we do. The Old Testament messianic prophecies emphasize how the Messiah will bring justice, mercy, and healing to the afflicted:

- "In love a throne will be established; in faithfulness a man will sit on it—one from the house of David—one who in judging seeks justice and speeds the cause of righteousness" (Isa 16:5).
- "Here is my servant, whom I uphold, my chosen one in whom I delight; I will put my Spirit on him, and he will bring justice to the nations. . . . In faithfulness he will bring forth justice; he will not falter or be discouraged till he establishes justice on earth" (Isa 42:1, 3–4).
- "The Spirit of the Sovereign Lord is on me, because the Lord has anointed me to proclaim good news to the poor. He has sent me to bind up the brokenhearted, to proclaim freedom for the captives and release from darkness for the prisoners, to proclaim the year of the Lord's favor and the day of vengeance of our God, to comfort all who mourn, and provide for those who grieve in Zion—to bestow on them a crown of beauty instead of ashes, the oil of joy instead of mourning" (Isa 61:1–3).

In keeping with these prophecies, when Christ preached his first sermon in his hometown at the synagogue in Nazareth, he quoted from Isaiah 61:1–2 (see Luke 4:16–21). He stopped just before citing "the day of vengeance," since that will happen at his second coming. Christ's earthly life and teaching embody justice and mercy poured out for the marginalized and afflicted. He forgave sin and preached the gospel at the same time as he healed the sick, the blind, the deaf, and the lame (Matt 11:4–5; Luke 7:22). He boldly and repeatedly stood up for the oppressed and confronted abusive authorities (Matt 23; John 8:1–11). He was deeply moved by human suffering (Matt 9:36; John 11:35). Christ demonstrated scandalous love for sinners and social outcasts. He touched and ate with lepers (Matt 8:2–3; 26:6), tax collectors, and various "sinners" (Matt 9:9–13; Luke 19:2–10). He allowed a "sinful woman" to touch him and kiss his feet (Luke 7:36–50). Jesus showed particular love, respect, and care for the marginalized, oppressed, and morally broken (Matt 21:31–32; John 4:4–26; 8:3–11). He violated patriarchal taboos by allowing women to travel with him as companions and students (Luke 8:1–3; 10:38–41). Jesus embodied justice and mercy to the marginalized and afflicted. He calls us to follow his example (John 20:21; 1 John 2:6).

Finally, we should note that the most radical New Testament instruction to live a life devoted to justice and mercy is given by Jesus himself (Matt 25:31–46). Drawing on Isaiah 58, Christ taught that the final "sheep and goat" judgment will be based not on verbal affirmations, theological statements, or pious religious practices. *Rather, it will be based on whether or not one fed the hungry, clothed the naked, and visited the imprisoned.* The righteous who are told they are inheriting the kingdom are affirmed by Jesus because they had fed, clothed, and visited him. His listeners are confused by this statement and ask: "Lord, when did we see you hungry and feed you, or thirsty and give you something to drink? When did we see you a stranger and invite you in, or needing clothes and clothe you? When did we see you sick or in prison and go to visit you?" (Matt 25:37–39). Jesus responds by saying, "Truly I tell you, *whatever you did for one of the least of these brothers and sisters of mine, you did for me*" (v. 40, emphases added). Those who are cast into judgment as goats failed to feed the hungry, clothe the naked, or visit the prisoners.

As we have already seen, the poor envisioned here who are hungry and naked epitomize those who are vulnerable and oppressed. The prisoners described here may well be those who have been persecuted for their faith. Some suggest this may refer to those imprisoned by the effects of abuse—those who are yet to be helped and healed. Based on other teaching throughout the New Testament, Jesus is not saying that one gets into heaven by practicing social justice. Rather, he is asserting that those who truly know him (his sheep) *will live out kingdom values—they will live out the gospel.* Serving the poor and afflicted demonstrates genuine commitment to Jesus. As D. A. Carson states regarding this passage in Matthew 25: "True disciples will love one another and serve the least brother with compassion; in doing so they unconsciously serve Christ. Those who have little sympathy for the gospel of the kingdom will remain indifferent and, in so doing, reject King Messiah."[18]

Based on Jesus's teaching, one cannot ignore the afflicted and rightfully claim to be his disciple. Justice and mercy for the abused and oppressed are essential to following Jesus's life and teachings.

Justice and Mercy for the Abused and Oppressed Brings Unique Blessings

Abby's justice and mercy work with the vulnerable and traumatized in Uganda is fulfilling yet challenging. It has been costly: she's suffered sickness, injustice, and countless painful losses that she could have easily avoided by staying in a comfortable American suburb. She is often asked if her work is hard. Her immediate, passionate answer is, "I can't imagine doing anything else! God has given us an amazing life! I actually feel sorry for people who don't get to do what I do. My life brings me joy." When Abby first moved to the slums of Kampala, she lived in a shipping container to be near the children she was serving. I'm sharing a blog entry written in 2009 from her hot, bug-infested shipping container that captures a small piece of the blessings that flow out of justice and mercy work. She wrote:

> There is a quote from a book by Gary Haugen, founder of International Justice Ministry that talks about bringing young girls into and out of brothels. It goes something like this, "when you walk into a brothel holding the hand of a little girl, the evil can almost tear you down, but when you walk out of a brothel freeing the hand of a little girl, the glory of God that is revealed can almost bowl you over . . ." When it comes to street children, it is exactly the same. I know what it feels like to hold the hand of a street child, take them to the hospital and then out to eat, making them feel special, and then have to walk back to the slum they came from, drop them off, and know that they are going to spend the night huddled up in a small ball in a dark corner somewhere trying to sleep, and it's a horrible, sickening feeling. But when you take the hand of a street child and tell them that today is the day, the day that they will never, ever have to go back to the streets, that you are going to get them something to eat, and then they are going to bathe. Then they are going to go home, to people who love them. And they will get to go to school. The glory of God revealed in that moment will take your breath away.

Like Abby, in our years of justice and mercy ministry God has repeatedly taken our breath away. You see, God promises particularly rich blessings for those who dedicate themselves to justice and mercy for the abused and oppressed. These abundant blessings prove this work is closest to God's heart. It is God's priority; he wants it to be ours. It is the indispensable mission of the church.

The following are just a few of God's rich promises.

"Blessed are those who have regard for the weak; the LORD delivers them in times of trouble. The LORD protects and preserves them—they are counted among the blessed in the land" (Ps 41:1–2; cf. Isa 56:1–2). This passage gives majestic promises of divine favor to those who use their power to support the vulnerable. This verse is very similar to Jesus's concise beatitude in Matthew 5:7, "Blessed are the merciful, for they will be shown mercy."

"Weak" in Psalm 41:1 (*dal*) refers to those who are low, poor, helpless (1 Sam 2:8; Ps 82:3). It is used by Amos of the weak whose heads are trampled on like "the dust of the ground" by powerful abusers (Amos 2:7; 5:11). David appears to write this lament psalm while suffering some type of illness (Ps 41:3–5). He reminds God that those who care for the weak are uniquely rewarded by God. He is counting on God to fulfill his promise since David needed these blessings (implying that he had been caring for the weak and could claim these rewards).

God promises to richly bless, deliver, protect, and preserve the one who has regard for the weak. The specific fulfillment of these blessings is unique to every person and situation. The point is that they are richly promised to the man or woman who prioritizes those who are vulnerable and suffering. "Whoever is kind to the poor [*dal*] lends to the LORD, and he will reward them for what they have done" (Prov 19:17). This is a radical proverb. When we show mercy to the vulnerable, we are doing it to God himself. He will richly reward those who show tangible mercy to the needy. This is similar to Luke 14:12–14, where Jesus instructs his audience to invite "the poor, the crippled, the lame, the blind" to their banquets. These destitute, suffering people can't reciprocate, but Jesus assures us that God will bless and repay those offering such care on the future resurrection day. The emphasis in both these texts is on tangible provision for those suffering from a lack of basic resources. As we have seen, Scripture does not view most poverty as the result of laziness or other character flaws but rather the result of systemic injustice and oppression. As Christopher J. Wright notes, oppression is "by far *the* major recognized cause of poverty" in the Hebrew Scriptures.[19] It is quite significant that the most common word used in the Old Testament for the poor is *ani*. It is used eighty times and most often denotes one who is oppressed by the rich and powerful (Isa 11:4; 32:7; Amos 2:7).[20] (Virtually the only place in the Old Testament where poverty is seen as a result of character flaws is in Proverbs, where the writer generally uses the word *mahsor* to describe the lazy poor; see Prov 6:11; 14:23; 21:17.) When we remember and aid the afflicted, God will remember and aid (bless) us.

I could cite many other biblical texts that promise unique blessings for those who prioritize justice and mercy for the abused and oppressed, but I've saved the best for last. Isaiah 58 (which Jesus draws on in Matt 25 when teaching about the final "sheep" and "goat" judgment) gives the most extensive list of blessings. The context is Israel's sinful hypocrisy. She went through the motions, observing daily religious practices such as fasting, yet God wasn't responding or blessing (Isa 58:1–3). God indicts Israel by highlighting the self-serving nature of her fasting. On the day Israel didn't eat to supposedly honor God, she dishonored the vulnerable. God's people were exploiting their workers and physically assaulting each other (vv. 3–4). In verses 6–7, God tells Israel what kind of fast he desires and will bless:

> Is not this the kind of fasting I have chosen:
> to loose the chains of injustice
> and untie the cords of the yoke,
> to set the oppressed free
> and break every yoke?
> Is it not to share your food with the hungry
> and to provide the poor wanderer with shelter—
> when you see the naked, to clothe them,
> and not to turn away from your own flesh and
> blood?

God's response to his own question is laser-focused on justice and mercy. These divine promises to those who heed this call are among the most effusive lists of blessings found anywhere in Scripture. God promises to the one who liberates the oppressed and cares for the afflicted (in vv. 8–12):

- "Your light will break forth like the dawn, and your healing will quickly appear."
- "Your righteousness will go before you, and the glory of the LORD will be your rear guard."
- When you call, "the LORD will answer." When you cry for help, he will say, "Here am I."
- "Your light will rise in the darkness, and your night will become like the noonday."
- "The LORD will guide you always; he will satisfy your needs in a sun-scorched land."
- "You will be like a well-watered garden, like a spring whose waters never fail."
- "Your people will rebuild the ancient ruins and will raise up the age-old foundations; you will be called Repairer of Broken Walls, Restorer of Streets with Dwellings."

This is a breathtaking list of blessings—healing, protection, fruitfulness, the divine presence, answered prayer, and restoration. God couldn't make it clearer that he delights in those who "pour [themselves] out" (v. 10 ESV) for the afflicted and make justice-and-mercy ministry a cardinal priority.

In summary, protecting the vulnerable and caring for the abused is one of the most significant moral obligations for all humans, particularly those who claim to follow the teachings of Scripture. However, not all Christian leaders clearly recognize or heed this biblical mandate. So how do pastors, trained in the Bible, change their paradigm? How do they come to recognize the reality of abuse and their responsibility to survivors? How can our churches become places of safety, protection, and care for the abused?

A CONCLUDING TESTIMONY

In the previous chapter, I shared how Pastor Brad compassionately listened to Sarah, the sex-trafficked young woman. Brad is now the vice president of a large mission agency. He has dedicated his life to serving Jesus and expanding God's kingdom through the local church. But his understanding of the church's mission has dramatically changed over the years. Brad grew up in the conservative evangelical church. He earned undergraduate and graduate degrees from a Christian university and a well-known evangelical seminary. He pastored evangelical churches for almost thirty years and spent decades immersed in institutions that declared Scripture as the inerrant, all-authoritative word of God. Yet he heard nothing about the biblical call to justice and mercy. Eventually, he realized he had utterly missed what Scripture *plainly* teaches—God unambiguously calls the church to prioritize justice and mercy for the oppressed and abused. This epiphany wholly transformed his life and ministry. What follows is Brad's story in his own words (and cited with his permission):

> For too long, my conservative evangelical background influenced my response (or lack thereof) to justice and mercy issues. Focused solely on vertical aspects of the gospel, the voices in my sphere proclaimed that attention to social issues was to stand opposed to God's "biblical" redemptive aims. In short, the good news was to be squarely centered on the eternal destiny of humanity. Societal maladies were to be handled by the "liberals" or, more candidly,

were of little concern considering "eternal" priorities. After all, Jesus said the poor would always be with us (Matt 26:11).

Of course, there were exceptions to the rule. If "our" political candidate needed us to rally or if our rights were viewed to be at risk, we could galvanize quickly. It seems we did believe in justice when viewing ourselves as the marginalized. I recall times when something inside me pushed back against this mindset, yet I did not pay attention. In the end, my heritage was not responsible for my inattention and inaction. I was culpable. The change began in the fall of 2008. I was serving on the pastoral staff of a church in Phoenix when I received an email invitation to attend a meeting to address underage human trafficking in our city. I was intrigued, but not really interested. The problem was the meeting was to be held less than a mile from my church. I could not think of an excuse to ignore the invitation. More significantly, I believe the Spirit of God urged me to attend. That Tuesday afternoon gathering caught me unaware and launched a deep transformation process within me. A mix of faith-based and wider community leaders were represented in both the audience and those presenting. Law enforcement, city leaders, and representatives from a Christian relief organization described the breadth of the problem and their collective response. It was clear a broad alliance had been formed to offer a compassionate, yet vigorous response to the need. This was further bolstered by the meeting being held at a church.

As I listened to accounts of child sex slavery and stories of those freed by law enforcement and assisted by beautiful individuals and organizations, I was stirred and inspired. The faith-based community was enthusiastically welcomed into the burgeoning coalition, which surprised me. Seldom had I seen such a wide range of people eager to work together toward a common objective. Our first responses say much about us. Given the complexities involved in societal issues, one can begin from any number of vantage points. What is the first thing that comes to mind? What are the initial words spoken? Is the first response concerning immigration about building walls, or is it to consider the trauma which induces travel along "the Devil's Highway" corridor of the Mexico-United States border?

While I have never heard God speak to me audibly, at times his call to me is no less clear. As the invitation was given for churches to become involved in the anti-trafficking movement, two thoughts simultaneously entered my thinking. The first was an overwhelming sense the church ought to be among the first to respond to the sexual exploitation of minors. The second—and it was as clear as if I had heard the words through a public address system—was if I did not care enough about this issue to become involved, I should pursue a different career. It was a moment of extreme clarity; a clarion call to extend pastoral care beyond the property lines of my church to the marginalized of my community. An invitation was extended to churches represented at the community forum. More faith-based communities were needed in the shared effort against child sex slavery in greater Phoenix. I immediately, inwardly committed myself and our church to the struggle that day. I did not know what that meant, but I knew I was "in" and that our congregation was somehow going to participate.

This began a decade-long pursuit of justice in the final years of my pastoral ministry in Phoenix from 2008–2019. The congregation I served graciously and enthusiastically allowed me to regularly highlight justice and mercy related themes and call for collective responses. We became thoughtfully involved in anti-human-trafficking efforts, foster family respite care, prostitution diversion, and other efforts to reach the sexually exploited. While we made our share of well-intentioned mistakes, our congregation grew in its love for the marginalized. These were among the most meaningful pastoral pursuits of my career.

The central Scripture passage in my journey has been Isaiah 58:6–12. While there are two thousand justice-related verses in the Bible, these seven have particularly informed my thinking. God's expectation of his followers to pursue justice for the oppressed and the promise of profound kingdom impact for those who do are complementary themes which have shaped my life for these past fifteen years. As I consider Isaiah 58, other biblical passages, and firsthand experiences since 2008, several lessons emerge:

1. Justice is not optional for followers of Jesus. "This is the kind of fasting I want" (Isa 58:6 NLT) sets bringing freedom and provision to the oppressed and needy as authentic worship, diametrically opposed to "the motions of penance" (58:5 NLT). Verse 6 is a precursor to the "pure" religion of James 1:27.

2. There is no competition between the vertical and horizontal aspects of the gospel; it all matters to God. God's kingdom purposes—including making things right for the marginalized—are to be pursued and experienced at some level in this life, while we anticipate full realization in the next.

3. Jesus's life demonstrates priority concern for the marginalized. The Gospels are replete with accounts of Christ's unswerving attention to those living in the shadows. His compassion for the oppressed is harmonious with the whole body of Scripture and reflects the Father's heart for the disenfranchised.

4. Justice-related activity often opens doors to share the gospel. Perhaps the "light" of Isaiah 58:10 extends beyond the realization of God's justice to a broader sense of his fame extending through the advocacy of his people. I have

engaged in many conversations about Jesus, faith, and spirituality that began with a shared interest in justice and mercy. While the evidence is anecdotal, this has happened too many times to be dismissed.

5. Engaging in justice-and-mercy ministry brings great peace and purpose because it reflects the heart of God. When I am active on behalf of the disadvantaged and abused, I feel congruence with a major theme of the Bible. Seldom have I felt surer about whether what I am doing is pleasing to God.

In this chapter, we have seen the robust divine mandate to care for the abused and oppressed. From a purely human perspective, this is an impossible task. In light of the prevalence and soul-shattering effects of abuse, how can one sustain a commitment to care for the abused? And in the end, is it even realistic to think that survivors can genuinely heal? The next and final chapter will explore God's commitment to heal, redeem, and restore. We will draw from the testimonies of abuse survivors themselves.

Chapter 11

GOD'S COMMITMENT TO HEAL, REDEEM, AND RESTORE

To what will you look for help if you will not look
to that which is stronger than yourself?
—C. S. LEWIS, *MERE CHRISTIANITY*

Praise be to the God and Father of our Lord Jesus
Christ, the Father of compassion and the God of
all comfort, who comforts us in all our troubles,
so that we can comfort those in any trouble with
the comfort we ourselves receive from God.
—2 CORINTHIANS 1:3–4

Celestia is one of the most Scripture-saturated people I know. She comes to God's Word for her daily sustenance. Then, because God doesn't waste anything, his Word—rooted deeply in her—feeds and comforts thousands more. For forty-two years, she has battled intractable pain from two degenerative diseases, one neuromuscular and the other neurological. She wakes every morning and trusts God for what she describes as a *million-dollar day*.

She recounts some of her journey in her own words:

I was a young counselor, naively unprepared for the ways I was about to be changed in this sacred work. I would arrive early to prepare every detail of my heart and office for the clients I quickly came to love. I knew God had sent each of them and carried a sober responsibility for their psychological and spiritual care. One by one, they came.

I would sit for hours in a well-worn green chair, listening. Each story was different yet eerily the same. As I leaned in to understand the source of their pain, I realized that it was most often rooted in an abuse of power by someone loved and trusted. Betrayal trauma is damaging enough all by itself, yet for most of my clients, the abuse that shattered their lives happened in a religious context. This spiritual layer of abuse took many forms—most of it involving faith leaders—parents, grandparents, Christian school teachers, pastors, or elders. It was horrifying to hear repeated stories of how these trusted authority figures used Scripture to shame and blame the actual victim(s) or, at best, not believe disclosures of abuse when their simple validation and advocacy would have made all the difference. A bit of courage could have saved the day.

In my clinical role, I was doing as much as possible to help yet not getting in front of the intergenerational fallout. I began to see that the systems impacting my clients needed education and transformation. I had a front-row seat to the problem but felt powerless to impact the larger community. My clients would leave my office and walk back alone into the same marriages, families, and churches that broke them.

It felt like a horror show. My soul was sinking. I was the helper, yet I needed help. It was 1996. I had so many questions and complaints: *Why wasn't there more support for churches and Christian organizations to understand, through a biblical lens, the non-intuitive effects of abuse?* Why wasn't there more accessible biblical *and* emotional support for survivors who couldn't afford high-quality Christian counseling? *Why weren't there more abuse prevention and aftercare resources that integrated Scripture, biblical data, and social science—all in one place?* **Why couldn't survivors get help in the safe churches they loved?** I felt complicit in it all. I needed direction and hope.

My ugly, unvarnished anguish finally erupted. I poured out confusion and grief as unfiltered prayer on the pages of my journal. My heart bled out on the right—God's words went on the left. I was well beyond faking anything pious or religious. If he didn't speak, I would turn the page and keep going. Light is the only cure for darkness. I knew: my Father of Light would come through in the end. When he spoke, I took detailed notes.

My chronological Bible reading was taking me through the minor prophets. I identified with their fiery passion for justice and deep sorrow over their people's suffering. Early one morning, I was reading Habakkuk and felt God's encouragement through the prophet's lament and God's responses to his pain. Like Habakkuk, I was stationed on my "watch post," which was my role as a counselor that gave me a unique view. I was hearing the stories most were not. And, like Habakkuk, I felt responsible for what I saw and now knew.

I copied the Lord's words in my journal: "I will take my stand at my watchpost and station myself on the tower, and look out to see what he will say to me, and what I will answer concerning my complaint. And the LORD answered me: '*Write the vision; make it plain on tablets, so he may run who reads it. For still the vision awaits its appointed time; it hastens to the end—it will not lie. If it seems slow, wait for it; it will surely come; it will not delay. . . .* The righteous shall live by his faith'" (Hab 2:1–3, 4 ESV, emphases added).

There's much more to tell, of course, but that is for another time. This was my starting place. For the first time in years, I saw a shaft of light through God's direction and promise to me. He had a plan that he would unfold one step at a time. I *was to do something with the stories I heard*—I didn't have to just sit with it anymore. Through this Scripture, he showed me that his people would come if I stepped out first. They would run with a community-based model of healing, which he would provide in his time. He was telling me to begin. To be patient. That the vision would be fulfilled because of his great, ever-abundant love.

As I write, Mending the Soul just celebrated her 21st birthday. Every year, thousands of people lock arms, working together to bring accessible trauma care in Jesus's name. Last year over 425,000 trauma survivors in Uganda and the Congo alone were served with MTS healing resources. Only God can do that! This is what I know: God delights in healing our brokenness. His word is our only sure source of truth and power. God's Spirit tells us what to do with it. He is always speaking to us. We just have to listen and follow. He does the rest.

Celestia's testimony illustrates numerous principles in this book: trauma survivors must saturate themselves in Scripture; God powerfully, lovingly speaks to his children through his Word; our intimacy with God is fostered when we bring our honest, raw pain and struggles to him in prayer. But beneath these essential principles is a bedrock conviction: despite all the pain created by leaders who fail to protect and aid the broken, our God is a benevolent healer and redeems pain. He will redeem all of it if we wrestle through it. God is infinitely more able and committed to healing and redeeming our wounds than we can imagine.

THE OVERARCHING THEME OF SCRIPTURE IS GOD'S PLAN TO HEAL, REDEEM, AND RESTORE

In chapter 1, Scripture is described as a *divine love letter*. From Genesis to Revelation, the Bible proclaims God's stunning commitment to restore shalom. We could trace this arc of restoration in numerous ways, particularly through the covenants that God initiated with his people and the dozens of prophetic promises of a coming Messiah. However, there is too much biblical data to reduce such a study to this final chapter.

A Shocking Genealogy

I've selected just one passage to illustrate this overarching healing and restoration theme. Matthew 1:1–17 records the genealogy of Jesus. It is compelling because it exposes the diverse, shocking ways God uses and transforms shame, abuse, and brokenness to restore his creation to its original beauty. At an initial glance, biblical genealogies are anything but stimulating reading. However, upon closer inspection, this genealogy is quite remarkable. It records not just Jesus's male ancestors but also five female descendants. In other biblical genealogies, women are rarely mentioned.[1]

All of the women mentioned in Matthew's genealogy are, from a Jewish perspective, scandalous and shameful: most are gentiles and thus not considered part of the covenant community of Israel. They were marginalized outsiders. All of these women had experienced deep sorrow and significant loss. Some had been shattered by abuse. This is simply not the "pretty" collection of matriarchs one would ever expect to produce the Savior of the world. By highlighting these five women, Matthew showcases God's commitment to healing and redeeming. Not only does God *not* recoil from those society deems unworthy and shameful, but he delights in using them to showcase his redemptive power and love.

Tamar, the "Prostitute" Daughter-In-Law

Tamar is the first of Jesus's ancestors mentioned in Matthew (1.3) and the first woman mentioned by name in the New Testament. Genesis 38 tells Tamar's story. Though Tamar was a probably a cursed Canaanite,[2] the patriarch Judah picked her to marry his son Er. Tragically, Er was evil and God struck him dead, leaving Tamar a widow. While Scripture gives us no details regarding the nature of Er's wickedness, it gives us all we need to know to feel gut-wrenching compassion for Tamar. One can only imagine the anguish and terror she experienced married to an evil man. While Er's death would have saved Tamar, it also created new challenges and burdens. Being a widow in the highly patriarchal world of the ancient Near East made her extremely vulnerable.

Furthermore, Tamar had no children, particularly sons, to carry on the family line. Having a future family lineage was extremely important in this culture. So, in keeping with ancient custom, Judah instructed the next-born son to sleep with his brother's wife. He could then fulfill his "duty to her as a brother-in-law to raise up offspring for your brother" (Gen 38:8). It isn't clear in the text whether Judah asked Onan to marry Tamar or simply to try to impregnate her. Onan was apparently happy to sleep with Tamar but strategized to keep her from getting pregnant. Impregnating Tamar would have reduced Onan's inheritance had she borne a son. Thus, "he spilled his semen on the ground to keep from providing offspring for his brother" (v. 9). God viewed Onan's callous greed as evil and struck him dead.

At this point, Judah promised Tamar that his next son, Shelah, would be given to her as a husband. However, Judah had no intention of doing so, fearing this son might die as well. Even though

Tamar was now part of Judah's household and under his care, he thoroughly dishonored Tamar by sending her back to her father. Susan Niditch notes the cumulative impact of Tamar's life experiences: "Tamar returns to her father's house, neither a virgin nor a wife nor a mother. She is on the fringes of the Israelite social structure, for nowhere does she properly belong."[3]

Tamar was in a scandalous and terrifying predicament in this ancient patriarchal world. She was utterly reliant on her deceitful, selfish father-in-law for protection and care, and yet he had callously sent her away. She was bound to an evil family, waiting for a husband who would never come. Yet she felt a duty to carry on her deceased husband's lineage by bearing a child. So she took matters into her own hands by disguising herself as a prostitute and positioning herself on Judah's route home. Her plan suggests that Judah's vulnerability to sexual temptation was predictable. He respected neither God nor women. The text states that as soon as Judah saw a woman he thought to be a prostitute, he immediately and crassly propositioned her: "Come, let me come in to you" (Gen 38:16 ESV). Tamar is depersonalized as a mere object for Judah's own sexual gratification. Sadly, being mistreated by males in this family was nothing new for Tamar. This is what she had known since joining the household. Most significantly, Judah, the patriarch of the family, didn't honestly know or care about Tamar. If Judah had known his daughter-in-law, her ruse would never have worked. But as David and Diana Garland perceptively note:

> Judah's blindness is not so surprising, however. He had never really seen Tamar as a person with needs and for whom he was responsible. He had made an early attempt to care for her by ordering Onan to lie with her. But evidently he never asked why no pregnancy ensued. He went through the motions just as Onan had. . . . He had never connected with Tamar, treating her as a

nonperson. It had been years since he sent her away. It is ironic that only now, when she was wearing a veil that he finally "saw" Tamar. As a sexual object—not a person—she attracted notice.[4]

Judah took the bait and had sex with her. Tamar's plot was successful, and she became pregnant with twin boys. Er's lineage would continue. Judah, upon hearing that his daughter-in-law was pregnant, harshly and hypocritically declared that she should be burned to death. Since Tamar was technically engaged, by custom, Judah declared his daughter-in-law an adulteress even though he had already determined not to give his youngest son Shelah to her in marriage. Little did Judah realize that in condemning her he was condemning himself. According to later Mosaic law, both parties in an adulterous relationship were to receive capital punishment (Lev 20:10). Once Tamar produced irrefutable evidence that Judah was the father of her child, he was forced to admit that Tamar was more righteous than him. While Tamar's scheme hardly sounds righteous to modern Western readers, one must consider the ancient world she lived in. She was not a prostitute in any real sense of the word. She was a woman on a bold mission to honor her deceased husband by giving him descendants. She was determined to overcome the strictures of an evil family that refused to fulfill their responsibilities. As Old Testament scholar Richard Davidson notes, in Genesis 38 "the biblical narrator positively characterizes Tamar."[5] Elsewhere in Scripture she is treated as honorable. She is cited in a blessing given to Ruth (Ruth 4:12), and King David honored Tamar by naming his daughter after her (2 Sam 13:1). There are many lessons we could draw from the life of Tamar. Her appearance in Jesus's genealogy highlights the fact that God's good redemptive plans are not thwarted by unjust marginalization, human evil, or family dysfunction. God delights in using humble, powerless people who have been shamed and pushed to the margins as agents of unimaginable blessing and healing.

259

Rahab, the Canaanite Prostitute

Rahab is the next woman mentioned in Matthew's genealogy (Matt 1:5). She is perhaps the most unexpected woman in the line of Jesus, being not just a cursed Canaanite but a prostitute (Josh 2:1–2). Prostitution was widely practiced in the ancient Near East and was socially acceptable to the extent that it was legal. But in these ancient communities, like the one Rahab lived in, prostitutes were generally held in low social esteem and "lived on the margins of society."[6] Rahab's inclusion in Jesus's genealogy is even more surprising, given that in Jewish and Christian tradition prostitution was forbidden (Lev 19:29; 1 Cor 6:16–18). It was considered highly shameful and sinful (Jer 3:1; Ezek 23:7). For instance, one could not give a gift to the temple if the proceeds were earned from prostitution; it was a polluted gift that God detested (Deut 23:18). Perhaps the supreme biblical condemnation of prostitution is found in Revelation, where it is used metaphorically of the supremely evil world power, Babylon, the source of earthly abominations (Rev 17:5).

However, Scripture does not focus on Rahab's demeaning occupation but on her faith (Heb 11:31; Jas 2:25). No one is beyond the scope of God's love and grace. God delights in honoring and using outcasts. The Gospel writers repeatedly showcase Jesus's love for the marginalized. He honored those whom society deemed shameful. He scandalized the religious elites by eating with tax collectors and "sinners" (Matt 9:10–13). He defended and praised a "sinful" woman, treating her with the utmost respect by allowing her to kiss his feet and anoint him with costly perfume (Luke 7:36–50). Jesus's religious opponents slanderously accused him of being "a friend of tax collectors and sinners" (Matt 11:19). In reality, this accusation was the greatest compliment they could have given him.

In summary, an ancient pagan prostitute such as Rahab is the last person one would expect in the line of the Messiah. And perhaps that is the point. God delights in redeeming, healing, and restoring, particularly those deemed most hopeless and worthless.

Bathsheba, the Voiceless Rape Victim

Bathsheba is the next woman noted in Matthew's genealogy (Matt 1:6). Notably, unlike the other four women, she is not referred to by name. Instead, she is listed simply as "the wife of Uriah" (ESV). Some might cynically argue that this wording demeans Bathsheba, viewing her simply as her husband's property. On the contrary, Matthew's wording strategically honors her, hinting at her victimization. Bathsheba has often been villainized and charged with seductively bathing on the roof of her home and luring King David into sexual sin. At best, she has been viewed as a willing adulterer. But this is not how Scripture describes what happened. Nowhere in Scripture is blame placed on Bathsheba. It falls squarely and solely on David. Second Samuel 11:1–12:25 recounts this incident. The focus throughout this passage is on David. Only once in the entire two chapters do we hear Bathsheba's voice, a mere three words in English, when she sends David a note, saying, "I am pregnant" (2 Sam 11:5). Even here, she is referred to as "the woman." Bathsheba is not pictured as a seductive vixen but as a voiceless, powerless victim.

The account of David and Bathsheba begins in 2 Samuel 11:1, right after David has had a great military victory over the Ammonites and Syrians. From the outset, David is the primary actor and agent. This chapter begins by ominously reporting that in the springtime, when kings lead their troops in battle, David is in Jerusalem. He is not just in Jerusalem in the spring but also in bed in the afternoon. The writer strongly implies that David is morally and psychologically unwell. He isn't where he should be, doing what he should be doing. This sets up the colossal tragedy that follows—David looks out his window and sees a beautiful woman bathing (v. 2). Ancient Israelites, lacking indoor plumbing, typically bathed on their roofs.

This was the usual custom. Bathsheba wouldn't have been seen by any of her neighbors. From his elevated view, only David could have seen her, and nothing in the text suggests she was aware of this. After seeing Bathsheba, David asks who the beautiful woman is. He is told that she is the daughter of Eliam, one of David's mighty men, and the wife of Uriah the Hittite (v. 3). This terse answer highlights two overlapping reasons David should have stopped dead in his tracks: she is married, and she is the daughter of one of David's most loyal "mighty men" (2 Sam 23:34). Sadly, in this moment morality, compassion, and loyalty were meaningless to David. He wanted what he wanted, and he would get it. So, he ordered his servants (possibly armed guards) to "take" (ESV) the woman to him in the palace (11:4). This Hebrew word used for "take" (*laqah*) is used elsewhere in Scripture for taking by force, capturing, and seizing.[7] When a monarch sent messengers to bring someone to him, they had little choice but to come.

Some have perceptively labeled what David did to Bathsheba as a "power rape."[8] As countless women from the dawn of human civilization have learned, there are many ways to force someone against their will into having sex. Blackmail, threats, or thunderous demands from all-powerful leaders can be just as effective as raw physical force. The biblical text nowhere condemns Bathsheba for having sexual relations with David. This chapter ends by telling the reader that "the thing *David* had done displeased the LORD" (2 Sam 11:27, emphasis added). The next chapter begins with God sending Nathan to confront *David*. Nathan uses a story in which Bathsheba is pictured as a powerless little lamb (2 Sam 12:4). Everything in this account speaks of Bathsheba's powerlessness and victimization.

Sexual abuse in all its forms is devastating. Bathsheba's losses were enormous. She lost her husband, her child, and life as she knew it. Yes, God, in his grace, gave her a new life as a queen in David's palace. She bore Solomon, a royal son. But her losses must not be minimized. As David and Diane Garland note: "No joyful wedding launched Bathsheba and David's family. Instead, they built a family on grief, on loss, on rape, on murder."[9] Even toward the end of her life, as David was near death, Bathsheba continued to face the devastating effects of others' choices, particularly her husband's. Because David was such a weak father, his son Adonijah arrogantly tried to wrestle the throne away from Solomon (1 Kgs 1:5–12). If he had succeeded, he would probably have had Bathsheba killed. Bathsheba's life hung in the balance due to powerful men's sinful choices.

In conclusion, Bathsheba's inclusion in Matthew's genealogy potently illustrates God's delight in redeeming the abused, empowering the powerless, and honoring the shamed. It turns out that Bathsheba was far more than the wife of Uriah and the helpless victim of a monarch. She played a critical role in bringing the Messiah into the world.

Ruth, the Hopeless Widow

The fourth woman in Matthew's genealogy is Ruth (Matt 1:5). For modern readers familiar with the story, the story of Ruth is typically remembered as a heart-warming romance with a very cheerful ending. It is all of that. But we must not lose sight of the fact that Ruth, like the previous three women, was an outsider who had suffered enormous losses. Apart from divine intervention, Ruth's story was bleak. Ruth was a Moabitess who had married a Judean man whose family had left their hometown of Bethlehem and traveled to Moab due to a severe famine. In the following decade, Ruth's husband, brother-in-law, and father-in-law all died. Her Moabite sister-in-law returned to their homeland of Moab. Ruth courageously chose to remain with Naomi, her mother-in-law, and return to Judah. Her future looked grim. She and Naomi were poor, landless widows reduced to gleaning in fields, hoping to gather enough grain the reapers had missed to be able to feed themselves. Ruth was highly vulnerable to being assaulted in the fields, something Naomi warned her about (Ruth 2:22; cf. 2:9).

Furthermore, Ruth was an outsider in a foreign land. Ruth's people group, the Moabites, owed their origins to an act of incest. After God's judgment on Sodom and Gomorrah, Lot's daughters, in their desperation to bear children, got their father drunk, hoping he would impregnate them. Their foul plan succeeded, and the firstborn daughter bore a son who became the father of the Moabites (Gen 19:30–37). This sordid story helps us understand why, in later Mosaic legislation, Moabites were not allowed to enter the Jewish assembly (Deut 23:3–4), and thus Jews were forbidden from marrying them. Despite being a disempowered gentile outsider with no reasonable hope for the future, God honored Ruth's godly character and faith. Like Tamar, Rahab, and Bathsheba, Ruth showcases God's delight in redeeming the hopeless.

Mary, the Unwed Mother

The final woman in Matthew's genealogy is Mary, the mother of Jesus (Matt 1:16). She is the only undisputed non-gentile listed in the genealogy. Like Ruth and Rahab, Mary exemplifies faith and obedience (Luke 1:38). Like the other women, her inclusion is unexpected. Mary was a poor, young teenager from an obscure village (Nazareth). And like most of the other women, her life was no doubt tainted with shame. While the Gospel accounts give sparing details regarding Mary's pregnancy, it is doubtful that her neighbors failed to do the nine-month math. She was engaged to Joseph, the final wedding ceremony had not been performed, and she was pregnant. There are hints later in the Gospels that Mary's pregnancy was scandalous. In John 8:41, when Jesus charges the religious leaders with not being true children of Abraham, they counter by asserting, "We are not illegitimate children," a not-so-subtle slander against Jesus's paternity. The fact that the inhabitants of Nazareth referred to Jesus as "the son of Mary" instead of the expected "son of Joseph" (Mark 6:3) also hints at Jesus's alleged illegitimacy. The shameful rumor that Jesus was conceived due to Mary's promiscuity persisted even after Mary's death. The second-century pagan philosopher Celsus suggested that Jesus was the illegitimate child of a Roman soldier named Panthera.[10] All this suggests that Mary experienced the stigma of sexual shame. Yet, God chose her to be the mother of the Messiah, the world's Savior. What a dramatic way to declare that God delights in using the powerless and the shamed to accomplish his greatest purposes.

I want to finish this chapter by sharing three powerful testimonies to illustrate how God heals, redeems, and restores.

GOD HEALS

Listen to your life. Listen to what happens to you because it is through what happens to you that God speaks. . . . It's in language that's not always easy to decipher, but it's there powerfully, memorably, unforgettably.
—FREDERICK BUECHNER, *LISTEN TO YOUR LIFE*

The New Testament presents the Christian life as an "already" but "not yet" experience. Healing begins when we come to Christ, but it will not be completed until we stand in God's presence (Rev 21:3–5). After training and caring for survivors for decades, we can testify that "not yet" does *not* mean "not much." We have repeatedly witnessed supernatural healing of the most extreme forms of complex trauma. From women in the US who were sold into prostitution by their parents, to massacre survivors in the Congo, to our own personal trauma healing, we testify that God is our healer. He delights in mending our brokenness and replacing our shame with dignity. He promises to "bind up the brokenhearted" (Isa 61:1) and to save those "crushed in spirit" (Ps 34:18). This rarely happens instantly. And it doesn't mean life goes on as if the abuse never happened. Healing from abuse trauma may mean that we carry some psychological scars. But as God does his healing work over time, our shame lessens and our dependency on Christ increases—and we can live whole, abundant, joyful lives of purpose. Healing from complex trauma rarely means we have no residual trauma scarring and triggers, but that the symptoms we carry no longer overwhelm us.

Many years ago, I was speaking at an abuse conference and struck up a conversation with a woman on the shuttle bus. Tina was a survivor of extreme domestic violence (she had to have her face surgically reconstructed after a severe beating). She recounted that she often shared her story at women's conferences like this one and would inevitably have nightmares before or after she spoke. She quickly responded when I sympathized with this: "Actually, I'm fine with the sporadic nightmares. I am in a very different place now than when my healing began. God has brought me so far. He has surfaced and healed many lies my abuser had drilled into me. I no longer carry the weight of shame. My trauma symptoms do not overwhelm me, and they don't define me. I know what to do when they surface." She said, "I'm glad that God has not completely removed my nightmares when I speak because they keep me connected to Jesus and to the hurting women he has called me to serve." Her compelling story is one of countless we have been privileged to hear. God delights in healing the broken.

GOD REDEEMS

Fear not, O Zion;
    let not your hands grow weak.

The LORD your God is in your midst,
    a mighty one who will save;
he will rejoice over you with gladness;
    he will quiet you by his love;
he will exult over you with loud singing.
I will gather those of you who mourn for the
    festival,
    so that you will no longer suffer
    reproach.
Behold, at that time, I will deal
    with all your oppressors.
And I will save the lame
    and gather the outcast,
And I will change their shame into praise
    and renown in all the earth.
(Zeph 3:16–19 ESV)

Tina's story demonstrates that God not only wants to heal abuse but wants to redeem it—use it for a bigger, restorative purpose. In his matchless wisdom and mercy, God delights in transforming the very things Satan and abusers perpetrate to destroy us. God loves to hijack the most painful, evil events and turn those very ashes into beauty (Isa 61:3). Evil is evil. We must not relabel or sanitize it. But God loves using the evil we've experienced to be a powerful source of redemption for others. This, in turn, gives new meaning to our suffering. In Scripture, Joseph epitomizes this principle. Born into a highly dysfunctional, polygamist family, he was mocked and scorned by his siblings. They eventually sought to murder him, but at the last minute his life was spared by being sold into slavery. In mere hours, he lost his freedom, family, homeland, and seemingly his future. Joseph spent years in an Egyptian prison for a crime he didn't commit. Despite all his losses and devastating trauma, God

THE HEALING ROLE OF SCRIPTURE

was working on his behalf. Later in life, after he had been restored to his abusive brothers, Joseph was able to look back on all that he had suffered and declare to his siblings who had committed great evil against him: "You intended to harm me, but God intended it for good to accomplish what is now being done, the saving of many lives" (Gen 50:20).

Unless you have experienced God's redemption of abuse, it may sound like a fairy tale. Many abuse survivors have a difficult time believing that these biblical principles of redemption apply to them. Their shame or the profound extent of their abuse may cause them to feel beyond the scope of healing and redemption. Thus, I find Alyssa's story particularly helpful.

We met Alyssa several years ago at a Mending the Soul trauma healing seminar we were conducting in Kigali, Rwanda. She wanted to learn the Mending the Soul model for teaching and mentoring in East Africa. Our training team had a wonderful time interacting with Alyssa. She is very engaged, compassionate, and attuned to others. She and her husband Mark are veteran missionaries with great wisdom and spiritual maturity. One could easily assume that Alyssa had a happy childhood and was a stranger to heartache and abuse. Nothing could be further from the truth. Alyssa embodies the redemptive power of God to heal from debilitating, chronic abuse and loss and to use it for great good. One of the primary ways God has redeemed Alyssa's family-of-origin pain is through the medicine of Scripture. Here is her condensed story (shared with her permission):

> I was a girl with too many fathers. Sixteen men auditioned for the role, yet none remained. My first father left me with his blue eyes. My second one taught me how to slurp Cream of Wheat and to separate marijuana seeds from their buds. He and I were committed to each other, but my mom found other men to enjoy,

so one night, my favorite dad returned me to my mom at an orgy. Then there was the father who moved us across the country in his 18-wheeler, high on handfuls of colorful pills. There was the young father whose age qualified him as my big brother and the one who cracked a wall with my mom's head. There was the father who slept most nights at the local bar and the big one who believed responsible parenting required beating me with his belt buckle.

Days before fleeing from the father with a gun, I had trusted in Christ to save me. He removed my shame for what I had done, but nothing had removed the shame from the things done against me. I survived my childhood, went to university, and began studying at a seminary. When I would discuss family structures with my classmates, their surprise at my history helped me see my story was not normal.

One of my classes required me to create a project based on a characteristic of God. Searching through the Old Testament, I began to notice the repeated mentions of "the fatherless." I studied every reference to see how God interacted with them and what this could teach me about his character. I learned that God's value for "the fatherless" was not based on their mother's moral choices or social position. Regardless of the mother, the lack of a father garnered special attention from God. In Psalm 10:14–18, I saw that the fatherless are among the afflicted and oppressed. God encourages them. He listens to their cries. He cares about their desires and defends them against those who would terrorize them. In Psalm 68:5, God reveals himself as the King of the universe who fathers the fatherless. He is not a distant authority but the founder of the world who claims unprotected children as his own.

When I was a child, I heard the whispers from good families who desired to keep their good children at a distance. I also listened to the shouts from upstairs windows when I walked down the streets of my small town. Everyone knew the shame of my deviant family. But as I studied the Scripture, my fatherless shame was dethroned by the God who faithfully claimed me as his child. I realized I am no longer listed among the outcasts and the shunned. The Bible showed me that I have a father who is present, faithful, and strong.

As I began trusting that God my Father would never leave me, he radically showed me that he listens to the desires and cries of the fatherless. A few years after the Scripture taught me that God is my Father, I was anxiously compelled to invite my birth father, the one with the blue eyes, to my upcoming wedding. This father came, but not alone. He was carrying his toddler son. Standing in my wedding gown in front of a man I could not distinguish in a crowd, I cried to God my Father, "Please, if there is any. . .!" I didn't know how to finish the request, but I desired that God my Father would protect this young boy. Thirteen months later, I received a phone call. The father with the blue eyes said, "Would you like to get to know your brother?" That same evening, this precious child moved into our home. A few days later, I was washing the dishes when he asked for my attention. I turned toward him, my eyes looking down to catch his. To my surprise, what started as his simple request became a new stage of my healing. I noticed his blue eyes reflecting my own and was overwhelmed with compassion for this little boy. In my heart, I cried out to God, "He didn't do anything to deserve this!" And my Father of the Fatherless responded to my heart, "You didn't either." God taught me lessons in his Word and brought me a child who looked like me. He answered the desires of this fatherless girl and set her in a family.

Satan did not have the last say in Alyssa's life. God is redeeming her horrific childhood. And he was using her story to heal and redeem her brother and countless others she now serves in Africa.

GOD RESTORES

I will restore to you the years
> that the swarming locust has eaten,
the hopper, the destroyer, and the cutter,
> my great army, which I sent
> among you.
You shall eat in plenty and be satisfied,
> and praise the name of the Lord
> your God,
> who has dealt wondrously with you.
And my people shall never again be put to
> shame. (Joel 2:25–26 ESV)

The context of Joel 2 is God's gracious commitment to heal and restore, even when the pain results from our sinful choices. (God sent a plague of locusts as corrective chastisement. Israel needed to turn from her destructive sin.) Since God is deeply committed to restoring us when our wounds are self-inflicted, he is every bit as committed to restoring us when others inflict our wounds. Often we experience a mixture—others sin against us, and we, in turn, make unwise and hurtful choices due to being wounded. God delights in restoration regardless of the cause of the destruction. Kelsey powerfully illustrates God's redemption of abuse survivors.

Kelsey is one of our Mending the Soul master trainers. Our Phoenix Seminary students and our African partners love her and give exuberant testimony of how her teaching has helped them. She is a true mental-health expert. She recently received a PhD in forensic psychology, doing her dissertation on evaluating the efficacy of the Mending the Soul trauma resources for former Congolese child soldiers. Kelsey has over twenty years of clinical experience working with trauma survivors in the juvenile justice system and in private practice. But despite all that training and experience, there was much more God wanted to teach her, much more God wanted to heal, and much more God wanted to restore. God used Scripture to be Kelsey's most powerful redemptive medicine! Here is her story (shared with her permission):

> I grew up in a physically and verbally abusive environment. I had three younger sisters. My parents' marriage was contentious, bitter, and dysfunctional. My mother had a severe trauma history from her childhood that prevented her from managing conflict in a healthy way. My father was aggressive and had an explosive temper. He was fired from nearly every job he had. My parents came to the Lord early in their marriage and became part of a legalistic Baptist church. Growing up, my dad could answer any question about the Bible and quote any verse. He was fond of Revelation and God's coming judgment. He would tell us Bible stories at night before bed. Ironically, my love of God's Word came from the seeds planted by my father's love of God's Word, although often taken out of context and twisted. He regularly listened to preachers on the radio. We'd be forced to listen to preaching on the way to church, crying in the car, as we'd just witnessed a physical fight between my parents or had been hit by my father. One of my earliest memories, which was uncovered decades later in a therapy session after I'd suffered a severe panic attack, was of my mother and us girls fleeing in our car as my dad chased us out of the house with a gun. We stayed at a shelter for some time.
>
> There were many occasions when my mother tried to leave my father. She sought counsel from pastors and elders at our different churches over the years, only to be told she had to stay because of the verse that said God hates divorce (Mal 2:16) and the passage in Ephesians about wives submitting to their husband's authority (Eph 5:22–24). They attempted Christian

counseling, only to be "affirmed" through Scripture that staying together was the biblical answer. My mother suffered greatly at the hands of well-intentioned but extremely misguided spiritual leaders. She fell into deep depression and made several suicide attempts that gravely impacted my sisters and me. My father would move out for brief periods, only to move back in, and the destructive cycle would commence again. In my early 20s, my mother finally divorced my father. They have lived separately ever since, remaining bitter and resentful toward one another. I cannot recall one kind or encouraging word between my parents the entire time I grew up. Over the years, my sisters and I wished and prayed my parents would get divorced, if only to end the ongoing cycle of violence and emotional turmoil in our home. But they were afraid to go against the "godly counsel" of the church.

In 2021, I began attending a new church that believes in the power of the Holy Spirit to heal miraculously. On one occasion in March of 2022, I sought prayer for physical healing. While being prayed for by some church members, one of the prayer partners asked how my relationship with my parents was. I wasn't sure what that had to do with my physical healing. He noted, gently and lovingly, that unforgiveness can, at times (not all the time), be the root of physical maladies. When he asked specifically about my relationship with my father, I stated that I hated him. Without judgment or using Scripture in a twisted way, he suggested I consider writing a letter of forgiveness to my father, not for my father's sake, but for mine. Where I usually would have bristled and become defensive, as Scripture had been used to coerce my mother into staying with my father, I felt a softening in my heart and knew this man was right in his suggestion. They continued to pray for my physical healing, but more than that, that I would be healed in my relationship with my father.

Several days later, with the continued prompting of the

Holy Spirit, I knew I needed to make time to write a letter to my father. I wrote over a page, thanking my father for the good things he instilled in me while wholeheartedly forgiving him for his wrongs. I felt free and light. I left the letter in the care of my mother to pass along to my father. In a strange turn of events, on the way to the hospital for a heart procedure, my father asked my mother to read the letter aloud to him over the phone; he feared reading it himself, not knowing what it might contain. My mother begrudgingly agreed. In the process of reading the words aloud, my mother was utterly undone by the spirit of forgiveness that was released by my words. Later that night, the Lord came to her in a dream and gently told her to give all her bitterness toward my father to him. She later said, "I had planned to live the rest of my life hating your dad. But it was a 'Saul to Paul' conversion. In one instant, all my bitterness and unforgiveness was gone." She felt the Lord telling her to help my father with his health issues. Overnight, my mother went from being critical, resentful, and bitter toward my father to being kind, patient, gentle, and loving. This sudden and complete change of heart rocked my entire family. Only the Lord could have done that level of "heart surgery" on my mother.

It surprised even my mother! She had no idea how she suddenly could be kind to my father. For the first time in thirty-eight years, I heard my mother speaking kindly to and about my father. They began getting along and spending time together, and my mother asked forgiveness from my father for how she had treated him over the years! My father told my sister that this change of heart in my mother had altered his world. His depression lifted, and he was "the happiest I've been my whole life. And it all started with that letter that Kelsey wrote."

Several months later, in September 2022, I got news of the most shocking miracle. After being divorced for nearly twenty years, my parents decided to remarry! This forever changed the trajectory of my family. My sisters and I, now all in our 30s, witnessed something no mind could conceive of: the power of forgiveness to set off a chain reaction that led to redemption that only Jesus could bring about.

I shared the testimony with my church, and they asked if they could record a video of my testimony to share. I willingly agreed. In response to that testimony, I regularly get people coming up to me and asking me to release the power of my testimony over them and their broken families. Just the other day, I had a man in my church share that watching the video of my family's healing gave him hope to pray for the same for his parents. He didn't know what was possible until he heard of God's faithfulness in my family.

The Scripture that God has given me in all this is Genesis 50:20: "You intended to harm me, but God intended it all for good. He brought me to this position so I could save the lives of many people" (NLT). The enemy meant to destroy our family through the abuse of my father, perpetuated by the misuse of Scripture in the church. But like Joseph, whom God redeemed from the pit and the prison to save the lives of many, God redeemed my family, and our testimony is being used to inspire and heal many. The comfort I have received from my heavenly Father has allowed me to comfort and bring hope to others with the same need (2 Cor 1:3–5).

As I reflect on my life and the years I cried out to God to save us from our situation, I now see he had a greater redemptive purpose. He heard the prayers of my childhood and "collected all my tears in [his] bottle" (Ps 56:8 NLT). God didn't condone our suffering, nor did he abandon us. He never left us. He protected us more than we will ever know this side of heaven. God indeed hated our suffering and will still hold my father accountable, but there is forgiveness. Forgiveness does not always equal reconciliation, although it did in my parents' case.

The abuse we suffered did not turn my sisters and me away from God. My sisters and I all follow and serve the Lord. He answered our prayers for salvation more than we could have ever imagined! My mother had resigned herself to a life of bitterness. He instead changed her heart in a way she never thought possible, giving her "beauty for ashes" (Isa 61:3 NLT). The kindness of God led her to repentance for her actions toward my father (Rom 2:4). While her actions did not cause my father's abuse, she took responsibility for her attitude and actions toward him in return. While my father doesn't "deserve" forgiveness or mercy from a human perspective, he received unmerited grace from my mother, which the Spirit of God empowered her to give. This is such a beautiful picture of what God has done for us. While we certainly never did (or will) deserve God's mercy and forgiveness, he freely gives it.

I can look back and see how Scripture was used to "poison" our family. But more significant than that, I can see how Scripture has been medicine to heal us! The power of God's words to heal, redeem, and restore is beyond human comprehension. He can do "far more abundantly than all that we ask or think!" (Eph 3:20 ESV). This verse is my anchor and my anthem to a hurting world!

INVITATION

Perhaps you, like Kelsey, have had Scripture weaponized against you. See this for what it is—a tragic, satanic distortion of God's love letter. Expect God to speak to you *from* his Word to heal the damage created *by* the perversion of his Word. Allow other brothers and sisters to accompany you in your healing journey. God is infinitely more committed to your healing than you can imagine. And until you take your last breath and stand in Jesus's presence, God will continue to heal the shattered pieces of your life. Your story matters and must be told.

Come! We welcome you into our Mending the Soul (MTS) family. Join a small group and heal in community. We're abused in relationships and will only heal in relationships. Then help us pass it on to the world.

> The place God calls you to is the place where your deep gladness and the world's deep hunger meet.
> —FREDERICK BUECHNER

> May God bless you
>   and keep you;
> may God's light shine upon you
>   and be gracious to you;
> May you feel God's presence within you always
>   and may you find peace.
>   (adapted from Num 6:24–26)

Appendix A

THE VALUE AND DIGNITY OF WOMEN

Learn this now and learn it well. Like a compass
facing north, a man's accusing finger always finds a
woman. Always. You remember that, Mariam.
—KHALED HOSSEINI, *A THOUSAND SPLENDID SUNS*

God made humans—men and women—in his image as relational beings.[1] Through our closest, most intimate relationships we can most closely see God. Male-female relationships in marriage have particular power to model the beauty of the Father, Son, and Spirit's intimacy. The covenant relationship of marriage is where God designed life to be created and nurtured. In light of the power of relationships, it's not surprising that Satan would strategize to pervert God's good plan. In a fallen world, relationships in general—and male-female relationships in particular—often reflect alienation and exploitation, which results in shame and pain. Genesis 3:16 predicted that the moment sin entered the world, men and women would experience discord and strife rather than loving unity. More specifically, the man would "rule over" the woman. Most Christian scholars recognize that "he will rule over you" does not reflect God's decree based on his desire. Instead, it's his prediction based on his perfect knowledge of the future. Due to human sinfulness and the tendency of those with greater power (physical, social, religious) to misuse that power against those who are weaker (Isa 1:15–17; Jer 22:3, 17; Ezek 22:7, 27–29), women are often the recipients of oppression and abuse. Throughout history, women have often been viewed as having little dignity or respect—as being inferior to men.

FEMALE INFERIORITY

Before we look at what Scripture has to say about women, we should note that in the ancient biblical world, Jews did not value women as they did men. The Mishnah, a second century AD collection of authoritative Rabbinic teachings, said this about women:

> Lots of meat, lots of worms; lots of property, lots of worries; lots of women, lots of witchcraft; lots of slave girls, lots of lust; lots of slave boys, lots of robbery. (m. Abot 2:7 [contrast Prov 31:10–31])[2]

One of the ancient Jewish religious books says this about women:

> Better is the wickedness of a man than a woman who does good; it is woman who brings shame and disgrace. (Sir 42:14 NRSV [contrast Rom 16:1–2])

One of the most respected ancient Jewish historians, a man who lived at the time the New Testament was being written, said this about women:

"Scripture teaches, 'A woman is inferior to her husband in all things.' Let her, therefore, be obedient to him." (Josephus, *Against Apion* 2.201 [contrast Gal 3:28; 1 Pet 3:7])[3]

Even though throughout history women have often been seen as having less worth and dignity than men, Scripture gives a completely different perspective. *It is essential that we form our views of women not from our culture but from God, the one who created men and women.* A survey of biblical teaching reveals that God has given women great value and dignity. We see this from the creation account, Jesus's treatment of women, and the teaching and practice of the early church. Let's begin where human history began: with the creation of the first man and woman.

CREATION

God looked at all he had made—including the woman—and pronounced it "very good" (Gen 1:31). The whole creation account teaches us that God made women with great value and dignity.

1. Man and woman are equally made in the image of God (Gen 1:26–27). When God created people in his own image and likeness, he created "male and female." Women are just as much made in the image of God as men. Actually, together as men and women we most fully show who God is.
2. Women are given great power by God over all of creation, which illustrates their value. The command to rule over creation is given to the man and to the woman jointly: "Let *them* rule over the fish of the sea. . . and over all the earth" (Gen 1:26 NASB; cf. v. 28, emphasis added).
3. The woman was made as an equal to Adam to serve *with*

him. No suitable helper is found for Adam, so God said, "It is not good for the man to be alone. I will make a helper suitable for him" (Gen 2:18). The Hebrew word for helper (*ezer*) does not mean a servant or slave for the man. This word is used twenty-nine times in the Old Testament, and almost every other time it refers to God being our helper (Exod 18:4; Ps 115:9; Hos 13:9). In the New Testament the Holy Spirit is said to be our "Helper" (John 14:16, 26; 15:26 ESV). So God is teaching us in the creation account that when he made the woman, he made an equal to complement the man—*not someone to serve the man but someone to serve* with *man as an equal.*

4. Adam saw Eve as a beautiful gift from God and as an equal. When God brought Eve to Adam he declared, "This is now bone of my bones and flesh of my flesh" (Gen 2:23). Adam was declaring that the woman was made from him and was his equal. She was not beneath him, nor was she inferior to him. The commentator Matthew Henry wrote, "The woman was *made of a rib out of the side of Adam*; not made out of his head to rule over him, nor out of his feet to be trampled upon by him, but out of his side to be equal with him, under his arm to be protected, and near his heart to be beloved."[4] The fall distorted healthy male-female relationships, tempting people to look at the other gender in unhealthy ways. In Genesis 3:16 God says that because sin had come into the world, the woman's desire will be for the man, but he will rule over her. This isn't a statement of God's desire but his prediction of what would happen in a fallen world. Women would be tempted to develop an unhealthy dependency on men (seeking to find in a man what only God can give), while men would be tempted to harshly rule over women.

JESUS'S TREATMENT OF WOMEN

Palestinian Jewish women in the first century couldn't give testimony in court, couldn't inherit property, weren't to be spoken to in public (even to family members), generally weren't allowed to study the law of Moses, and were almost universally understood to be inferior to men. Jesus went against the customs of his day by viewing and treating women with the greatest respect and kindness. Jesus repeatedly and forcefully rejected first-century Jewish patriarchy. Jesus touched (Mark 5:25–34; Luke 7:36–50), empowered (Matt 21:31; John 4:4–42), and taught women (Luke 10:38–42). The ancient rabbis said you shouldn't do any of these things because women were inferior to men. They said you shouldn't teach women the Scriptures; you shouldn't talk to women in public, even to your own mother; you shouldn't spend time with women, even your wife, for that was a waste of time. But Jesus did all of these things despite the fact that his ancestors said women were not to be valued this way.

1. Mark 5:25–34: Jesus touched the woman with a hemorrhage. He showed great compassion and respect to this woman.
2. Luke 7:36–50: Jesus allowed a "sinful" woman to kiss and anoint his feet. Again, Jesus is most kind and respectful to a woman despised by others. Jesus is criticized by the religious leaders for looking at "sinful women" with love and respect.
3. John 4:4–42: Jesus conversed with and received a drink from a Samaritan woman (which in Jewish tradition would have made him unclean, showing what a sacrificial act this was on Jesus's part). Jesus made one of his most explicit messianic claims to this immoral Samaritan woman, showing amazing respect for her.
4. Luke 10:38–42: Jesus praised Mary for sitting at his feet as a disciple, listening to his teaching, while Martha carried

out the traditional female domestic tasks of serving others. Jesus looked at women as spiritual equals who were worthy of studying the Scriptures alongside men.

5. John 20:17: Jesus chose women to tell of the resurrection. In other words, God chose women to be the first witnesses of the greatest event in human history. What is amazing about this is at this very time in Jewish society, a woman could not give testimony in court, because the Jewish leaders said that women were too emotional and not rational enough to be reliable witnesses. Jesus did not look at women that way. He trusted and valued them.

6. Luke 8:1–3: Jesus allowed women to join men as close disciples who traveled with Jesus. Among Jesus's earthly disciples we know seventeen by name, and eight of them were women and were part of his circle of devoted disciples: Mary his mother, Mary Magdalene, the other Mary, Mary and Martha of Bethany, Joanna, Susanna, and Salome.

THE EARLY CHURCH

In the early church, women were viewed as spiritual equals who should be valued and respected for their spiritual service alongside men.

1. Women waited in the upper room alongside the male disciples for the coming of the Spirit (Acts 1:14).
2. Women received the Spirit (Acts 2:2–4); Peter quotes Joel regarding women in the last days prophesying (Acts 2:17; Joel 2:28).
3. Women were authoritative spiritual leaders, for they delivered prophetic revelation (Acts 2:15–18; 21:8–9; 1 Cor 11:5).

4. Women were influential spiritual ministers in the early church (Acts 16:11–40; 18:26; Rom 16:1–15; Col 4:15).

   a. Priscilla was a key church leader and taught Apollos (Acts 18:26). Her name appears before that of her husband Aquila.

   b. Women helped found the Philippian church (Acts 16:11–40).

   c. Three women were leaders of house churches: Chloe (1 Cor 1:11), Nympha (Col 4:15), and Apphia (Phlm 2).

5. Paul treated women as equal partners in ministry (Rom 16:1–15; Phil 4:2–3). He mentions twelve by name (see Rom 16).

   a. He refers to four women as those who "worked very hard in the Lord" (Rom 16:6, 12: Mary, Typhena, Tryphosa, and Persis). This same description of working hard is used of the special work of the gospel ministry, including his own apostolic ministry (1 Cor 4:12; 15:10; Gal 4:11; Phil 2:16).

   b. He refers to them as coworkers (Phil 4:2–3: Euodia and Syntyche; Rom 16:3–4: Priscilla).

OTHER PASSAGES MISUSED TO TEACH THE INFERIORITY OF WOMEN

What about biblical passages that instruct women to submit to men (Eph 5:24; Col 3:18; 1 Pet 3:1) and say that husbands are created to be the "head" (1 Cor 11:3; Eph 5:23)? Don't these show that women are inferior to men?

It's our sinfulness that causes us to read these passages and conclude that men are superior and women are inferior. Headship doesn't mean *superiority*. We can prove this from Scripture. *The husband's role as "head" of his wife is not about power over her, but instead it's about responsibility for her.* Husbands and male pastors have a great responsibility to care well for the women God has placed in their lives. While the New Testament does affirm male leadership in the home and in the church, it's radically different from the common ancient (and modern) views of women as inferior to men.

1. Women are declared absolutely equal to men (Gal 3:28; 1 Pet 3:7). Peter goes so far as to say that husbands are to live with their wives and treat them with respect as the weaker partner (probably a reference to their physical weakness) and as heirs of the gracious gift of life, so that nothing will hinder the husbands' prayers. In other words, God so values women and expects their husbands to do the same that if the husband doesn't respect and value his wife and live with her in an "understanding way," God will not answer that man's prayers.

2. The husband is no longer declared the ultimate authority, Christ is (Col 3:18). Furthermore, Christ declared that hierarchical power structures, in which the ruling classes assert their authority over those under them, is the way of pagans, not Christians. Spirituality is expressed in humble service rather than in ruling over others. Notice how plainly Jesus teaches this in Matthew 20:25–28:

> Jesus called them together and said, "You know that the rulers of the Gentiles lord it over them, and their high officials exercise authority over them. Not so with you. Instead, whoever wants to become great among you must be your servant, and whoever wants to be first must be your slave—just as the Son of Man did not come to be served, but to serve, and to give his life as a ransom for many.

3. Godly Christian leaders use their position to meet others' needs rather than their own (Gal 5:13; Phil 2:3–4).

   In several passages that affirm male leadership, mutual deference is emphasized. Yes, wives are to submit to their husbands, but Paul also says husbands are to submit to their wives (1 Cor 7:1–5; Eph 5:21). Godly leadership in the home and the church means putting others' needs—including our wives' needs—above our own. This is the idea of Philippians 2:3–8:

   > Do nothing out of selfish ambition or vain conceit. Rather, in humility value others above yourselves, not looking to your own interests but each of you to the interests of the others.
   >
   > In your relationships with one another, have the same mindset as Christ Jesus:
   >
   > Who, being in very nature God,
   >   did not consider equality with God something
   >   to be used to his own advantage;
   > rather, he made himself nothing
   >   by taking on the very nature of a servant,
   >   being made in human likeness.
   > And being found in appearance as a man,
   >   he humbled himself
   >   by becoming obedient to death—
   >   even death on a cross!

4. Since male headship is explicitly said to be patterned after the Father's headship over the Son (1 Cor 11:3), and the Father exercises his headship over the Son by strategically honoring, loving, and sharing authority with the Son (John 5:18–24), husbands and male church leaders should give the utmost

attention to finding ways to strategically honor, nurture, and lift up women.

5. Most importantly, in a context clarifying what male headship means, men are to love their wives as Christ loved the church. This is specifically explained by Paul in Ephesians 5:25–33 in terms of sacrificing, nurturing, and caring for her even to the point of death. Men are to be to their wives what Jesus is to the church—"in the same way" they are to love their wives as their own bodies.

SUMMARY

In our sinful world, women are often treated with disrespect because they are seen as inferior to men. God's Word shatters this view of women. We're to view women as God does: precious equals made in God's image who deserve love and respect. To treat women as inferiors, to dishonor them, or to mistreat them is to dishonor the God whose image they bear. Dishonoring women also dishonors Jesus who loves women, respects them, and died for them. He is the model for how husbands are to treat their wives.

Appendix B

LIES EXPOSED, GOD'S TRUTH REVEALED

Satan lies to us, and his lies are engineered to distort the best of what God's created in us.[1] Jesus declares this about Satan: "He was a murderer from the beginning, not holding to the truth, for there is no truth in him. When he lies, he speaks his native language, for he is a liar and the father of lies" (John 8:44). The toxic shame that he creates in us as a result of our abuse or abandonment is pervasive and seems frighteningly real. God's Word—which contains the truth about God's love for us and the beauty he's created in us—is our only guide for identifying and healing these destructive and deceptive beliefs about ourselves, and others. Read through the lies below—some of them may be familiar to you. The Scripture references show why these statements, if spoken by Christians, are lies. So reflect on the truths of these Scripture passages. Once you understand and begin to embrace God's truth, you can begin to rebuild your relationship with God and with others.

LIES ABOUT GOD

- **I can't trust God because he allowed me to be abused.**

  THE TRUTH:

  Isaiah 63:9—*When I suffer, God suffers. He cares for me as his child, and because of his love and pity, he's working on my behalf.*

  Psalm 5:5–6—*God hates the abuse I experienced, and he will severely judge my abuser unless he or she repents.*

- **God despises me.**

  THE TRUTH:

  Psalm 103:10, 12–13—*God does not deal with me according to my sins. He removes my sin as far as the east is from the west. He's my loving Father who is understanding and compassionate toward his weak children.*

  Romans 8:31–39—*God loves his children (including me) with a perfect love. Because he gave up his Son, Jesus, for me, no one can condemn me or accuse me. God is the one who declares me forgiven and sees me as his own, chosen child. Nothing whatsoever can separate me from the love of God.*

- **God is distant and uninterested in me.**

  THE TRUTH:

  Psalm 34:18—*God is near me when I am brokenhearted and saves me when I am crushed in spirit.*

  Matthew 10:30—*God cares and knows everything about me— even the number of hairs on my head.*

- **God is disgusted with me when I fail. Sooner or later, he'll leave me.**

  THE TRUTH:
  Zephaniah 3:17—*God delights in me as his child even though I still sin. God rejoices and sings over me and calms me with his love.*

  Hebrews 13:5–6—*God has promised that he will never leave me or forsake me.*

  Hosea 11:8–9—*Just as God never gave up on sinful Israel but continued to love her even when she failed him, God will never leave me, even when I fail.*

- **God wants to punish me and is angry with me.**

  THE TRUTH:
  Romans 8:1—*There is no condemnation for me because I am in Christ Jesus.*

  Romans 5:1—*Because I have been justified by faith, I have peace with God through my Lord Jesus Christ.*

- **God will only accept me if I'm good.**

  THE TRUTH:
  Titus 3:5—*I'm not saved by works of righteousness, but instead it is his mercy that has saved me.*

  Luke 15:1–32—*Because Jesus is a friend of sinners and seeks out the lost, I know that Jesus loves and accepts me not based on my goodness but based on* his *goodness.*

- **Sooner or later God will reject me, too.**

  THE TRUTH:
  Philippians 1:6—*I can be certain that God began a good work in me and will bring it to completion at the day of Christ's return.*

  Psalm 94:14—*God promises that he will never reject or forsake his people, and that includes me, because I've trusted in Jesus to be my Savior.*

- **God loves others more than me. I'm unlovable.**

  THE TRUTH:
  1 John 4:10—*This is love: not that I first loved God but that he first loved me and gave his Son to satisfy God's anger toward my sin.*

  Ephesians 2:4–7—*Even when I was dead in my sin, God loved me, because he is so rich in mercy. He delights in me because of Jesus, and he'll continue in the coming ages to show his rich grace and kindness toward me.*

- **God can't forgive some of the things I've done.**

  THE TRUTH:
  1 John 1:9—*If I confess my sin, God is faithful to forgive all my sin and cleanse me from all unrighteousness.*

  Psalm 32:1–2, 5—*No matter what terrible sins I have committed, God has promised to completely forgive and cleanse me as soon as I confess my sin to him.*

LIES ABOUT OTHERS

- **Others say I'm worthless, so I must be.**

  THE TRUTH:

  Romans 8:31–39—*God declares me to be his precious child. He gave his Son for me, proving how much worth I have to him. God unconditionally loves me, and nothing in heaven or on earth can separate me from his love.*

  1 Peter 2:9—*I am part of God's royal priesthood, his chosen nation and special possession. I do not need to listen to false voices that slander me and say I have no worth.*

- **In order to be accepted by others, I must be perfect.**

  THE TRUTH:

  1 Thessalonians 5:14—*Godly believers help the weak and are patient with everyone.*

  Colossians 3:12–14—*Healthy Christians don't expect perfection from others—instead, they love as God does. Thus, they are kind, forgiving, and patient with imperfect sinners like me.*

- **People will only hurt you or leave you. No one can be trusted.**

  THE TRUTH:

  Proverbs 17:17—*There is a true type of friend who loves you at all times and stays with you in times of trouble.*

  Proverbs 18:24—*Some friends are unreliable, but there are true friends who stick closer to you than a blood brother.*

- **Women are all the same; they only want your money.**

  THE TRUTH:

  Proverbs 31:10–12—*A godly woman is completely trustworthy— she loves God and her family and always does good to her husband.*

  Proverbs 12:4—*Some women are untrustworthy and can bring harm, but a godly woman brings great blessing to her husband.*

- **No sane person would ever want me.**

  THE TRUTH:

  Ephesians 2:10–19—*I am God's beautiful handiwork. He has given me gifts with which to bless others. Even though some people are not interested in me because of my background, gender, or ethnicity, in Jesus I have new brothers and sisters. We're fellow members of God's household. So godly fellow believers will want to know me and have healthy relationships with me.*

- **Men only want me for sex.**

  THE TRUTH:

  1 Timothy 5:1–2—*While some men only want to take from women, godly men treat women like me with respect and complete purity.*

- **Sooner or later people will find out the truth about me and reject me.**

  THE TRUTH:

  Luke 7:34–50—*Jesus is a friend of sinners like me, and he loves us even though he knows the truth about us.*

  James 5:16—*In a healthy Christian community, I can be honest about my struggles. When I confess my sins, others will pray for me and help me.*

1 John 4:10–11—*Jesus's followers have been loved by God despite their sin and are to love other people the same way they have been loved. So a godly believer will not reject me when he or she learns the truth about my struggles.*

LIES ABOUT MYSELF

- **I must have deserved my abuse.**

THE TRUTH:
Psalm 11:5–7—*No one deserves to be abused, because God hates abuse and evil abusers. God loves it when people are treated properly, and he will judge abusers.*

- **I have nothing to offer others.**

THE TRUTH:
1 Corinthians 12:7–11—*God has given me spiritual gifts with which to bless the body of Christ.*

1 Corinthians 12:14–30—*Even though I may feel that my gifts and abilities are small and unimportant, God says that I'm needed by the body of Christ just as much as those with showy, powerful abilities.*

- **I'm only important if I'm beautiful, superior, or successful.**

THE TRUTH:
1 John 3:1—*I am important and have worth because I am a child of the King.*

1 Samuel 16:7—*Humans look on outward appearance, but God looks on the heart.*

- **I should never have been born.**

  THE TRUTH:
  Psalm 139:13–17—*God uniquely created me while I was still in my mother's womb. He delights in me.*

  Jeremiah 29:11—*God has good plans for my life.*

  Ephesians 3:20—*God wants to do more than I can dream of in my life, because he's the one working in me.*

- **I must do everything right to be accepted.**

  THE TRUTH:
  Ephesians 1:3–5—*Even though I was spiritually dead in my sins and following the path of the world and Satan, God by grace chose me before the world began, and because I have trusted in Jesus, God has adopted me to be his own son or daughter.*

  Romans 15:7—*Healthy Christians accept each other as God accepts us: by grace and not by our works.*

- **I deserve to be punished.**

  THE TRUTH:
  Isaiah 53:5–6—*Jesus suffered the punishment I deserved—my sin was laid on him so that I could and do have peace with God.*

  Romans 8:1—*There is no condemnation or punishment for me, because I have a relationship with Jesus.*

- **I can't be a Christian if I've done _____.**

  THE TRUTH:
  1 Corinthians 6:9–11—*Even if I was sexually immoral, a*

drunkard, or a thief, because I've trusted Jesus, God has cleansed me from my sins and declares me to be righteous.

1 Timothy 1:13–16—*Even if I was the chief of sinners and blasphemed God and murdered his people, Jesus came for sinners and saved me because of my faith in Jesus.*

- **I'm evil.**

THE TRUTH:
Romans 1:7—*I, like all others who have placed their faith in Jesus, am loved by God, and he calls me one of his holy people.*

Romans 3:21–26—*God has justified me and made me righteous in Christ. This means that when God looks at me, he doesn't look at me as evil but sees Jesus's righteousness given to me.*

- **I'm a worthless sinner.**

THE TRUTH:
John 15:15—*I am a friend of Jesus, because Jesus calls his followers his friends.*

Colossians 3:12—*Because I have trusted in Jesus, God says I'm part of his chosen people, holy and dearly loved.*

- **I'm a hopeless case; I can never change.**

THE TRUTH:
Philippians 4:13—*I can do all things through Christ who gives me strength.*

Ephesians 1:13–14—*The Holy Spirit permanently lives in me to sanctify me. This is God's proof that God will complete his good work in me.*

- **I'm inferior to others and always will be.**

  THE TRUTH:
  Romans 8:15–17—*God has adopted me as his own child. I am his heir and a joint heir with Jesus. So I am special because I am a child of the King and have the King's blessings.*

- **I'm disgusting and sinful because I have sexual desires.**

  THE TRUTH:
  Genesis 1:26–28; 2:24–25—*God is the one who gave me my gender and made me a sexual being. Sexual desire in itself is normal.*

  1 Corinthians 7:1–5 and Hebrews 13:4—*The satisfaction of my sexual desires in marriage with my spouse is healthy and blessed by God when it expresses our love for each other.*

Pay attention to the truth of God's beautiful design revealed in his Word. No matter the lies that Satan might whisper in a survivor's ear, God's truth remains. We may cling to that amid the darkness of trauma. For healing to occur, we must acknowledge the truth about God, others, and ourselves.

NOTES

Chapter 1: The Richness of Scripture

1. J. Lenow, J. Cisler J, and K. Bush, "Altered Trust Learning Mechanisms among Female Adolescent Victims of Interpersonal Violence," *Journal of Interpersonal Violence* 33 (2019): 159–79, and Johanna Hepp et al., "Childhood Maltreatment Is Associated with Distrust and Negatively Biased Emotion Processing," *Borderline Personality Disorder and Emotion Dysregulation* 8 (2021), available at https://doi.org/10.1186/s40479-020-00143-5.

2. m. Yadayim 3:5.

3. Walter Bauer, Frederick W. Danker, William F. Arndt, and F. Wilbur Gingrich, *A Greek-English Lexicon of the New Testament and Other Early Christian Literature*, 3rd ed. (Chicago: University of Chicago Press, 2000), 206. In the New Testament *graphē* is often used of Scripture in its entirety (Matt 21:42; John 10:35; Rom 15:4; 2 Pet 1:20), as it is in 2 Tim 3:16.

4. The Greek word *pherō* means here "to carry along" and is the same verb used in Acts 27:15 of the terrible storm that drove or carried the ship through the sea.

5. The quoted texts include Pss 2:7; 45:6–7; 102:25–27; 104:4.

6. Matt 21:42; Luke 24:27.

7. See also Gal 1:11–12; 1 Thess 2:13; Rev 1:10–11.

8. Eckhard Schnabel, "Pharisees," in *The New Interpreters Dictionary of the Bible*, vol. 4, ed. Katherine Doob Sakenfeld (Nashville: Abingdon, 2009), 486. Paul's description in Acts 22:3 of his Pharisaical roots, that he was educated with an *akribeia*, or precise, strict understanding of the law, lends weight to this understanding of the meaning of "Pharisee."

9. For a very insightful discussion of some of the ways Revelation 22:1–5 pictures the reversal of the fall and a completion of and advancement on the shalom experienced in Eden, see G. K. Beale, *Revelation: A Shorter Commentary* (Grand Rapids: Eerdmans, 2015), 497–505.

10. See, e.g., Neh 9:17; Pss 103:8; 145:8; Jer 32:18–19; Lam 3:32; Dan 9:4; Joel 2:13; Jonah 4:2; Nah 1:2–3.

11. Michael Goheen and Craig Bartholomew, *The True Story of the Whole World: Finding Your Place in the Biblical Drama* (Grand Rapids: Brazos, 2020). Goheen and Bartholomew give a fuller version of their model in *The Drama of Scripture: Finding Our Place in the Biblical Story*, 2nd ed. (Grand Rapids: Baker Academic, 2014).

12. Goheen and Bartholomew, *True Story of the Whole World*, x, quoted from "Our World Belongs to God: A Contemporary Testimony," Christian Reformed Church (Grand Rapids: Faith Alive Resources, 2008), para. 18.

13. Derek Kidner, *Psalms 73–150* (Downers Grove, IL: InterVarsity Press, 1975), 452.

14. Most likely Ps 119:1–2 harkens back to the summary of the entire book of psalms found in Ps 1:1–3: "Blessed is the one / who does not walk in step with the wicked / or stand in the way that sinners take / or sit in the company of mockers, / but whose delight is in the law of the

NOTES

Lord, / and who meditates on his law day and night. / That person is like a tree planted by streams of water, / which yields its fruit in season / and whose leaf does not wither— / whatever they do prospers."

15. By "live out" I am referring to the wide range of attitudes and actions the author uses to describe his relationship with and response to Scripture, including delighting in (vv. 16, 92), meditating on (vv. 15, 27), setting his heart on (v. 30), loving (v. 140), putting his hope in (v. 43), memorizing (v. 11), obeying (v. 8), reciting (v. 13), doggedly following (v. 33), and rejoicing in (v. 162).

16. For a treatment of this concept as applied to biblical teaching on sexual morality for singles, see Steven Tracy, "Chastity and the Goodness of God: The Case for Premarital Sexual Abstinence," *Themelios* 31 (2006): 54–71.

17. Cornelius Plantinga, *Not the Way It's Supposed to Be: A Breviary of Sin* (Grand Rapids: Eerdmans, 1995), 14.

18. For further development, see Steven and Celestia Tracy, *Mending the Soul: Understanding and Healing Abuse*, 2nd ed. (Grand Rapids: Zondervan, 2023), 41–44, 80–83.

19. See also the abuse and threats identified or implied in Ps 119:21, 61, 69, 86, 146–50.

20. E.g., Gen 12:10–15; 21:9–21; 1 Sam 2:22; 2 Sam 11; Jer 20:1–2; 26:8; Mic 2:8–9.

21. Individual lament psalms include Pss 3, 4–7, 13, 17, 22, 26, 31, 35, 39, 40–43, 52, 54–55, 58–59, 64, 69, 70–71, 77, 83, 86, 88, 109, 142–43. Communal lament psalms include Pss 12, 44, 60, 74, 79–80, 89, 94, 126, and 137.

22. My presentation was published as "Abortion, the Marginalized, and the Vulnerable: A Social Justice Perspective for Reducing Abortion," *Cultural Encounters* 6 (2010): 23–33.

Chapter 2: Principles for Interpreting Scripture: Part 1

1. Donald Bloesch, *Holy Scripture: Revelation, Inspiration and Interpretation* (Downers Grove, IL: InterVarsity Press, 1994), 179.

2. The presenter at this conference was Richard B. Hays. He brilliantly articulates his hermeneutics of suspicion and trust in "Salvation by Trust? Reading the Bible Faithfully," *The Christian Century*, February 26, 1997, 218–23.

3. While this African pastor's interpretation of Psalm 45 is much more common among African than Western Christians, there are Americans who make this same argument. See "Why Christian Women Should Bow to Their Husbands," Biblical Gender Roles, Sept. 7, 2022, https://biblicalgenderroles.com/category/biblical-obeisance.

4. Some believe Paul is only prohibiting women in this congregation from interpreting prophecies; see 1 Cor 14:29. The prohibition against women may well be an occasionally generated one based on disorder in the assembly, perhaps led in this case by some particularly unruly Corinthian women (see 14:31–33, 34, 40).

5. See James White, "Harold Camping," Christian Research Institute, April 14, 2009, www.equip.org/articles/harold-camping.

6. Origin developed the widely utilized quadriga, which views Scripture as having four layers of meaning: the literal (plain), moral (how we are to act), anagogical (what relates to our heavenly future), and allegorical (that which relates to doctrine).

7. Scott Smith, "The Hidden Throne of Israel & The Blessed Mother," The Scott Smith Blog, July 24, 2017, www.thescottsmithblog.com/2017/07/the-hidden-throne-of-israel-blessed.html.

8. Augustine, *The Good of Marriage* 3, 15.

9. Rebecca Davis, "Jesus Didn't Have Boundaries, So I Shouldn't Either," heresthejoy.com, January 31, 2022, https://heresthejoy.com/2022/01/jesus-didnt-have-boundaries-so-i-shouldnt-either.

10. Daniel New, "The Old Testament Shepherd Was No Wimp," February 2004, www.danielnew.com/dn021504.shtml.

11. Matthew Mantooth, "The Call of Our Shepherd's Psalm 23," Sermons by Logos, https://sermons.logos.com/sermons/46839-the-call-of-our-shepherd's-psalm-23.

Chapter 3: Principles for Interpreting Scripture: Part 2

1. Manfred Brauch, *Abusing Scripture: The Consequences of Misreading the Bible* (Downers Grove, IL: Intervarsity Press, 2009), 15–16.
2. We should note that Scripture ultimately has two authors, human and divine (2 Pet 1:21). In arguing for the identification of the human author's most likely meaning, I am not asserting that the human author fully understood what the Holy Spirit was guiding him to write. It is uncertain how fully the prophets and psalmists understood that their prophecies applied to Christ, the ultimate Son of David. The point here is that we must begin with identifying the author's most likely intended meaning and work from there based on the entirety of Scripture.
3. *ESV Study Bible* (Wheaton, IL: Crossway, 2008), s.v. Genesis 41:57.
4. Doug Phillips, "The Return of the Daughters: A Vision of Victory for the Single Woman of the 21st Century," a documentary film directed by Anna Sophia and Elizabeth Botkin (Western Conservatory of the Arts and Sciences, 2007), cited by Rebecca Davis, *Untwisting Scriptures That Were Used to Tie You Up, Gag You, and Tangle Your Mind, Book 2: Patriarchy and Authority* (Greenville, SC: Pennycress, 2021), 41–43. It should be noted that Phillips resigned from the now defunct Vision Forum after an admission of an inappropriate relationship and allegations of sexual abuse.
5. Numerous biblical texts undermine this type of patriarchy. For instance, Adam *and* Eve were given authority to rule over creation (Gen 1:28). Fathers *and* mothers have parental authority in the home (Prov 6:20). In the early church men *and* women received divine revelations (Acts 2:15–18). For additional biblical data, see appendix A.
6. For a survey of various evangelical understandings of the role of the Mosaic law in the life of the New Testament believer, see Stanley N. Gundry, ed., *Five Views on Law and Gospel* (Grand Rapids: Zondervan, 1996).
7. Gordon D. Fee and Douglas Stuart, *How to Read the Bible for All Its Worth*, 4th ed. (Grand Rapids: Zondervan, 2014), 174.
8. Leland Ryken has written a series of short books on various biblical genres. See, e.g., his volumes in the Reading the Bible as Literature series published by Lexham Press.
9. Fee and Stuart, *How to Read the Bible*, 110.
10. Aminata Coote, "Ahasuerus & Vashti: Signs of a Disrespectful Wife," Hebrews12Endurance.com, https://hebrews12endurance.com/ahasuerus_and_vashti.
11. Rebecca Hopkins, "Like Father, Like Son? Allegations Surface Against Father of Accused Oregon Megachurch Pastor," The Roys Report, September 2, 2021, https://julieroys.com/jon-courson-alleged-sexual-misconduct-applegate.
12. Scott Duvall and Daniel Hays, *Grasping God's Word: A Hands-On Approach to Reading, Interpreting, and Applying the Bible*, 3rd ed. (Grand Rapids: Zondervan, 2012), 375.
13. T. J. Malcangi, "Here's What God Promises Through Psalm 91 . . . You Need to Watch This," www.youtube.com/watch?v=3vJcWscgcao.
14. Bill Fullilove, "When the Psalms Promise Too Much," The Washington Institute, https://washingtoninst.org/when-the-psalms-promise-too-much. See also Luke 21:16–18: "You will be betrayed even by parents, brothers and sisters, relatives and friends, and they will put some of you to death. Everyone will hate you because of me. But not a hair of your head will perish."
15. Tremper Longman III, *Proverbs*, Baker Commentary on the Old Testament Wisdom and Psalms (Grand Rapids: Baker Academic, 2006), 231.
16. An example of a proverb that is always true is Prov 11:1: "The LORD detests dishonest scales, but accurate weights find favor with him." Other Scripture helps us make this assessment.
17. "Abuse in the Family," Bay Area Ministers of Reconciliation, https://ministersofreconciliation.org/abuse-in-the-family.
18. "Abuse in the Family."
19. Pat Robertson, *Bring It On: Tough Questions, Candid Answers* (Nashville: Thomas Nelson, 2002), 53–54.

NOTES

Chapter 4: Passages on Marriage

1. Much of the following discussion of Ephesians 5:24 is drawn from Steven Tracy, "What Does 'Submit in Everything' Really Mean? The Nature and Scope of Marital Submission," *Trinity Journal* 29 (2008): 285–312.
2. Ruth Tucker, *Black and White Bible, Black and Blue Wife: My Story of Finding Hope After Domestic Abuse* (Grand Rapids: Zondervan, 2016), 22.
3. Lundy Bancroft, *Why Does He Do That? Inside the Minds of Angry and Controlling Men* (New York: Putnam, 2002), 50–59, 62–64.
4. For specific accounts from professionals (theological, mental health, law enforcement) as well as abuse survivors of how biblical-submission teaching is often used to justify abuse, see the video produced by Day of Discovery, *When Love Hurts: Understanding and Healing Domestic Abuse, Part 2: When the Bible Is Used to Abuse*, 4-Part DVD (Day of Discovery/Our Daily Bread Ministries, 2007).
5. For a development of this thesis with research documentation, see Celestia and Steven Tracy, *Mending the Soul*, 35–40. Given the fact that in the evangelical world the vast majority of church leaders (pastors and elders) are male, one can argue that men are also more likely to perpetrate spiritual abuse. For a development of global violence against women from a Christian perspective, see Elizabeth Gerhardt, *The Cross and Gendercide: A Theological Response to Global Violence Against Women and Girls* (Downers Grove, IL: InterVarsity Press, 2014), and Elaine Storkey, *Scars Across Humanity: Understanding and Overcoming Violence Against Women* (London: SPCK, 2015).
6. Wayne Mack, *Strengthening Your Marriage*, 2nd ed. (Phillipsburg, NJ: P&R, 1999), 18, 20.
7. Stuart Scott, *The Exemplary Husband: A Biblical Perspective* (Bemidji, MN: Focus, 2000), 77.
8. Douglas Wilson, *Reforming Marriage*, 2nd ed. (Moscow, ID: Canon, 2005), 24, 80.
9. Wilson, *Reforming Marriage*, 80.
10. Douglas Wilson, *Fidelity: How to Be a One-Woman Man*, 2nd ed. (Moscow, ID: Canon, 1999), 84.
11. Wilson, *Fidelity*, 88–89.
12. On the complex relationship between domestic violence and patriarchy, see Steven Tracy, "Patriarchy and Domestic Violence: Challenging Common Misconceptions," *Journal of the Evangelical Theological Society* 50 (2007): 573–94.
13. Lou Priolo, *The Complete Husband: A Practical Guide for Improved Biblical Husbanding*, 2nd ed. (Phillipsburg, NJ: P&R, 2017), 248.
14. Douglas Wilson, *Federal Husband* (Moscow, ID: Canon, 1999), 32.
15. Mark Chanski, *Manly Dominion in a Passive-Purple-Four-Ball World* (Merrick, NY: Calvary, 2004), 171.
16. Debbi Pearl, *Created to Be His Help Meet* (Pleasantville, TN: No Greater Joy Ministries, 2004), 77.
17. Elizabeth George, *A Woman After God's Own Heart* (Eugene, OR: Harvest House, 1997), 70, 73.
18. Nancy Wilson, *The Fruit of Her Hands: Respect and the Christian Woman* (Moscow, ID: Canon, 1997), 28, 40, 45.
19. Beneth Peters Jones, *Ribbing Him Rightly: The Ministry of the Christian Wife* (Greenville, SC: BJU, 2000), 24–25.
20. Linda Dillow, *Creative Counterpart: Becoming the Woman, Wife, and Mother You've Longed to Be*, rev. ed. (Nashville: Thomas Nelson, 2003), 141.
21. H. Dale Burke, *Different by Design: God's Master Plan for Harmony Between Men and Women in Marriage* (Chicago: Moody, 2000), 102; Dorothy Patterson, *The Family: Unchanging Principles for Changing Times* (Nashville: Broadman & Holman, 2002), 42–43.
22. Beth Impson, *Called to Womanhood: The Biblical View for Today's World* (Wheaton, IL: Crossway, 2001), 125–26.
23. Martha Peace, *The Excellent Wife: A Biblical Perspective*, rev. ed. (Bemidji, MN: Focus, 1999), 157–59, 185.

24. 1 Cor 14:3; Col 3:18; Titus 2:5; 1 Pet 3:1, 5.
25. There is no question the household code begins in v. 21 because v. 22 does not have a stated command in the original Greek. It simply reads "wives to their own husbands as to the Lord." The verb in this sentence is supplied from v. 21.
26. Wayne Grudem, *Evangelical Feminism and Biblical Truth: An Analysis of More than 100 Disputed Questions* (Sisters, OR: Multnomah, 2004), 191.
27. Wayne Grudem, *Systematic Theology: An Introduction to Biblical Doctrine*, 2nd ed. (Grand Rapids: Zondervan, 2020), 593.
28. In 1 Clement the author uses the same Greek word for "submit" that Paul uses in Ephesians 5 (*hypotassō*). Believers are specifically told to submit to the Lord's will (1 Clem. 34.5). Church members are told to submit to the leaders (1.3), and factious individuals told to submit to the presbyters (57.1). But he also uses *hypotassō* to urge each individual to submit to his neighbor (38.1) and all members of the body to work together and unite in mutual submission (37.5). This is very significant early attestation of the concept of leaders (church and husbands) having some unique authority, but that authority is limited in scope and balanced by a mutual submission.
29. Since Jesus only mentions leaving wives, some might draw the hasty conclusion that the primacy of following Christ over family extends only to the husband as the head of the family and not to the wife. But Jesus need not list every single family member to establish this point. Note that parallel or similar accounts of this teaching in Matt 10:37–38 and Mark 10:29–30 list various family members but mention neither husband nor wife; they are assumed.
30. On kinship and identity in the ancient Jewish world, see David A. deSilva, *Honor, Patronage, Kinship and Purity: Unlocking New Testament Culture* (Downers Grove, IL: InterVarsity Press, 2000), 158–73.
31. Plutarch, *Moralia* 140.19, translation by Frank Cole Babbitt, Loeb Classical Library (Cambridge: Harvard University Press, 1928).
32. Plutarch, *Moralia* 140.14, 16; 139.9; 142.32.
33. Carolyn Osiek comments on the manner in which the Ephesian household code compares to Greco-Roman codes. She argues that in the Ephesian code "the dominance-submission pattern is still there, but it has been radically changed, from treatise on male dominance to exhortation to mutual relationships in Christ" ("The Bride of Christ [Ephesians 5:22–33]: A Problematic Wedding," *Biblical Theology Bulletin* 32 [2002]: 31).
34. Kurt Aland, ed., *The Greek New Testament*, 4th ed. (New York: United Bible Society, 1998).
35. Not only is the submission command in Colossians and Ephesians given directly to the wife, but in both instances the middle voice is used, which highlights the voluntary nature of the command and softens it (for arguments for the implied verb in Eph 5:22 being middle voice and not passive, cf. Harold H. Hoehner, *Ephesians: An Exegetical Commentary* [Grand Rapids: Baker Academic, 2002], 731–32). Spicq writes, "The use of the middle voice . . . emphasizes the voluntary character of the submission and alleviates whatever might be humiliating about subordination" (Ceslas Spicq, "ὑποτάσσω," *Theological Lexicon of the New Testament*, ed. and trans. James D. Ernest, 3 vols. [Peabody, MA: Hendrickson, 1994], 3:424).
36. Paul uses a different verb, *hypakouō*, in Eph 6:1, 5 and Col 3:20 of children and slaves. Most commentators affirm that *hypakouō*, unlike *hypotassō*, denotes obedience, and therefore the usage of the latter for wives is significant (Craig Blomberg, "Women in Ministry: A Complementarian Perspective," in *Two Views on Women in Ministry*, rev. ed. [Grand Rapids: Zondervan, 2005], 174; Marcus Barth, *Colossians*, Anchor Bible [New York: Doubleday, 1994], 433–35, 440–42).
37. Many conservatives will find appealing to broad themes of Scripture without having a specific supporting proof text to be far too subjective and hence an unacceptable moral guideline (particularly if the husband is appealing to a specific biblical text to support his position). In response, I would emphasize that since many of the moral issues of our day are not addressed directly in Scripture, we must apply scriptural principles in broad ways. While this

is a somewhat subjective process, so are other central aspects of the Christian life, particularly life in the Spirit (cf. Rom 8:14; Gal 5:15, 25).

38. In Scripture, Jonathan would be a good example of a godly individual whose authority (his father, King Saul) did not want him to have a relationship with David. Jonathan, however, disobeyed his father and maintained his deep friendship with David (1 Sam 19–20).

39. Contra Dillow, who argues that a wife can only disobey her husband if he commands her to do something that directly contradicts Scripture, since "an individual's conscience is not always a reliable guide, and neither is the feeling of being led by the Lord" (*Creative Counterpart*, 141). James R. Slaughter also seems to say that a wife must obey her husband even when it violates her conscience, such as participating in a sexual practice she finds distasteful ("Submission of Wives [1 Pet 3:1a] in the Context of 1 Peter," *Bibliotheca Sacra* 153 [1996]: 74). Martin Lloyd-Jones, on the other hand, even though he was a traditional complementarian who strongly emphasized male authority in the home, explained that "submit" in "everything" does not mean a wife should violate her own conscience (*Life in the Spirit in Marriage, Home, and Work: An Exposition of Ephesians 5:18 to 6:9* [Grand Rapids: Baker, 1973], 126).

40. Dan Allender gives a helpful personal illustration of a time that his wife refused his direct order when he was being harsh with their son. Allender notes that her refusal to submit to his harsh parenting protected their son and stimulated his repentance (*How Children Raise Parents: The Art of Listening to Your Family* [Colorado Springs, CO: WaterBrook, 2005], 196).

41. We noted in chapter 3 that Old Testament narrative stories are not necessarily positive examples for emulation, but the fact that Abigail is treated positively in Scripture and that God blessed her greatly strongly suggests that her actions in 1 Samuel were wise and godly.

42. For a more detailed analysis of this topic, particularly the relevance of 1 Pet 2:13–25, which is often used to counsel wives to follow the example of Jesus and submit to abusive husbands, see Steven R. Tracy, "Domestic Violence and Redemptive Suffering in First Peter," *Calvin Theological Journal* 41 (2006): 279–96.

43. Note the way Abigail's refusal to submit to Nabal's implied command not to support David and his men kept David from killing him (1 Sam 25:1–35). Various Scripture passages affirm God's judgment on unrepentant abusers (Isa 10:1–2; Ezek 22:11, 21; Joel 3:19; Amos 4:1–3; Mic 2:1–2; 3:9–12; Matt 18:5–6).

44. *Kephalē* can mean "source of life or nourishment," which may well be the meaning in Eph 4:15 and Col 2:19. For a further explanation of the meaning of *kephalē*, see my explanation in William and Aida Spencer and Steve and Celestia Tracy, *Marriage at the Crossroads: Couples in Conversation about Discipleship, Gender Roles, Decision Making and Intimacy* (Downers Grove, IL: IVP Academic, 2009), 60–64.

45. Michelle Lee-Barnewall, *Neither Complementarian nor Egalitarian: A Kingdom Corrective to the Evangelical Gender Debate* (Grand Rapids: Baker Academic, 2016), 155–56.

46. Early in my academic career I affirmed the eternal subordination of the son; see Steven Tracy, "1 Corinthians 11:3: A Corrective to Distortions and Abuses of Male Headship," *The Journal for Biblical Manhood and Womanhood* 8 (2003): 17–22. I now strongly reject this view.

47. The following is drawn from Tracy and Spencer, *Marriage at the Crossroads*, 65–71.

48. One of the best biblical surveys of the Trinity, which gives several hundred different biblical texts that show the overlap and mutuality in the Old Testament and New Testament descriptions, actions, and ministries of the Father and Son, is Edward Bickersteth, *The Trinity: Scripture Testimony to the One Eternal Godhead of the Father, and of the Son, and of the Holy Spirit* (Grand Rapids: Kregel, 1959). This is a reprint of a nineteenth-century work by an English minister, who was responding to an increasingly popular Unitarianism that denied the Son was divine and equal to the Father in his being and attributes.

49. The Father chose believers for salvation (Eph 1:4; 2 Thess 2:13–14; 1 Pet 1:2), sent the Holy Spirit to indwell believers (John 14:16, 26), and judges, disciplines, and sanctifies believers (John 15:1–2).

50. Larry Crabb cogently argues that, beginning with the first human sin recorded in Gen 3:1–13,

males are inclined to be sinfully silent when they should take the risk and initiate—that is, speak (*The Silence of Adam* [Grand Rapids: Zondervan, 1995]).

51. The grammar of the passage clearly indicates purpose (the use of the conjunction *hina* with the subjunctive verb). Other Scripture passages such as Phil 2:9–11 develop the theme of the Father lifting up Christ, giving him power and authority, and decisively working so that all created beings would honor him. On the Father giving the Son authority (a concept that many gender traditionalists seem to deny), we should note that the Father gives the Son "all authority in heaven and on earth" (Matt 28:18), and the Son is called "God Almighty" (*pantokratōr*), the all-powerful, authoritative One who rules and judges and is to be worshiped (Rev 1:8; cf. 17:14).

52. J. I. Packer, *A Quest for Godliness: The Puritan Vision of the Christian Life* (Wheaton, IL: Crossway, 1990), 269; cited in "Divorce and Remarriage," submitted to the PCA 20th General Assembly, p. 192n24.

53. Wayne Grudem, *What the Bible Says About Divorce and Remarriage* (Wheaton, IL: Crossway, 2021), 38–53; John Frame, *The Doctrine of the Christian Life* (Phillipsburg, NJ: P&R, 2008), 780–81; Russell Moore, "Divorcing an Abusive Spouse Is Not a Sin," *Christianity Today*, March 24, 2022, www.christianitytoday.com/ct/2022/march-web-only/russell-moore-divorce-marriage-domestic-violence-abuse.html.

54. David Instone-Brewer finds four grounds for divorce and remarriage affirmed in both Old and New Testaments: adultery, emotional and sexual neglect, abandonment, and abuse. He draws heavily from Exod 21:10–11 and ancient rabbinic understandings of this text, as well as Deut 24:1–4 (*Divorce and Remarriage in the Bible: The Social and Literary Context* [Grand Rapids: Eerdmans, 2002]; *Divorce and Remarriage in the Church: Biblical Solutions for Pastoral Realities* [Downers Grove, IL: InterVarsity Press, 2003]). I respect his position but find 1 Corinthians 7:15 to be a clearer biblical basis for divorce for abuse.

55. Steven Tracy, "Is Porneia (Sexual Sin) Limited to Sexual Intercourse?," available on the Mending the Soul Ministries website under Additional Resources (www.mendingthesoul.org).

56. The definitive New Testament Greek lexicon notes that *lysis* refers to "release, separation, (in marriage) a divorce" and gives 1 Cor 7:27 as an example of its use to refer to divorce (Bauer et al., *Greek-English Lexicon of the New Testament*, 605).

57. Moore, "Divorcing an Abusive Spouse."

58. Grudem, *Divorce and Remarriage*, 42.

59. William Perkins, *Christian Oeconomie: Or, A Short Survey of the Right Manner of Erecting and Ordering a Familie According to the Scriptures*, trans. Thomas Pickering (London, 1609), 107, cited in a special report given to the twentieth general assembly of the Presbyterian Church of America in 1992 entitled, "Report of the Ad-Interim Committee on Divorce and Remarriage," 191.

60. Grudem, *Divorce and Remarriage*, 46.

Chapter 5: Passages on Children

1. Vic Ryckaert, "Son Had 36 Bruises. Mom Quoted the Bible as Defense," *Indy Star*, August 31, 2016, www.indystar.com/story/news/crime/2016/08/31/son-had-36-bruises-mom-quoted-bible-defense/88998568.

2. Kathryn Joyce, "Horror Stories from Tough-Love Teen Homes," *Mother Jones*, July/August 2011, www.motherjones.com/politics/2011/08/new-bethany-ifb-teen-homes-abuse. The Texas attorney general was unimpressed with Roloff's quip and responded that he was more concerned with bottoms "that were blue, black, and bloody." For an explanation of how abusive Christian reform schools continue to exist and thwart state laws, see Nile Cappello, "How Christian Reform Schools Get Away with Brutal Child Abuse," *Vice*, December 5, 2017, www.vice.com/en/article/vbzexd/how-christian-reform-schools-get-away-with-brutal-child-abuse.

3. William Webb, *Corporal Punishment in the Bible: A Redemptive-Movement Hermeneutic for Troubling Texts* (Downers Grove, IL: InterVarsity Press, 2011), 58, 74.

4. Webb unpacks the eighteen cultural/transcultural criteria in *Slaves, Women & Homosexuals: Exploring the Hermeneutics of Cultural Analysis* (Downers Grove, IL: InterVarsity Press, 2001).

5. While I strongly disagree with Wayne Grudem's model of male authority in the home and the church, he is a brilliant and very articulate scholar. I find his negative critique of Webb's hermeneutic to be extremely insightful, well argued, and devastating to Webb's model. I share his concern that Webb's trajectory hermeneutic nullifies in principle the moral authority of Scripture. See Wayne Grudem, "Should We Move Beyond the New Testament to a Better Ethic? An Analysis of William J. Webb, *Slaves, Women & Homosexuals: Exploring the Hermeneutics of Cultural Analysis*," paper presented on November 19, 2003 at the Evangelical Theological Society 55th Annual Meeting, Atlanta, Georgia, available at www.waynegrudem.com /should-we-move-beyond-the-new-testament-to-a-better-ethic.

6. On homicide and overall child-abuse rates, see the American SPCC, "National Child Maltreatment Statistics," AmericanSPPC.org, https://americanspcc.org/child-maltreatment -statistics/#:~:text=Annual%20estimate%3A%201%2C820%20children%20died,involve %20at%20least%20one%20parent. See also Dan Hurley, "Why Doesn't the US Have an Accurate Count of Child Abuse Deaths?," *The New Yorker*, December 12, 2019, www.newyorker.com/news/news-desk/why-doesnt-the-us-have-an-accurate-count-of-child -abuse-deaths.

7. Rebecca Wilson, et al., "Trends in Homicide Rates for US Children Aged 0 to 17 Years, 1999 to 2020," *JAMA Pediatrics* 177 (2023): 187–97.

8. Michael and Debi Pearl, *To Train Up a Child: Child Training for the 21st Century* (Pleasantville, TN: No Greater Joy Ministries, 1994). The Pearls claim on their No Greater Joy website that this book has sold over 625,000 copies. This book has been extremely influential with conservative Christian parents, particularly homeschoolers.

9. Erik Eckholm, "Preaching Virtue of Spanking, Even as Deaths Fuel Debate," *The New York Times*, November 7, 2011; see also Rachel Held Evans, "The Abusive Teachings of Michael and Debi Pearl," Rachelheldevans.com, March 23, 2013, https://rachelheldevans.com/blog /the-abusive-teachings-of-michael-and-debi-pearl. For an exposition of the flawed theology of *To Train Up a Child*, see Steve Smith, "To Train Up A Child . . . Abuser (Part 2)," January 11, 2014, https://libertyforcaptives.com/2014/01/11/to-train-up-a-child-abuser-part-2.

10. Paul Wegner, "Discipline in the Book of Proverbs: 'To Spank or Not to Spank?,'" *Journal of the Evangelical Theological Society* 48 (2005): 719.

11. Wegner, "Discipline in the Book of Proverbs," 719–26.

12. Deuteronomy 21:18–21 gives instructions for parents of rebellious adult children to hand the son over to the civil authorities, who in turn adjudicate and may carry out capital punishment on the rebellious son (though there is no record of this ever being carried out in ancient Israel). The text makes it clear that this is not a case of mere disobedience but of recalcitrant rebellious "evil" that threatened to corrupt the whole community. This punishment reflects a "very last resort" against a most pernicious community threat (Christopher J. H. Wright, *Deuteronomy*, New International Bible Commentary [Peabody, MA: Hendrickson, 1996], 236).

13. Michael and Debi Pearl, *To Train Up a Child*, 59; see also 46.

14. Personal conversation with Paul Wegner, August 8, 2023; see also Wegner, "Discipline in the Book of Proverbs," 728.

15. On the complex emotional, relational, and spiritual effects of child abuse, see Steven and Celestia Tracy, *Mending the Soul*, 113–202.

16. Andrew T. Lincoln, *Ephesians*, Word Biblical Commentary 42 (Dallas, TX: Word, 1990), 406.

17. Jennifer Greenberg, "Honoring Your Father When He's Evil," The Gospel Coalition, June 18, 2021, www.thegospelcoalition.org/article/honoring-father-evil.

18. See Matt 2:18; 15:26; 1 Thess 2:7. Hoehner notes that the use here of *teknon* instead of *huios* indicates a close relationship with the parent and implies a dependent relationship (*Ephesians*, 786).

19. C. Leslie Mitton, *Ephesians*, The New Century Bible Commentary (Grand Rapids: Eerdmans, 1973), 210.

20. Greenberg, "Honoring Your Father When He's Evil."

21. Amber Hunter Jesse, "Where I'm From," *Freedom Steps*, Released September 2012. Used by permission.

Chapter 6: Passages on the Church

1. Documentation of Karen's story and The Village Church's response can be found online: Amy Smith, "Karen Hinkley's Response to The Village Church 5/23/15 Email Sent to 6000 'Covenant Members' about Her and Jordan Root," Watchkeep, May 27, 2015, https://watchkeep.org/2015/05/karen-hinkleys-response-to-the-village-church-5-23-15-email-sent-to-6000-covenant-members-about-her-and-jordan-root. What follows comes from this document.

2. Smith, "Karen Hinkley's Response."

3. Smith, "Karen Hinkley's Response."

4. Smith, "Karen Hinkley's Response."

5. Smith, "Karen Hinkley's Response."

6. Sarah Eekhoff Zylstra, Morgan Lee, and Bob Smietana, "Former Member Accepts Acts 29 Megachurch Apology in Church Discipline Case," *Christianity Today*, June 10, 2015.

7. John Bevere, *Under Cover: Why Your Response to Leadership Determines Your Future*, 2nd ed. (Nashville: Emanate, 2018), 165. The title is indicative of Bevere's flawed theology of church leadership, in which being under the "cover" or authority of church leaders brings great blessing, while being out from under their covering exposes one to demonic "witchcraft curses" (based on his experience of the testimony of witches and a misinterpretation of 1 Sam 15:22–23, which is actually about rebellion against God, not rebellion against human authorities). See pp. 73–86.

8. Bevere, *Under Cover*, 164, 175–76.

9. Bauer et al., *Greek-English Lexicon of the New Testament*, 434.

10. A. J. Coetsee, "Practical Principles for Church Leaders and Church Members from Hebrews 13," *Unio cum Christo* 2 (2016): 197.

11. T. Smith, "An Exegesis of Hebrews 13:1–17," *Faith and Mission* 7 (1989): 74.

12. Over and over Paul calls his readers to follow his example (1 Cor 11:1; Phil 3:17; 4:9; 2 Thess 3:7). He taught his disciples Timothy and Titus to exercise the same leadership strategy (1 Tim 4:12; Titus 2:7). Paul persuaded by appealing, not demanding (1 Cor 1:10; 2 Cor 10:1; 1 Thess 2:3). He appealed to his love for his disciples, not his inherent authority as the basis for their response (1 Cor 4:14–16; 2 Cor 7:1–5; 1 Thess 2:6–8).

13. Diane Langberg, *Redeeming Power: Understanding Authority and Abuse in the Church* (Grand Rapids: Brazos, 2020), 10–11, 152. An excellent resource for understanding spiritual abuse and creating healthy church environments that resist abuses of power is Scot McKnight and Laura Barringer, *A Church Called Tov: Forming a Goodness Culture* (Carol Stream, IL: Tyndale, 2020).

14. "Benny Hinn – Touch Not the Anointed," YouTube, https://youtu.be/c2SRIA0yFeA. See also Pastor Chris Oyakhilome, "Touch Not My Anointed," AffirmationTrain.org, October 7, 2020, www.affirmation-train.org/touch-not-my-anointed.

15. Julie Roys, "Hard Times at Harvest," *World Magazine*, December 29, 2018; Bob Smietana, "When Does Church Conflict Become Spiritual Abuse?," *Baptist Standard*, August 2, 2022.

16. Daniel Silliman, "RZIM Will No Longer Do Apologetics," *Christianity Today*, March 10, 2021.

17. For instance, see Chris Moody's account of Mark Driscoll (who left his previous church in Seattle after church leaders accused him of being unfit for ministry due to his bullying and misuse of power) creating a cult-like environment in his church in Scottsdale, Arizona, which reportedly requires complete loyalty, even to the point of severing relationships with friends and family members whom Driscoll deems unhealthy or disloyal to the church. See Chris Moody, "Mark Driscoll's Safe Space: How The Embattled Pastor Built A New Church And Became An Online Influencer," The Roys Report, October 3, 2023; available at: https://julieroys.com/mark-driscolls-safe-space-how-embattled-pastor-built-a-new-church-became-an-online-influencer.

18. Rebecca Davis, *Untwisting Scriptures That Were Used to Tie You Up, Gag You, and Tangle Your Mind, Book 3: Your Words, Your Emotions* (Greenville, SC: Pennycress, 2021), 22–23.

19. *Psithyristēs* and *psithyrismos* respectively (Bauer et al., *Greek-English Lexicon of the New Testament*, 1098).

20. Andy de Ganahl, "Caring for Elders, Part 2: Protection – 1 Timothy 5:19–21," The Pastor's

Brief, November 7, 2019, www.thepastorsbrief.com/post/caring-for-elders-part-2-protection-1-timothy-5-19-21.

21. Wright, *Deuteronomy*, 224.

22. See Isa 1:23; 3:13–15; 58:3; Jer 5:23–32; 22:1–3; Ezek 45:8–9; Amos 4:1–2; 5:7–13; Mic 3:1–3.

23. Exod 22:21–27; Lev 25:8–54; Deut 15:1–11; 24:14–17.

24. Peter C. Craigie, *The Book of Deuteronomy*, New International Commentary on the Old Testament (Grand Rapids: Eerdmans, 1976), 269.

25. McKnight and Barringer, *Church Called Tov*, 51 (emphasis theirs).

26. While this text does not spell out the specific actions of receiving and weighing the alleged victim's account, they are assumed as the requisite means for a judicial decision.

27. Michael Kruger notes that of all the procedural objections made by abusive spiritual leaders, the one trumpeted most loudly is that Matthew 18 wasn't followed. Before long the conversation is no longer about the crime but about the procedure, and the abusive pastor ends up claiming to be the victim, and the real victim is portrayed as the pastor's abuser, Michael J. Kruger, *Bully Pulpit: Confronting the Problem of Spiritual Abuse in the Church* (Grand Rapids: Zondervan, 2022), 81.

28. William D. Mounce, *Pastoral Epistles*, Word Biblical Commentary 46 (Nashville: Thomas Nelson, 2000), 312.

29. Raymond F. Collins, *I & II Timothy and Titus* (Louisville: Westminster John Knox, 2002), 146n80.

Chapter 7: Passages on Abuse Victims

1. Cheryl, "Forgiving & Turning the Other Cheek Is Bad for Your Physical & Mental Health. How Turning the Other Cheek Messed Me Up Physically & Mentally," MindKind Mom, July 14, 2017, https://mindkindmom.com/forgiving-turning-the-other-cheek-is-bad-for-your-physical-mental-health.

2. Alex Lickerman, "The Problem with Turning the Other Cheek," ImagineMD, October 10, 2010, https://imaginemd.com/blog/the-problem-with-turning-the-other-cheek. Lickerman understands "turn the other cheek" to involve an "extreme form of pacifism in which we willingly allow ourselves to come to harm rather than taking measures to protect ourselves that require us to harm someone else."

3. J. Scott Duvall and J. Daniel Hays, *Grasping God's Word: A Hands-On Approach to Reading, Interpreting, and Applying the Bible*, 3rd ed. (Grand Rapids: Zondervan, 2012), 283.

4. Leland Ryken, *How to Read the Bible as Literature . . . and Get More Out of It* (Grand Rapids: Zondervan, 1984), 100.

5. Dan Lacich, "Provocative Bible Verses: Turn the Other Cheek," The Provocative Christian, January 23, 2009, https://danlacich.com/2009/01/23/provocative-bible-verses-turn-the-other-cheek.

6. Erik Raymond, "Love Endures All Things," The Gospel Coalition blog, August 28, 2015, www.thegospelcoalition.org/blogs/erik-raymond/love-endures-all-things.

7. Erik Raymond, "Love Believes All Things," Gospel Coalition blog, August 26, 2015, www.thegospelcoalition.org/blogs/erik-raymond/love-believes-all-things.

8. Julie Roys, "John MacArthur Shamed, Excommunicated Mother for Refusing to Take Back Child Abuser," The Roys Report, March 8, 2022, https://julieroys.com/macarthur-shamed-excommunicated-mother-take-back-child-abuser. See also Kate Shellnutt, "Grace Community Church Rejected Elder's Calls to 'Do Justice' in Abuse Case," *Christianity Today*, February 9, 2023, www.christianitytoday.com/2023/02/grace-community-church-elder-biblical-counseling-abuse. Shellnutt gives evidence that GCC's mistreatment of Eileen Gray is part of a larger pattern of injustice toward abuse survivors, particularly domestically abused women and children.

9. Sarah Einselen, "Head of Counseling at John MacArthur's School: Wife Should Endure Abuse

Like Missionary Endures Persecution," The Roys Report, April 5, 2022, https://julieroys.com/head-counseling-john-macarthur-school-wife-endure-abuse.

10. Bill Gothard, in discussing abused wives, states, "There is no 'victim' if we understand that we are called to suffer for righteousness." He cites 1 Peter 2 for biblical support (Bill Gothard, *Supplementary Alumni Book*, vol. 5 [Institute in Basic Youth Conflicts, 1979], 10), cited by James Alsdurf and Phyllis Alsdurf, *Battered into Submission: The Tragedy of Wife Abuse in the Christian Home* (Downers Grove, IL: InterVarsity Press, 1989), 88. Debi Pearl similarly tells abused wives, based on 1 Peter, that "the chain of authority must remain intact" even if that involves abuse. Furthermore, "you were called by God for the very purpose of suffering for him" (Debi Pearl, *Created to Be His Help Meet* [Pleasantville, TN: No Greater Joy Ministries, 2004], 263).

11. The following discussion of 1 Pet 2:18–23 is largely drawn from Steven Tracy, "Domestic Violence in the Church and Redemptive Suffering in First Peter," *Calvin Theological Journal* 41 (2006): 279–96. Used with permission.

12. Robert L. Wilken, *The Christians as the Romans Saw Them* (New Haven: Yale University Press, 1984), 62–67. Wilken notes that later pagan critics such as Minucius Felix criticized the Christians for failure to observe the civic practices, but this was as much a religious criticism as it was social: "You do not go to our shows, you take no part in our processions, you are not present at our public banquets, you shrink in horror from our sacred games" (*Octavius* 12).

13. David Balch argues that a primary apologetic function of the household code in 1 Peter was to reduce the sociopolitical tension between society and the churches by urging Christians to conform to the expectations of Greco-Roman society (David L. Balch, *Let Wives Be Submissive: The Domestic Code in 1 Peter*, Society of Biblical Literature Monograph Series 26 [Atlanta: Scholars Press, 1981], 87–88).

14. While some translations such as NASB euphemistically translate the verb used in v. 20 (*kolaphizō*) as "harshly treated," it most often refers to physical abuse—i.e., of literally striking with the fist, beating (Matt 26:67; Mark 14:65), which is how it is being used here.

15. K. Bradley notes that in the early Roman Empire, slaves were technically given some legal recourse to file a complaint regarding abusive treatment, but it was exceedingly difficult for them to access this protection, and it was rarely if ever given (K. R. Bradley, *Slaves and Masters in the Roman Empire: A Study in Social Control* [Oxford: Oxford University Press, 1987], 123–37).

16. The famous first-century Roman poet and satirist Juvenal criticizes the woman who, because her husband turns his back on her at night, has the household slave stripped and beaten by a professional torturer while she puts on her makeup, gossips with friends, and reads the gazette (Juvenal, *Satires* 6.474–85). This illustrates the vulnerability of household slaves to being abused due to their daily proximity to the master and his family.

17. Seneca, *Epistles* 47.5.

18. Richard P. Saller, *Patriarchy, Property and Death in the Roman Family* (Cambridge: Cambridge University Press, 1994), 102; see also Sarah B. Pomeroy, *Goddesses, Whores, Wives, and Slaves: Women in Classical Antiquity* (New York: Schocken, 1975), 190–204.

19. Martin Hengel, *Crucifixion* (Minneapolis: Fortress, 1977), 51–63.

20. Pliny, *Letters* 3.14.

21. Bradley, *Slaves and Masters*, 122–23.

22. Holt Parker, "Loyal Slaves and Loyal Wives: The Crisis of the Outsider Within and Roman Exemplum Literature," in *Women and Slaves in Greco-Roman Culture*, ed. Sandra Joshel and Sheila Murnaghan (New York: Routledge, 1998), 152–70.

23. Even here there is some irony, since the only time the Old Testament recounts Sarah calling Abraham "lord" is in Gen 18:12 when Sarah somewhat sarcastically refers to her lord being too old to have a child.

24. Caryn Reeder, "1 Peter 3:1–6: Biblical Authority and Battered Wives," *Bulletin for Biblical Research* 25 (2015): 528.

25. Ibid., 528.

26. Augustine, *Confessions* 9.19. While Augustine wrote a few centuries after 1 Peter was written, the social conditions of wives was very similar.

27. Reeder, "1 Peter 3:1–6," 534.

28. Carol J. Adams, *Woman-Battering* (Minneapolis: Fortress, 1994), 88.

29. In commenting on 1 Pet 2:21, John Calvin notes the importance of clarifying the exact manner in which Christ is our example. He warns that unless we make this clarification, we will end up imitating Christ in an absurd manner, seeking to imitate his activities that were inimitable (John Calvin, *Commentaries on the Catholic Epistles* [Grand Rapids: Baker, 1981], 89).

30. See Clinton Arnold, *The Colossian Syncretism: The Interface between Christianity and Folk Belief at Colossae* (Grand Rapids: Baker, 1996). While the Colossian opponents were promoting ascetic self-abuse, not abuse from other people, the principle remains the same—suffering is not to be sought out; avoidable suffering is not redemptive.

31. On the need for abuse victims to establish personal safety and stabilization to begin the process of healing, see Steven and Celestia Tracy, *Mending the Soul*, 216–28.

32. Paul Hegstrom, *Angry Men and the Women Who Love Them* (Kansas City: Beacon Hill, 1999), 43–57; Eva Lundgren, "I Am Endowed with All the Power in Heaven and on Earth: When Men Become Men through 'Christian' Abuse," *Studia Theologica* 48 (1994): 33–47.

Chapter 8: Passages on Spiritual Life

1. Bauer et al., *Greek-English Lexicon of the New Testament*, 38. This same usage of *akouō* is found in the previous chapter (Matt 17:5): "This is my Son, whom I love; with him I am well pleased. *Listen to* him!"

2. For a detailed discussion of what biblical forgiveness does and doesn't mean for abuse survivors, see Steven and Celestia Tracy, *Mending the Soul*, 266–91.

3. Ed Welch, "The Angry Person: Always the Last to Know," Christian Counseling and Educational Foundation, April 14, 2016, www.ccef.org/angry-person-always-last-know.

4. For instance, see the individual lament psalms found in Pss 35:4–8; 58:6–11; 69:19–28; 109:1–31; 139:19–22. While these passages cited do not explicitly use the word anger, anger is indisputably present. Otherwise, these texts would make no sense.

5. One of the best summary surveys of the applicability of these psalms for New Testament believers is given by Bruce Waltke and Fred Zaspel, *How to Read and Understand the Psalms* (Wheaton, IL: Crossway, 2023), 308–16.

6. Alasdair Groves and Winston Smith, *Untangling Emotions* (Wheaton, IL: Crossway, 2019), 171.

7. John and Janie Street, *The Biblical Counseling Guide for Women* (Eugene, OR: Harvest House, 2016), 22.

8. Nancy DeMoss Wolgemuth, *Lies Women Believe: And the Truth That Sets Them Free*, 2nd ed. (Chicago: Moody, 2018), 75–76.

9. NIV alternate reading. The Hebrew word translated here as "God" or "angels" (NIV primary reading) is *elohim* and overwhelmingly refers to God elsewhere in the Hebrew Scriptures.

10. Heath Lambert, "Understanding Fear," Biblical Counseling Podcast, August 27, 2018, https://biblicalcounseling.com/resource-library/podcast-episodes/til-169-understanding-fear.

11. Groves and Smith, *Untangling Emotions*, 32.

12. Bauer et al., *Greek-English Lexicon of the New Testament*, 632.

13. For a detailed explanation of the neurobiology of trauma, see Steven and Celestia Tracy, *Mending the Soul*, 148–75.

14. Gavin De Becker, *The Gift of Fear: Survival Signals that Protect Us from Violence*, rev. ed. (New York: Little Brown and Company, 2021).

15. Tristen Collins and Jonathan Collins, *Why Emotions Matter* (Beaumont Press, 2019), 70. See also Matthew Elliott, *Faithful Feelings: Rethinking Emotion in the New Testament* (Grand Rapids: Kregel, 2006), 204.

16. As cited by James B. Adamson, *The Epistle of James*, New International Commentary on the New Testament (Grand Rapids: Eerdmans, 1976), 116n113.

17. Cornelius Plantinga, *Not the Way It's Supposed to Be: A Breviary of Sin* (Grand Rapids: Eerdmans, 1995), 21.

Chapter 9: God's Response to Abuse

1. Primo Levi, *Survival in Auschwitz: If This Is a Man* (New York: Orian, 1959), 64.
2. Celestia was in and out of the hospital for four months. The Infectious Disease Department at Mayo never was able to determine the source of the infection. For over six months, Celestia had lengthy Vanco infusions through a PICC-line every twelve hours. Angels in the form of nurses cared for her so that she could come home between surgeries. The infection was eventually defeated, and she slowly regained her strength over the next year. Dr. Morrey's son, also an orthopedic surgeon who treated her along with his father, shared later that he was fasting and praying during this time and that his family prayed for her around their dinner table. God provided just what Celestia needed. He showed himself to her in a myriad of ways. She describes her arm as her ninety-degree blessing, because the small range of motion she has left is exactly the bend she needs to type.
3. G. R. Lewis, "Impassibility of God," in *Evangelical Dictionary of Theology*, ed. Daniel Treier and Walter Elwell, 3rd ed. (Grand Rapids: Baker, 2017), 422.
4. James Dolezal, "Strong Impassibility," in *Divine Impassibility: Four Views of God's Emotions and Suffering*, ed. Robert Matz and A. Chadwick Thornhill, Spectrum Multiview Book Series (Downers Grove, IL: InterVarsity Press, 2019), 13, 23.
5. For an explanation and negative critique of open theism's response to theodicy (the defense of the goodness of God in light of evil and suffering), see Steven Tracy, "Theodicy, Eschatology, and the Open View of God," in *Looking into the Future: Evangelical Studies in Eschatology*, ed. David W. Baker (Grand Rapids: Baker, 2001), 295–312. Two other helpful negative critiques of open theism are Millard Erickson, *What Does God Know and When Does he Know It* (Grand Rapids: Zondervan, 2003), and Bruce Ware, *God's Lesser Glory: The Diminished God of Open Theism* (Wheaton, IL: Crossway, 2000).
6. See, for instance, Rob Lister, *God Is Impassible and Impassioned* (Wheaton, IL: Crossway, 2013), 36, 260. Lister's treatment is insightful, and I agree with much of what he has written. However, I find quite unsatisfactory the way he equivocates regarding God's suffering. He refuses to clarify how God suffers. I agree with him that God never "involuntarily suffers," but Lister never responds to the question of whether God voluntarily suffers (258). Lister discusses one of the key texts that describes God's suffering over human suffering (Isaiah 63:9 "in all their affliction he was afflicted," ESV) and confusingly states "whatever this affliction is that God joins them in, it is not ultimately an affliction against his will" (213). Depending on how one defines "will" I might agree with his statement, but again why the reluctance to affirm what Scripture clearly states, namely that God suffers?
7. Donald Bloesch, *God the Almighty: Power, Wisdom, Holiness, Love* (Downers Grove, IL: InterVarsity Press, 1995), 210. See also Richard Bauckham "'Only the Suffering God Can Help': Divine Passibility in Modern Theology," *Themelios* 9 (1984): 6–12, and John Peckham, "Qualified Passibility," in *Divine Impassibility*, 98–102. Steven Duby argues that the concept of God's self-limitation that would lead to vulnerability and pain is a mythological assertion. He argues this based on God's self-sufficiency affirmed in Acts 17:24–25 and God's incorruptibility affirmed in Romans 1:23, in *Jesus and the God of Classical Theism: Biblical Christology in Light of the Doctrine of God* (Grand Rapids: Baker, 2022), 355. Duby's insistence that if God freely chose to be vulnerable it would necessarily diminish his perfection is based on a reductionistic understanding of God's independence and a flawed definition of corruptibility. It is well-argued logically but fails to account for extensive biblical data.
8. John Stott, *The Cross of Christ* (Downers Grove, IL: InterVarsity Press, 2006), 323, cited by Peckham, "Qualified Passibility," 100.
9. David Lamb, *The Emotions of God: Making Sense of a God Who Hates, Weeps, and Loves* (Downers Grove, IL: InterVarsity Press, 2022), 16–18.

NOTES

10. Even a qualified impassibilitist such as D. A. Carson argues that one cannot deny God having emotion by insisting "that all the biblical evidence to the contrary is nothing more than anthropopathism. The price is too heavy. You may then rest in God's sovereignty, but you can no longer rejoice in his love" (D. A. Carson, *The Difficult Doctrine of the Love of God* [Wheaton, IL: Crossway, 2000], 59).

11. Erickson, *What Does God Know*, 17–19. Erickson draws heavily on a study of *naham* by H. Parunak, "A Semantic Survey of NHM," *Biblica* 56 (1975): 512–32.

12. John Oswalt, *The Book of Isaiah, Chapters 40–66*, New International Commentary on the Old Testament (Grand Rapids: Eerdmans, 1998), 606.

13. Lamb, *Emotions of God*, 94–96; see also Christopher J. H. Wright, *The Message of Jeremiah*, The Bible Speaks Today (Downers Grove, IL; InterVarsity Press, 2014), 118–21.

14. Nicholas Wolterstorff, *Lament for a Son* (Grand Rapids: Eerdmans, 1987), 81.

15. For a basic overview of how various worldviews respond to the "where is God" question, see Steven Tracy, "Where Is God in the Midst of the Suffering of Abuse?," *Africanus Journal* 2 (2010): 45–52.

16. Jerome Neyrey, "Despising the Shame of the Cross," *Semeia* 68 (1996): 113.

17. See Steven Tracy, "Abuse and Shame: How the Cross Transforms Shame," in *Honor, Shame and the Gospel: Reframing Our Message and Ministry*, ed. Werner Mischke and Chris Flanders (Littleton, CO: William Carey, 2020), 101–14.

18. Cicero, *Pro Rabirio Perduellionis Reo*, trans. H. G. Hodge, Loeb Classical Library 198 (Cambridge: Harvard University Press, 1927), 466–67.

19. For an excellent discussion of the theological significance and affirmation of Jesus's resurrected body having scars, see Peter Widdicombe, "The Wounds and the Ascended Body: The Marks of the Crucifixion in the Glorified Christ from Justin Martyr to John Calvin," *Laval théologique et philosophique* 59 (2003): 137–54.

Chapter 10: God's Mandate to Protect the Vulnerable and Care for the Abused

1. See Joshua Pease, "The Sin of Silence: The Epidemic of Denial About Sexual Abuse in the Evangelical Church," *The Washington Post*, May 31, 2018, www.washingtonpost.com/news/posteverything/wp/2018/05/31/feature/the-epidemic-of-denial-about-sexual-abuse-in-the-evangelical-church.abuse in the evangelical church

2. See "The Statement on Social Justice & the Gospel," which has been signed by over 17,400 people, particularly Christian leaders. It is available at: https://statementonsocialjustice.com.

3. Kevin DeYoung and Greg Gilbert, *What Is the Mission of the Church: Making Sense of Social Justice, Shalom, and the Great Commission* (Wheaton, IL: Crossway, 2011), 40–41.

4. They also argue that justice is a "prosaic" category in the Bible (DeYoung and Gilbert, *What Is the Mission*, 175–76).

5. John MacArthur, "Social Justice and the Gospel, Part 1," Grace to You, August 26, 2018, www.gty.org/library/sermons-library/81-21/social-justice-and-the-gospel-part-1.

6. Christopher J. H. Wright, *Old Testament Ethics for the People of God* (Downers Grove, IL; InterVarsity Press, 2004), 257.

7. Peter Gentry and Stephen Wellum, *Kingdom Through Covenant: A Biblical Understanding of the Covenants* (Wheaton, IL: Crossway, 2012), 577; Wright, *Old Testament Ethics*, 257.

8. Abraham Heschel, *The Prophets* (New York: Harper Collins, 1962), 276. Hemchand Gossai in his in-depth study of the language of the Hebrew prophets concludes that *tsedeq* and *mishpat* are "fundamentally" relational terms; see Hemchand Gossia, *Social Critique by Israel's Eight-Century Prophets: Justice and Righteousness in Context* (Eugene, OR: Wipf & Stock, 1993), 310.

9. DeYoung and Gilbert, *What Is the Mission of the Church*, 146–47.

10. See Owen Strachan's minimization of injustice against African Americans, titled *Christianity and Wokeness: How the Social Justice Movement Is Hijacking the Gospel and the Way to Stop It* (Washington, DC: Salem Books, 2021), 116–21, and Scott David Allen's treatment of George

Floyd's murder, *Why Social Justice Is Not Biblical Justice* (Grand Rapids: Credo House, 2020), 95–97.

11. For instance, Tom Nettles in a thirty-two page chapter titled, "Biblical Justice and Social Justice," says virtually nothing about defending the vulnerable. His "biblical" response to injustice is that this is an unjust world, those who suffer injustice should endure like Jesus (1 Pet 2:19); "it will be worth it all when we see Jesus," and "be patient"; see Tom Nettles, "Biblical Justice and Social Justice," in *By What Standard: God's World . . . God's Rules*, ed. Jared Longshore (Cape Coral, FL: Founders, 2020), 60–61, 64–65, 68–70, 88–89. Given his understanding of justice, it is unsurprising that in a torturous argument from silence, Nettles argues that Jesus did not consider slavery to be evil perhaps because "the relation of master and slave was not condemnable" (69–70).

12. For a good overview of the biblical use of *hesed*, see Michael Card, *Inexpressible: Hesed and the Mystery of God's Lovingkindness* (Downers Grove, IL: InterVarsity Press, 2018).

13. Heschel, *Prophets*, 265.

14. Bruce K. Waltke, *An Old Testament Theology* (Grand Rapids: Zondervan, 2007), 914.

15. It is noteworthy that the Greek word used here translated "distress" is *thlipsis*, and it often denotes suffering as a result of oppression (Bauer et al., *Greek-English Lexicon of the New Testament*, 457).

16. John Stott, *Human Rights and Human Wrongs: Major Issues for a New Century*, 3rd ed. (Grand Rapids: Baker, 1999), 39.

17. Abby Tracy, "Street Kids," September 20, 2008. The concept of believers being God to the needy comes from one of the early apostolic fathers; see *Epistle to Diognetus* 10.

18. D. A. Carson, "Matthew," in *Expositor's Bible Commentary*, ed. Frank E. Gaebelein, 12 vols. (Grand Rapids: Zondervan, 1984), 8:522.

19. Wright, *Old Testament Ethics*, 170.

20. Francis Brown, Samuel Rolles Driver, and Charles Augustus Briggs, *Enhanced Brown-Driver -Briggs Hebrew and English Lexicon* (Oxford: Clarendon, 1977), 776; J. David Pleins, "Poor, Poverty," in *Anchor Bible Dictionary*, ed. David Noel Freedman, 6 vols. (New York: Doubleday, 1992), 5:408.

Chapter 11: God's Commitment to Heal, Redeem, and Restore

1. First Chronicles 2:4 and 3:5 are the only exceptions; Tamar and Bathsheba are mentioned. Other biblical genealogies are found, e.g., in Gen 5:1–32; 11:10–32; Ruth 4:18–22, and 1 Chr 1–3. The other biblical genealogy of Jesus is found in Luke 3:23–38 and contains no females.

2. See Gen 9:24–25; cf. Gen 28:1.

3. Susan Niditch, "Genesis," in *Women's Bible Commentary*, 3rd ed., ed. Carol Newsom, Sharon Ringe, and Jacquelyn Lapsley (Louisville: Westminster John Knox, 2012), 42.

4. David E. Garland and Diana R. Garland, *Flawed Families of the Bible: How God's Grace Works Through Imperfect Relationships* (Grand Rapids: Brazos, 2007), 113.

5. Richard M. Davidson, *Flame of Yahweh: Sexuality in the Old Testament* (Grand Rapids: Baker Academic, 2007), 233; also 235, 306. See also Carolyn Custis James for an excellent discussion of Tamar's positive character ("Tamar the Righteous Prostitute," in *Vindicating the Vixens: Revisiting Sexualized, Vilified, and Marginalized Women of the Bible*, ed. Sandra Glahn [Grand Rapids: Kregel, 2017], 31–48).

6. Marten Stol, "Prostitution," in *Women in the Ancient Near East* (Berlin: de Gruyter, 2016), 416, 418.

7. For instance, *laqah* is used of the evil sons of Eli seizing meat in the temple (1 Sam 2:16), of the evil sons taking bribes (1 Sam 8:3), and of Ezekiel being lifted up between heaven and earth by a lock of his hair (Ezek 8:3). See Sarah Bowler, "Bathsheba: Vixen or Victim?," in Glahn, *Vindicating the Vixens*, 96–97.

8. Richard Davidson gives eighteen different arguments to support his assertion that this was a "power rape" by a powerful monarch, whose citizens were expected to come when he said come

(*Flame of Yahweh*, 523–32); cf. also Bowler, "Bathsheba," 81–100, and Larry Spielman, "David's Abuse of Power," *Word and World* 19 (1999): 251–59.

9. Garland and Garland, *Flawed Families*, 177.

10. Origin, *Contra Celsum* 1.69.

Appendix A: The Value and Dignity of Women

1. This appendix is condensed from Steve and Celestia Tracy, *By His Wounds: Trauma Healing for Africa* (Phoenix: Mending the Soul Ministries, 2014), 196–203.

2. Jacob Neusner, *The Mishnah: A New Translation* (New Haven, CT: Yale University Press, 1988), 676.

3. William Whiston, trans., *The Works of Josephus* (repr., Peabody, MA: Hendrickson, 1987).

4. Matthew Henry, *Matthew Henry's Commentary on the Whole Bible: Complete and Unabridged in One Volume* (Peabody: Hendrickson, 1994), 10.

Appendix B: Lies Exposed, God's Truth Revealed

1. Taken from Steve and Celestia Tracy, *By His Wounds: Trauma Healing for Africa* (Phoenix: Mending the Soul Ministries, 2014), 99–105.

SCRIPTURE INDEX

PROVERBS

ROMANS

1 CORINTHIANS

SUBJECT INDEX

CONTINUE THE JOURNEY

Healing is a sacred process. It doesn't end when you finish the last page of a book. It continues as God gently restores what has been broken. None of us are meant to walk this path alone. We need safe places to share our stories, companions to encourage us, and resources to guide us as we grow. Our prayer is that you will keep pressing into your story so that you can experience more of God's love.

Mending the Soul is dedicated to creating those safe spaces. For over two decades, we've equipped survivors, faith leaders, churches, and communities around the world to respond with wisdom, compassion, and truth to the wounds of abuse and trauma.

To help you deepen your journey, we've prepared companion resources:

- Study Guide: with reflection and discussion prompts for individuals and groups
- Prayer Journal: a space to bring your heart to God in prayer, lament, and hope
- Additional Resources: supplementary articles, guides, and tools to strengthen both your healing and the healing of your community

We invite you to explore these resources, join a small group, and continue the work God has begun in you. Visit www.mending thesoul.org/to-heal-or-harm.

MENDING *the* SOUL
THE DIFFERENCE IS VISIBLE